Cycles of Becoming

ALEXANDER RUPERTI was born in Germany of Russian parents in 1913, and was educated in both England and Germany. While in England, he attended Alice Bailey's Arcane School and was affiliated with the Astrological Lodge where he studied with C.E.O. Carter. He began practicing astrology professionally in 1937. In 1939, he finished his osteopathy and physical therapy training and then moved to Switzerland, where he still resides. There he maintained a full-time practice in osteopathy, physical therapy, and healing, using the birthcharts of many patients in order to understand the basic problem behind the physical complaint. Greatly impressed by Dane Rudhyar's pioneering work (*The Astrology of Personality* in 1936), he began to teach a positive, holistic approach to astrology in 1939 and continued such courses for many years thereafter. He was probably the first person to promote such a modern, psychological type of astrology in Europe. After extensively touring the United States in 1975, and encouraged by the great interest in his ideas and the excellent response to his lectures, Mr. Ruperti retired from his practice in the healing arts in order to devote more time to astrological writing. Although his articles have appeared in a number of astrological journals, *Cycles of Becoming* is his first book to be published in America.

CYCLES

OF

BECOMING

The Planetary Pattern of Growth

Alexander Ruperti

CRCS PUBLICATIONS

Asbill Court Building
111 G Street, Suite 29
Davis, California 95616

Library of Congress Cataloging in Publication Data

Ruperti, Alexander, 1913-
   Cycles of becoming.

   Bibliography: p.
   1. Astrology. 2. Cycles--Miscellanea. 3. Biological rhythms--Miscellanea. I. Title.
BF1725.R86   133.5   77-84029

ISBN 0-916360-07-5 pbk.

INTERNATIONAL STANDARD BOOK NUMBER:
   0-916360-07-5 (paperback)

LIBRARY OF CONGRESS CATALOG CARD NUMBER: 77-84029
Published simultaneously in the United States
and Canada by CRCS Publications

Distributed in the United States &
Internationally by CRCS Publications

Cover Design: Original painting (Untitled) by Mark Douglas Arroyo
Text Design: Joanne Case & Kathleen Mullins

Acknowledgements

I would like to give special thanks to Batya Stark for her invaluable help and persistent encouragement in the preparation of this book. Her translation of my condensed style into a more readable form as well as her understanding of what the reader, especially if an astrologer, would want to know from such a book, have added greatly to whatever merits it may have.

A final word of appreciation goes to James Feil who took on the job of the final copy-editing of the text.

To my friend and teacher, Dane Rudhyar,
whose wisdom put my feet on a path to the light.

Contents

CYCLES OF BECOMING

Introduction

During the last fifty years, and especially since Einstein proposed that "everything is related to everything else in a space-time continuum," the reality of time values has taken on an increasing importance in man's explanations of reality. This means that, for the physical sciences, the reality of time has become a fourth dimension added to the three dimensions of space in terms of which one seeks to explain the universe. For the scientist, therefore, time is still part of an explanation of reality based on space values and an extension of them. "Space values," when related to a human being, are those values which determine his *place* in the universe: first of all as a member of the human species, then of a particular race and physiological type. A human being, interpreted in terms of "space" values, has no *individual* characteristics; he is simply a member of a certain collectivity or group and is judged in terms of characteristics which are found predominant within that collectivity or group.

Traditional astrology also explained man in terms of such space values. A person born on a given date was not seen as an individual but as an expression of the human qualities related to the zodiacal Sign in which the Sun, Moon and planets were found on his birthday. Space-bound astrology evolves through an expansion of the variety of relationships that can be established between our knowledge of human nature and astrological symbols.

The establishment of statistical probabilities in many fields is also an expression of spatial, i.e., relational values, in which one predicts the behaviour of the parts in terms of the whole which contains them. This statistical technique is used, for example, in Gallup polls, in the establishment of insurance or life-annuity premiums, and in every case where the individual is judged solely in terms of the overall behaviour of the group to which he belongs physically, socially, economically, and so on. As Bertrand Russell says (*The Analysis of Matter*, page 191):

> Statistics, ideally, are accurate laws about large groups; they differ from other laws only in being about groups, not about individuals.

The time element in life is understood differently by the scientist, the philosopher and the psychologist. For the scientist, time has no creative meaning; it is mathematical and linear — past, present, future. But a philosopher like Bergson (*Creative Evolution*) understood time as "duration" and showed that our experience of time is subjective — a minute may seem like an hour or an hour like a minute, according to the nature of our experience at the time. And the psychologist Jung, when speaking of his "synchronicity principle," attributed a particular quality to each moment of time. If we apply the time concepts of Bergson and

Jung to man's life, we can postulate that the moment of his birth can reveal much concerning the individual qualities he may display during his life-span. His heredity and environment will establish the "space" values through which he must manifest his individual "time" values. Astrologically, the birth-chart thus becomes the space-time structure which can reveal how and at what rhythm the individual potential contained in the birth-moment can become a spatial reality.

A further distinction between the scientists' understanding of time and that which progressive thinkers are trying to reinstate can be seen in the different ways in which one can explain evolution. For the scientists, evolution proceeds in a straight line, from the amoeba to man, whereas before the scientific era, the notion of cycle and of cyclic process predominated. We have to thank the Church for the unfortunate repudiation, for theological reasons, of the concept of a cyclic progression in evolution, at the Council of Constantinople in the Fifth century A.D. Since the concept of cycle has been deemed heretical since that date, it is not surprising that the leaders of academic thought have difficulty in accepting its importance today. However, biologists have been obliged to accept the fact that many phenomena in the lives of animals, birds, sea creatures and plants recur in cycles. Studies in physiology reveal cyclic patterns in the functioning of the organs and the body systems, and research into human behaviour and development reveals set ages for the appearance of specific life crises, both physical and psychological, common to all men and women. Even our economic growth is governed by the cyclical ups and downs of the stock market.

Whereas occult traditions and what today is called the "humanistic" approach to astrology define a cycle as a structured sequence of phases in the development of some life process, most people think of a cycle simply as a repetitive eternal return to a same starting-point. If a cycle is reduced to a closed circle of repetitive events, it cannot have the creative, evolutionary meaning it possesses when understood to be the expression of a creative process. And yet, as a matter of fact, both interpretations of a cycle are correct. The *structure* of a cycle in time, i.e., its duration, repeats itself. A day cycle repeats itself every twenty four hours; the lunation cycle, on which the month is based, repeats itself at each New Moon; the year cycle repeats itself every twelve months. But those who limit their understanding of the significance of a cycle to such a repetitive sequence of time values — days, months or years — forget that what *happens* during a given day, month or year, does *not* repeat itself exactly. The way we act and the meaning we find in a particular experience during a given cycle represent the creative, individual element; the nature of the cycle and the cycle's phase which corresponds to the experience enable one to understand better the significance of what one does and experiences at the time.

All our life activities are structured by the day, month and year cycles, but we forget that these cycles are founded on astronomical data used by astrologers since very ancient times. The great stumbling-block to the acceptance of the astrologer's use of astronomical cycles to interpret what is happening on earth and in human nature is the fact that astrology uses the planets' cycles as well as the day, month and year cycles. Scientists cannot understand how it is possible to relate planets to events in human lives because, for them, the planetary "cause" and the "human event effect" do not belong to the same order of phenomena. They have left man out of the universe they study; they do not seek to give a *human meaning* to what they find by their measurements. They want to be "objective," and so they detach themselves from the object of their study and come to believe that what they find in the universe is outside of them, an expression of absolutely valid and true "laws" beyond the human equation. They have forgotten that they are human beings and that therefore, whatever the source of their knowledge of the universe, this scientific knowledge is and will ever remain *human* knowledge. They do not seem to realize the extent to which their mental conditioning limits their methods of investigation; the answers they find — and have found — may be "true" in terms of and within the limits of the point of view they adopt, but they are certainly not "true" explanations of *total* reality because the scientific method is built upon the systematic *exclusion* of all that the method cannot cope with. So, if scientists are incapable of finding any connection between the solar system and both inner and outer events in a human life, this does *not* mean that there is no connection, but simply that the connection is of an order other than that which the scientific method can establish.

Astrologers study the sky because it gives them an experience of universal order. They do not seek to detach themselves from the universe and its rhythms as the scientists do, but rather identify themselves with these rhythms. Ancient astrologers explained the relationship of Man to the universe in terms of the law of correspondences — "as above, so below"; the medieval alchemist-astrologers explained the statement "man is made in the image of God" as meaning that the structural patterns of the manifested universe are expressions of an all-inclusive harmonic order operating within galaxies, solar systems, men and atoms alike. Thus for the astrologer both the celestial bodies in our solar system *and* human nature follow the *same* law and rhythm of development; in order to live a spiritually significant life, therefore, human beings should try to live in harmony with the laws which govern the universe and the planets. Planets and human beings should be synchronous in their manifestation of the power and purpose of the whole universe. Because a human being is a constellation of the same powers that form the planets in the sky, we should try to live our lives according to the rhythmical cyclic movement of the planets which, taken together, symbolize the basic functions of the total human being. But since these basic functions are common to *all* human beings, if we would individualize ourselves, we must *use* these common human functions, qualities and capacities in an individual manner.

The astrological thesis is that the planetary picture found in our birth-charts, related to the particular moment and place of our birth, will enable us to get a perspective on the particular manner in which we should use these human functions in order to grow in an individually meaningful and significant way. The rhythm and the time-table of this potential individual development will be keyed to the rhythm of the planetary cycles from the birth-moment onwards. This book is an attempt to help the reader to understand the significance of these cycles, so that he or she may live consciously according to this cyclic rhythm on the path toward personal maturity. These cycles will not reveal concrete events; there is no determinism involved; but their phases will reveal the *types* of experiences which should attract our conscious attention if we would get the maximum out of our lives. They will enable us to understand better the meaning of what happens at any moment in relation to the overall purpose of our life.

Today, many people have lost a sense of order and the feeling that there is meaning and value in their lives. The psychologist Viktor Frankl in his book *Man's Search For Meaning* has shown that such a sense of order and meaning is more vital to both children and adults than food or clothing. Many people are haunted by the experience of their inner emptiness, of a void within themselves, caught in that situation which Frankl calls "the existential vacuum." So it is important that something be done to restore this sense of meaning if we would curb the alarming growth of neurosis, frustration and boredom. Modern science is incapable of doing this since its methods are not adapted to our individual differences. But astrology, rightly understood and applied, is a sort of "counter-science" which can meet the demand for an objective understanding of both the cycles of human experience and of the specific meaning of a person's life at a given moment. In this way even tragedy, when seen as a phase within an over-all pattern of growth, may be understood as a temporary crisis which can lead to self-transcendence and a more meaningful life. It is probably for this reason that astrology has today become more popular than ever, in spite of academic scorn and even occasional persecution.

As a final word of introduction, I would like to state that there is nothing fated or predetermined in the suggested meanings that I have given to the phases of the various planetary cycles. The reader is at all times free to make a choice between accepting or rejecting them, to fulfill the potentiality or else to forfeit it. But he or she must take the entire responsibility for the results of the choice; astrology is not responsible for them. I have presented the interpretations from the point of view which considers that men and women are beings whose main concern is trying to fulfill a meaning or purpose in life and to actualize values rather than to adapt happily and successfully to what our modern chaotic society and environment offers. A life without tension would be a meaningless life, a loss of self in boredom and emptiness. It is much more important to concentrate one's energies toward the struggle to attain what one considers to be a worthwhile goal and to *time* one's efforts according to the phases of the planetary cycles, so that one may do what life asks of him at the right moment however difficult it may be. As Frankl wrote in *Man's Search For Meaning:*

> As each situation in life represents a challenge to man and presents a problem for him to solve, the question of the meaning of life may actually be reversed. Ultimately, man should not ask what the meaning of his life is, but rather must recognize that it is *he* who is asked. In a word, each man is questioned by life; to life he can only respond by being responsible... responsibleness is the very essence of human existence. So one should not search for an abstract meaning of life. Everyone has his own specific vocation or mission in life; everyone must carry out a concrete assignment that demands fulfillment. Therein he cannot be replaced, nor can his life be repeated. Thus, everyone's task is as unique as is his specific opportunity to implement it.

One can hardly present more clearly the spirit in which the reader is asked to approach the material presented in this book. I only hope that what I say in the following pages may help each person toward a more meaningful use of his or her potentials — and of astrology, if so inclined.

I

The Humanistic Approach

Since the dawn of time itself, Man has measured his life by the cycles of the planets — from sunrise to sunrise and from one new Moon to the next he has reckoned his existence by the heavens. Indeed, it is this conscious awareness of Time which separates the human being from all other living creatures. His alone is the ability to see time as a continuum of past, present and future — for Man alone is the conscious awareness that his days are numbered. Humanistic astrology is the first approach to astrology to use the concept of cycles as the foundation for the understanding and interpretation of its basic symbols: Houses, Signs, planets and aspects. This is more than a "new technique" of interpretation; it is a new approach. For thousands of years astrology has been based on a belief in the existence of cosmic forces, planetary rays or vibrations which *directly* influence life on this planet and force individuals to do certain things or to experience certain events. Even today, despite the individual's abhorrence to viewing himself as a victim of the universe, this belief system remains among most astrologers.

There is an attempt to water down the inherent determinism of astrology with the currently popular cliche, "The stars do not compel, they impel"; however, the difference between "compel" and "impel" is vague at best. The belief system remains. In that philosophy the cyclic inter-relationship of the planets has no significance, and neither does the periodical order of the universe. It is precisely that periodical order inherent in all cyclic inter-relationships of the planets which makes their use in relation to human life relevant and significant to the Humanistic astrologer.

WHAT IS A CYCLE? A cycle is a form-structure of time. It is the context in which change takes place. All of existence is structured by time, and all activity takes place in time. A cycle is the life-span of any given entity. Although a cycle has a recognizable beginning and end, it is erroneous to interpret it as a perpetual starting point — beginning, end and new beginning. Such a view of cycles in astrology will lead one to consider them as repetitive sequences of *events*. This is not a true picture of reality; for although the *pattern* of its unfoldment from beginning to end repeats itself, the *contents* of a cycle — the changing states, events or experiences within its span — are never exactly repeated. A day is a recognizable cycle. It is a time structure the form of which is determined by one axial rotation of the Earth every 24 hours. Concurrently, the day is a portion of the lunation cycle described by the phases of the Moon and measuring the Sun/Moon relationship from one new Moon to the next; and both of these cycles are circumscribed within other cycles. It is this interrelationship among cycles which describes the total uniqueness of each moment and at the same time links them together in a rhythmic order. These time values revealed in the solar system — the greater Whole of which our Earth is a part — act upon the time values of the individual. Astronomy provides us with the data, and astrology interprets these data with reference to the processes of life on Earth and particularly within the individual.

A cycle, being a "whole of activity," contains a middle as well as a beginning and an end, and there are recognizable phases of development as it unfolds. As soon as a particular moment is identified as being part of a cycle, it becomes inextricably related to both the beginning and the end of that cycle. Any specific moment within a cycle is considered part of the "middle," a working out of the impulse which began the cycle, and is directed toward the consummation or *purpose,* of that cycle. Thus, all moments within a cycle stretch back to the cyclic root and at the same time forward toward the cyclic seed. This simultaneous impulse forward and backward involves any particular moment with all the other moments of the cycle. Rudhyar calls this TIME-INTERPENETRATION. It is the fourth dimension of time. Rudhyar stresses the fact that such an inter-penetration of root, seed and all other moments of a cycle means far more than the ordinary concept of cause-and-effect, which is based upon a rigid sequence of separated moments of time. Every moment in time is a part, aspect or phase of an all-encompassing reality—the Whole, and has its essential meaning *only* with reference to this Whole. Thus every apparently separate unit is involved with and participates in every other unit within the time span of a cycle. This is so because in any cycle the effect also acts upon the cause and *every present moment is pulled by the future as well as pushed by the past.* The entire cycle is implicit in every moment of it.

Astrology as a study of cycles then becomes a study of the interconnections between all these factors — between the future and the past in every present moment; between the universal macrocosm and the individual microcosm. The birthchart is the starting point of the individual's life cycle. It is poised between the ancestral past — the karmic roots; and the potentially individualized future — the dharmic life-purpose. It is the pattern or plan of what Jung called the individuation process, revealing in symbolic language how each person can fully become what he potentially is.

WHAT IS A CRISIS? Cycles are measurements of change. In order for any purpose to be realized, change must take place, and change necessarily involves crises. Many have difficulty with the word *crisis;* confusing it with "catastrophe." They study astrology in the belief that prior knowledge of "bad aspects" or "malefics" will enable them to avoid crises. A crisis, however, is not a terrible calamity. It derives from the Greek word KRINO, "to decide", and means simply a *time for decision.* A crisis is a turning point — that which precedes CHANGE. In order to avoid a crisis one would have to avoid change itself, an obvious impossibility.

Although all matter, both living and inanimate, is constantly changing, only Man has the capacity for conscious decision. In order to evolve, he must abandon instinctive behavior serving only survival or social compulsions in favor of conscious choice. The barrier to conscious choice is the "ego," that which society has told an individual that he should be, as opposed to the experience of Self, which tells him what he really is. It is in conforming to the societal role that one assumes habitual patterns of behavior. Then, when a time for decision (crisis) arrives, one allows those patterns to determine the choice, rather than using guidelines which issue from one's own personal truth.

Unfortunately, the temptation to avoid making a decision in hopes that the need will disappear and things will remain at a comfortable "normal" is always present. Sometimes this technique appears to work, and the thread of the *status quo* seems unbroken; however, no matter how small the decision or how insignificant the crisis, this avoidance is a spiritual defeat. A refusal to decide, or a waiting for circumstances or other people to make the decision, does not absolve the individual from responsibility. Each time a decision is not made, the instinctive, unconscious patterns are deepened. What was a groove in childhood later becomes a rut and finally a grave. This repeated lack of conscious decision can build up the tension in a situation until it finally explodes. One may then be obliged to react to difficult or painful circumstances which could have been avoided if he had met the earlier and lesser crises with objectivity and courage. The resultant catastrophe is not the necessary outcome of crises, but of decisions avoided. Thus to humanistically oriented astrologers, crises are not external events, even though external events may precipitate them or condition their development. Crises, both large and small, are essentially opportunities for growth — the only opportunities we ever really have. One must strive continually to be awake and free of the unconscious habit patterns which hinder spiritual growth. Thus, he will be able to use crises for his individual purposes.

The challenge of confrontations is endless. Some of these turning-points are biological (such as adolescence and menopause) and are met at specific ages, while others are individual and may occur at any time during the life-span. The potential for the latter is inherent in the natal chart, and the interpretation of effects and responses will depend on the age of the person at the time of the crisis (see Chapter II — "The Age Factor"). An astrologer can deduce the timing and nature of potential future crises from the transits and progressions. If one expects a specific type of change, transition period or crisis of growth, he or she can prepare to meet it *consciously and with open eyes*, and may gain more from it in terms of personal maturity and spiritual unfoldment. Such knowledge may also help one to avoid overly rash or hasty decisions. Also, the sense of despair which often arises in the midst of a crisis can be dispelled by the astrologer's ability to predict the cycle's end.

Foreknowledge can also have negative effects, however. The anticipation of an impending crisis very often induces fear and anxiety — the primary causes of all evil. Ideally this negative approach should be less likely from the humanist point of view, since its aim is spiritual development rather than materialistic enrichment or comfort. The humanistic astrologer should know, moreover, that crises are not isolated events, but phases of individual growth. He should interpret them with reference to the smaller or greater cycles within which they occur — as phases of these cycles. The phase to which the crisis corresponds will reveal its meaning and purpose in terms of the nature, scope and purpose of the cycle as a whole. Humanistic astrology will therefore be able to bring a sense of direction, orientation and purposefulness to every crisis. The ability to envision what could and should develop in the future (i.e., the aim and purpose of the complete cycle) even while one is in the midst of a chaotic current situation is not aided by most astrological textbooks. It must be learned by facing experiences in terms of the fourth dimension of time — that is, by seeing the whole cycle in every living moment and by approaching that present moment in a clear and conscious manner.

Although humanistic astrology can greatly assist in the understanding of future crises, this approach may be even more valuable in understanding those crises which have already occurred. Such hindsight is the best preparation for constructively and significantly meeting the crises of growth yet to come. Yet, like any technique, its value depends on the person using it — his courage, his wisdom and his spiritual vision. No one can see, whether in a birth-chart or in the person himself, anything which is beyond the scope of his own understanding. An astrologer can only get out of a birth-chart what he puts into his own life.

PROGRESSIONS AND TRANSITS — THE PATHS OF UNFOLD-
MENT. When I first became interested in astrology over forty years ago,
there was a controversy raging among astrologers concerning the
relative value of progressions (or directions) and transits which still
persists. The current pseudo-scientific trend in astrology has led many
astrologers to give up their use of progressions and directions, and to
rely exclusively on transits. Other astrologers use both sets of measure-
ment but confuse them, considering progressions, directions and
transits to all refer to external events. The humanistic astrologer uses
both progressions or directions and transits but defines them as distinct
categories. Since this book deals primarily with transits, there will be no
lengthy discussion of progressions and directions. Suffice it to say that,
in the humanistic view, they refer essentially to an *internal* or *subjective*
process of the growth of individual potential. They deal with the gradual
transformations which occur as the purpose and character of the
individual revealed in the natal chart are realized through the process of
life itself. Progressions show how the entire natal structure unfolds *of
itself,* according to the individual need and rhythm of development, so
that what is an abstract archetypal identity at birth may progressively
become a fully actualized and integrated person. There is no outside
pressure involved here; that is provided by the transits. Progressions
deal with the transformations of the rhythm of the Self itself, while
transits refer to the impact of the environment as a whole upon the Self.

Although one is not free to change one's potential of existence (the
birth-chart), an individual is free to decide what he will do with that
potential. The fulfillment of possibilities could be easily accomplished if
human beings lived in individual vacuums — isolated and independent
one from another. But as in fact we are all part of a collective environment, our individual success in realizing our individual potential is
dependent on that collective. Planetary, racial, social, cultural and
familial considerations all exert constant and powerful pressures,
especially in the early years; while they provide the raw materials for the
growth of the conscious mind and for the necessary development of a
sense of self, they also tend to obscure, stifle, distort or adulterate the
birth potential. These external pressures are measured by the transit
cycles, which show how the conscious mind may be developed by
experiencing a multitude of impacts and relationships. Self-actualization must be a conscious process, and it is only through the *conscious use* of
the confrontations revealed by the transit cycles that this can be
achieved. These confrontations, however, also produce all manner of
tensions, fears, inhibitions, ambitions and desires, which nearly always
belie the birth potential and tend to make the individual into what in
essence he is *not.* Some of the confrontations may cause pleasure,

happiness or even exaltation, while others can cause pain, misery and depression. When the transits reproduce planetary positions and aspects contained in the natal chart, they tend to strengthen the basic factors in the essential nature of that person. When, on the other hand, the transits upset the birth pattern too strongly, the pressures may tend to disintegrate the personality.

The birth potential — the archetypal essence of Self — remains what it is throughout the life. It is the permanent factor in every individual — the seed-form of his being and destiny. Everything that surrounds that individual in life (described by the transit cycle) will tend to change the quality of his essential being. Day by day his integrity will be challenged. All of those factors to which the transits refer will draw him away from the essence of his true identity, regardless of motivations and intentions. The best, the highest and the noblest of these forces — even love — will tend to change the true experience of Self and its inherent destiny.

To sum up: progressions deal with the internal unfoldment of personality, while transits refer essentially to the external impact of society and of the cosmos upon that personality. *Neither of the two should be considered alone.* Man reacts through transits only as well as he acts through *progressions.* A person is born as a seed of unique potential, and that seed should normally unfold into the realization of a fulfilled personality. The universe, however, does not stop at that moment of birth. All things which come thereafter in the universe astrologically in the form of transits will also exert an influence upon that unfolding personality and he must react to them. This is the eternal way. Man is not bound by fate. New situations arise within the universe at every successive moment, but no man is compelled to respond to them in a predetermined way. Therein lies his freedom, but he must choose it.

The degree and quality of *resistance* an individual will have to the pressures and forces of his environment is difficult to ascertain. In addition to the socio-cultural traditions, racial or nationalistic loyalties and the subtle or harsh commands of public opinion as expressed through the mass-media (especially in its advertisements), a person is also bombarded by solar and cosmic radiation, atmospheric pressure, the pull of gravity, and a host of pollutants which he breathes and ingests. All of these influences beat down upon the individual — strike at his skin, his senses, his mind and his electro-magnetic field (or aura) with unrelenting force. As long as the individual can resist these impacts he will live as a relatively separate organism. When the sum-total of these forces exhaust his ability to withstand them and he becomes too tired to hold himself separate from that surrounding cosmic and social ocean, he lets go. The ocean then rushes into the void of his separateness and he drowns; he goes insane or he dies. The capacity for courage cannot be measured by a birthchart, and no one can know fully the depth of his own ability to resist — much less that of another. And quite apart from this personal quality of resistance, the pressure may be relieved because other people help one to carry his burdens. There are many incidents of a person being saved from an accident or even death by the love of another. Such help is, however, merely a stop-gap measure, and may eventually cause the person being helped to lose his ability to help himself. Ultimately every individual must learn to stand alone.

So many contingencies exist that exact prediction of inner or outer events on the basis of critical transits alone is impossible. Man must be attacked from without (transits) at a time when he is weak within (progressions) and otherwise unsupported, if his resistance against the constant pressure of society and the universe is to collapse. This relationship between progressions and transits must not be forgotten. A person need not follow some predominant collective trend because of a transit in force at the time, unless it corresponds to, or enables him to fulfill, some individual need revealed by his progressions. *An individual may change his life consciously* at any time as the result of a socially-motivated decision. Thus, the individual and collective-social factors are constantly inter-related; and as a consequence, astrologers should use both progressions *and* transits.

Why do some astrologers emphasize transits and others progressions? Rudhyar once gave a psychological explanation for this. He noted that just as there are two basic types of human beings, there are two basic types of astrologers: extroverts and introverts. The extrovert centers his attention and interest in the outer world and his inter-personal relationships, while the introvert centers his on the subjective world of self, placing the greatest importance on what happens within his own individual being. The extroverted astrologer, therefore, would be the one who relies on the use of transits, while the introverted astrologer would stress the use of progressions. This difference of opinion is basically a difference of psychological and organic structure, and as a result it cannot be resolved into a common consent by mere intellectual discussion. According to Jung, these two types can never understand one another completely. Nevertheless, the humanistic astrologer must be able to realize that both of these points of view represent together the two halves of a complete truth and must learn to use both transits and progressions.

In addition to this inherent individual psychological predisposition, a proclivity towards extroversion exists in Western civilization as a whole. Collective values and collective fate weigh heavily on each individual in a so-called "modern" society, and especially on those living in large cities, where the almost total dependency of one person upon the collective is a dominant factor in his life. A technological society is designed by and for extroverts — for people who by nature place the greatest significance on their relations with the external world. It is not surprising, therefore, to find most astrologers putting the accent on transits and on the prediction of events, since they are asked to deal primarily with the concrete world and the individual's outward success or failure — with all that is dear to the extroverted mentality.

Yet another reason for the contemporary astrologer's preference for transits is the desire to be recognized by the scientific community. In this, transits — the actual day-by-day positions of the planets — represent astronomical data, as opposed to the purely symbolic nature of all forms of progressions and directions, and are more scientifically palatable. As the event-oriented astrologer is often a follower of some "scientific" system of thought, this predilection for transits seems logical, even though a scientifically acceptable explanation of *how* the birth-chart remains a sensitive plate capable of registering planetary impacts throughout the life will always remain a nearly insurmountable difficulty.

The holistic astrologer does not study the heavens in hope of finding ways of avoiding undesirable situations. At the same time, he can no more discount transits than he can ignore the external world which they represent. The study of the unfolding of personality is a subtle balance of progressions and transits — of the external and the internal. A humanistic astrologer must understand and use transits in a way which is fundamentally different from his event-oriented colleague. While accepting the fact that we are all subject to the constant pressures of the outer environment, he must postulate that, as individuals, we are capable of resisting that pressure *if* we are inwardly strong enough.

THE STUDY OF TRANSITS. As seen from Earth, the pattern of the solar system is constantly changing. The term "transits" refers to those changes — the astronomical raw data which astrology seeks to interpret. By definition, "transit" means "moving or passing through or across"; the Sun, Moon and planets all move through the zodiac and pass across specific points of reference. In practice, astrologers regard the transits primarily in their angular relationship to the natal positions of the Sun, Moon, planets and Angles of the birth-chart, although in the strictest sense, they should refer only to the passage of a planet *over* a natal position — hence to the conjunction.

The traditional astrologer views the natal chart as a fixed structure which remains unchanged throughout the life, and uses transits to explain how the life to which that birth-chart refers constantly changes. He does this by calculating the aspect between the transiting planet and the natal position, stipulating that the transit causes changes in the operation of the natal planet's function. The nature of these changes is supposedly determined by the character of the transiting planet. For example: When transiting Mercury aspects a natal planet, a mental stimulation should occur which enhances that person's reasoning faculties. A transit of Venus should cause an intensification of the feeling nature, while Mars is supposed to activate an aspected planet with energy (anger or aggression if Mars is viewed as a malefic). A Jupiter transit will expand and bring opportunities for growth and good luck, and a Saturn transit should inhibit or contract (or bring bad luck or loss if deemed a malefic). A Uranus transit will inspire, transform or bring radical changes; while a Neptune transit should shroud experience in a poetic mist and bring unclarity; and a Pluto transit is supposed to cause a break from past traditions.

At this point an astrologer may ask himself: Why should a transiting planet necessarily "produce" any effect at all? The traditional explanation of "planetary influences" postulates that within each individual there are "sensitive points" or "centers" to which the planetary positions at birth correspond; these sensitive points are somehow activated by the transits. This hypothesis is the quintessence of event-oriented astrology. The tendency here is to isolate each transiting aspect from the others, which may be a logical procedure if very specific events are being sought. However events, thus considered, acquire almost unavoidably a tinge of predestination, and the results of this approach can be frightening to both astrologer and client.

When an astrologer sees that an eclipse is going to fall on his solar return, or a conjunction of traditionally malefic planets will square his natal Sun, it is difficult for him to avoid manifestations of subconscious, if not conscious, fear. Almost every astrologer, before becoming humanistic in his orientation, has learned the rudiments of astrology from the usual text-books and from teachers who have emphasized the concept of "planetary influence". This concept, accepted by generations of astrologers, will persist on the unconscious level. Although one may be intellectually drawn to humanism, on the deeper feeling levels he will still be subject to the notion of "influences". Thus, when such powerful transits are noted, and because they are objective and concrete manifestations of what can be seen in the sky, they are felt to be fateful and unavoidable phenomena, however much one might resist that feeling on the conscious level.

Whatever one may try to do to avoid the projected danger, he cannot make the transit itself disappear. The transit *will* take place, and if one truly "believes" in astrology, then some event related to established meanings of eclipses or malefic planets is bound to occur. Otherwise, the astrological thesis of some form of correspondence between planets and men would be false. Astrology cannot have it both ways. The more astrologers emphasize the impersonal, scientific reasons for astrological correspondences, the greater the potential psychological danger in astrological counseling.

But can the doctrine of "planetary influences" be truly called scientific, when it does not take into consideration the astronomical facts in the interpretation of transits? A transit refers to an astronomical change which is literally taking place in the sky. These changes have nothing to do intimately with us as individuals; indeed, they would take place even if no life existed on Earth. The presence of planets as shown in the current ephemeris at any time in a given Sign can therefore only refer to a *general trend* in effect during the time of their transits. The duration of the trend varies according to the length of time which a given planet remains in a given Sign. Also, as all the planets are continuously moving at different speeds and aspecting each other in the sky, they create a complex ever-changing pattern which must be interpreted *as a whole*. For this reason the tendency of beginners, of astrological text-books and of many professional astrologers to isolate each aspect of each transiting planet to each natal planet or angle and to study them separately will never give a picture of living reality.

Just as the ever-changing celestial pattern is a fact, so also is it a fact that an individual is part of the world around him, and that his individual destiny is influenced by the general trends at any given time. Because of this, an individual must eventually deal with collective factors — with the way people *in general* will tend to think, feel or act. When transiting planets aspect his natal or solar chart, that person is stirred by a general trend; and whether he likes it or not, he is subjected to the pressures of the collective. What happens as a result is not *directly* related to his individual life-destiny — it is not the *exteriorization* of a phase of his individual development, even though it may change his individual life. This latter possibility is more likely to occur when the progressions *and* the transits point in the same direction.

Transits call attention to the fact that individuals do not live in a vacuum. One cannot isolate himself from the universe. He is obliged to respond in some way to all changes in the social, cultural, and political world as well as changes in the biosphere. The task of a humanistic astrologer is to respond to the universe — to transits — in an individualized manner and to show his clients how to do likewise. No one is obliged to passively follow some predominant collective trend because of a transit in force at that time. The results will then depend on his subjective condition and on his capacity to *resist* external pressures.

For this reason, humanistic astrology emphasizes the principle that one need not consider a supposedly "bad" transit as denoting the impact of a force *external* to man. Although the astrological situation may be correlated to, or synchronous with, an event having an external cause — a traffic accident, being on a hijacked plane or involved in a street riot, or losing one's job because of the economic collapse of the company — it must not be taken for granted that the astrological configuration refers to the occurrence in its external aspect. The humanistic astrologer views the astrological configuration as referring to *what takes place within the individual*. It is the internal response that is important, whatever the external event may be. Exact prediction is not important; but rather, the creation within oneself of a positive, courageous and conscious attitude in the face of an experience necessary to one's psychological and spiritual development. Whatever the outward crisis may be, it must be understood as a necessary phase of growth. One often cannot change the external situation, so what matters is how he faces up to it and what *meaning he gives to the experience*. The only true freedom exists in an individual's ability to give to his crises either the meaning of growth and fulfillment, or the meaning of hopeless frustration and disintegration. We, and not the planets, are responsible for the results of all life-confrontations. The astrologer's task, therefore, is not to set himself up as some sort of oracle, but rather to assist others to gain a better understanding of their birth potential, and to reach their full stature as mature, spirit-radiating beings.

It is psychologically important that one should avoid stressing any *single* transit, particularly the so-called "bad" ones. In the humanistic approach one studies *trends* rather than events — the *cyclic phases* rather than sharply defined aspects. Humanism addresses *the whole life-destiny* rather than a particular issue considered outside the context of the whole life. To practice astrology in this way will not make of one a startling fortune-teller, and that is essential if one is to give to others — and to oneself — sound and meaningful psychological assistance.

TRANSITS AND THE BIRTH PATTERN. The natal chart is a description of the transits at the moment of birth as seen from a specific point on Earth. It is related to the continuing movement of the planets in the same way that each successive moment of present time is related to the whole of Time — past and future. As the planetary pattern at birth reveals who and what that person potentially *is*, any modification of that pattern is a distortion of that essential being. In *The Practice of Astrology**, Dane Rudhyar explains this aspect of the individual's problem when facing transits. He observed that as the planets move on in the heavens after birth, the distortion becomes increasingly more generalized, except at such times as the same aspects between certain planets found in the natal chart are repeated in the sky, or when a planet returns to its birth position.

---

*Chapter 10, pp. 103-113.

To illustrate this point, we can take the example of a birth-chart containing a conjunction of Mars and Jupiter. In this example, the character and purpose of the Mars-Jupiter relationship is defined as a conjunction. Life, however, as reflected in the sky day after day, will tend to alter this definition by changing that relationship progressively from a conjunction to a sextile, then a square, a trine and so forth. Life and the external world, as described by the transits, thus tends to throw the basic pattern of Self out of balance. When, on the other hand, Mars and Jupiter return to their natal positions — Mars every two years and Jupiter every twelve years — there will be a strengthening of the natal Mars/Jupiter individuality as the natal configuration is re-emphasized. The same will be true when a transiting Mars/Jupiter conjunction occurs. This transiting re-enforcement of a natal configuration will not necessarily result in an event. It will, however, on the psychological level, give one a feeling of freedom to be oneself — a feeling that the external world agrees with one's internal experience of Self.

An example of this is a person born with Mars in Aries. That natal placement reveals a characteristic tendency toward impetuous, pioneering behavior which will be retained throughout the life. Such a person would probably have strong powers of initiative, a fiercely competitive nature, impatience with obstacles and a temper which explodes easily. He also may drive a little faster than most people. Some of these natural characteristics are not condoned by society — "It's not nice to lose your temper," "Don't push," "It's illegal to drive fast." These are the strictures with which he has had to fall into agreement, even though they are foreign to his basic nature. Every two years Mars will transit the sign Aries. This one and a half month (average) accent on Aries will refer to a *general trend* of human reactions all over the world insofar as the Mars function is concerned. Of course, this does *not* mean that *everybody* will rush around impetuously, fighting, pushing or getting angry. There will, however, be a general tendency toward shorter tempers and higher speedometer readings; and the individual with a natal Mars in Aries will fit smoothly into the general pattern.

THE GENERIC CYCLES. Quite apart from the aspects which transiting planets make to the planets and angles of a natal chart, an astrologer can also isolate a specific planet and study its individual cycle, relating the transiting planet to its own natal position. Each "return" of a transiting planet to its natal position symbolizes a new beginning according to the nature of that planet. Having absorbed the lessons of the previous cycle, the return is a step up the ladder of development to a new and higher level. Only when the lessons of the previous cycle have not been learned, or the necessary development has not taken place is the new cycle a bizarre repetition of itself. These are called "generic" cycles

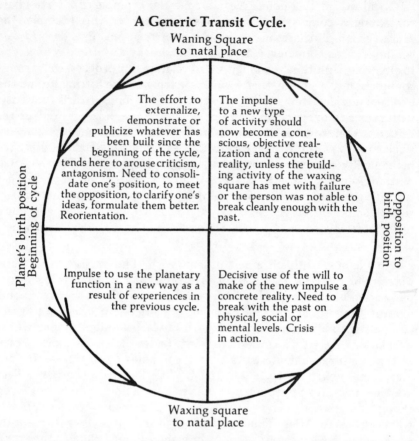

A Generic Transit Cycle.

Waning Square
to natal place

The effort to externalize, demonstrate or publicize whatever has been built since the beginning of the cycle, tends here to arouse criticism, antagonism. Need to consolidate one's position, to meet the opposition, to clarify one's ideas, formulate them better. Reorientation.

The impulse to a new type of activity should now become a conscious, objective realization and a concrete reality, unless the building activity of the waxing square has met with failure or the person was not able to break cleanly enough with the past.

Planet's birth position
Beginning of cycle

Opposition to
birth position

Impulse to use the planetary function in a new way as a result of experiences in the previous cycle.

Decisive use of the will to make of the new impulse a concrete reality. Need to break with the past on physical, social or mental levels. Crisis in action.

Waxing square
to natal place

because they relate specifically to the genus *homo*, meaning MAN; and the crises which they describe are those common to all human beings by virtue of the fact that they have reached a specific age. The starting point for a generic cycle is the birth position; and in the course of an 84-year life span every planet except Neptune and Pluto will make at least one complete circuit of the birth-chart and return to its natal position.

The generic cycles do not describe external events, but rather the stages of an inner process of growth, development and decay specifically related to the nature of the planets. Although the crises which they describe are generally painful — either physically as in the instance of cutting one's first teeth; or emotionally, as in the experience of adolescence — they are not only natural, but necessary phases of development. These are the crises which people complain about the most, and control the least; for even with extraordinary measures there is no way an individual can avoid experiencing them, except by dying.

TRANSITS AND THE HOUSES. In studying a transit in relation to the basic life-purpose of an individual — which is to say how a person should *use* that planet in an individualized manner — it is important to relate the transit to the particular birth-chart. Since everyone born on a given day will have nearly the same solar chart, and everyone born at the same time will have the exact same solar chart, the specifically unique and individual characteristic of a birth-chart is the cross of Horizon and Meridian and the Houses of the natal chart. These angles depend not only on the date and time of birth, but also on the geographic location. This is why the humanistic astrologer considers the Houses to be the single most important factor in describing *individual* values. A truly personal approach to transits has to be made in the context of the four Angles of the Natal chart.

Of all the Houses, the First House is the most individual. For this reason, the individual cycle of a planet begins when that planet transits the Ascendant for the first time. Whatever happens *before* a planet first reaches the Ascendant will refer to a sort of "pre-natal" or preparatory phase in terms of the function of that planet. It is only as the planet reaches the Ascendant that the energies associated with it will gradually begin to assert themselves *in an individualized manner* in the life-destiny of that person. The time of these cyclic beginnings will vary according to the natal House position of the planet and its speed. In most instances the first planet to transit the Ascendant will be the Moon. This transit occurs some time during the first twenty-eight days of life and expresses the first emergence of personality as an awareness of Self. The Sun and the planets up to and including Saturn (i.e., those planets which are visible in the sky) will transit the Ascendant some time during the first twenty-eight years of life; while it may take Uranus as long as 84 years to cross the Ascendant. Neptune and Pluto move so slowly that they may not transit the Ascendant at all within a given lifetime. In the case of Uranus, Neptune and Pluto, therefore, the individualized response to their challenges will begin at the time they reach the first angle of the birth-chart during their passage through the zodiac.

TRANSITS AND THE QUADRANTS. The axis of Horizon and Meridian divides the birth-chart into four quadrants. Dane Rudhyar has established a correspondence between these four sectors of the natal chart and the four seasons of the year.* The Ascendant corresponds to the winter solstice; the Nadir, to the Spring equinox; the Descendant, to the summer solstice; and the Midheaven, to the fall equinox. A transiting planet passing from the Ascendant to the Descendant will therefore move through the six Houses which represent the North of the chart. This motion parallels the northward movement of the Sun in declination

---

American Astrology magazine: August, 1942.

The Meaning of the Four Quadrants

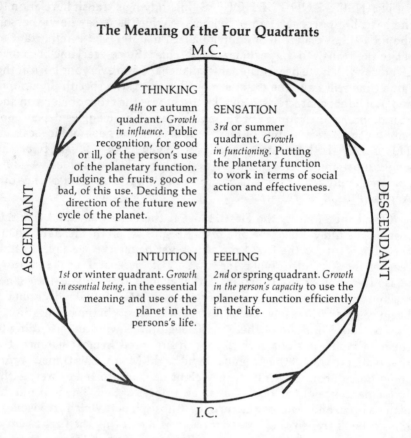

M.C.

THINKING

4th or autumn quadrant. *Growth in influence.* Public recognition, for good or ill, of the person's use of the planetary function. Judging the fruits, good or bad, of this use. Deciding the direction of the future new cycle of the planet.

SENSATION

3rd or summer quadrant. *Growth in functioning.* Putting the planetary function to work in terms of social action and effectiveness.

INTUITION

1st or winter quadrant. *Growth in essential being,* in the essential meaning and use of the planet in the persons's life.

FEELING

2nd or spring quadrant. *Growth in the person's capacity* to use the planetary function efficiently in the life.

ASCENDANT

DESCENDANT

I.C.

from the winter to the summer solstice. The transiting planet then proceeds upward to the Midheaven — the South point of the chart and returns again to the Ascendant. Humanistic astrologers therefore describe the four quadrants of the birth-chart as the winter, spring, summer and autumn quarters.

Rudhyar has given a general meaning to transits through each of these quarters. This meaning will, of course, be modified according to the particular nature of the transiting planet and will be discussed at length in the following chapters on the separate planetary transit cycles.

The Winter Quarter: The period during which a planet transits through the first three Houses of the birth-chart is a time of maximum subjectivity. Just as a seed appears to lie dormant in winter, the new impulse, born out of the preceding cycle of experience, appears to sleep. Everything that has been achieved or experienced during the cycle just past, and especially in the external, social experiences which marked its last half, must be assimilated. Growth is internal and subjective, and nothing at all may be apparent on the surface. Below, on the foundations of the old cycle, new power, new faculties and a new cycle of destiny are being prepared. The planetary function should now be used ever more consciously in the light of one's own personal development — to illuminate and clarify the individual sense of who and what one really is. This is the basic challenge of a transit through the first quadrant. The keynote of the period is: *Growth in essential being.*

The Spring Quarter: As a planet crosses the Nadir and moves through the 4th, 5th and 6th Houses, the inner workings of its life-function are adapted to the new and present needs of the personality and destiny. Now they begin to show external results. What was subjective is now becoming objective, just as the seeds which germinated through the winter sprout and grow in the Spring. New ways of using that planetary function are discovered, learned and mastered. These are the tools which will later enable the individual to fully manifest that life-function. In addition to manifestation on the internal and purely personal biological and psychological levels, the new expression of the life-function will affect social levels as well. The planetary function should now be used in an ever-expanding externalization. The keynote of this period is: *Growth in capacity.*

The Summer Quarter: When a planet moves through the 7th, 8th and 9th Houses of the natal chart, the new capacities which have developed throughout the preceding quarter of the transit cycle crystallize clearly through social action. The person has the tools and must now employ them with ever-increasing skill and effectiveness. As the individual uses them in his relationship to the objective world, he or she will realize with increasing clarity the part which that planet plays within his or her own personality. He will be able to use this function consciously to further his outer destiny. His social activity should become ever more distinctive and personalized. The high-point in this process of growth is reached when the transiting planet comes to the Midheaven. The keynote for this period is: *Growth in functioning.*

The Autumn Quarter: This is the time of the harvest. After the natal Midheaven is reached and the transiting planet moves through the 10th, 11th, and 12th Houses, the external, social operation of that planetary function is publicly acknowledged. This recognition will bring either social advantages or retribution to the user. Whatever was sown by personal exertion (or the lack of effort) during the preceding phases of the cycle will now be reaped. Efforts are judged and rewarded according to the value standards of society at that time. In this quadrant one meets and must accept the results of his past actions in order to extract the essential meaning of success and failure. Whatever the fruits — whether positive or negative — they will decide the direction which the new cycle will take. The seed of the future cycle is formed here. When the Ascendant is reached, a sort of "Judgment-day" is experienced. The seed of the new cycle is sown and the direction and significance of the new cycle is set. Either consciously or unconsciously, in freedom or in bondage to the past, the new cycle begins. The keynote of this final period is: *Growth in influence.*

In addition to its developmental dimension, each quadrant also refers to a basic psychological function. The humanistic correspondence established by Rudhyar in *The Astrology of Personality* links the Ascendant to the intuition, the Nadir to feeling, the Descendant to sensation, and the Midheaven to thought. Accordingly, whenever there is a transit accent on a specific Angle or quadrant, there will be a corresponding emphasis on the *use* of the psychological function linked to it. This applies to all planets, including the transiting Sun and Moon. Special attention should be paid to the New Moon in relation to the conscious development of the function related to the natal quadrant in which it falls. This type of quadrant interpretation can be used to give a personal meaning to the generic transit cycles because it is based on the individual birth-chart. Additionally, during certain periods of the life one of the four basic psychological functions can become especially prominent through multiple planetary emphases on the corresponding quadrant and should receive conscious attention to its development at that time.

THE LIFE CYCLE — THE HOLISTIC APPROACH. Any serious study of the transit cycles in a person's life necessitates that the astrologer plot them out for the whole life — that is to say, for a life span of 70 to 84 years. In this way one can establish the high spots in that life and also the length of time between them. One must never forget that the potential of any current transit cycle is conditioned by what happened or was realized during the preceding cycle. The past cycle — the lived-through portion of the life — must be analyzed before there can be an understanding of any present situation. The whole life must be the background upon which to examine any particular moment.

As Pluto and Neptune cannot complete their cycle during a life span, one must begin by noting the quarters of the chart which will be emphasized by their transit motion, as well as the major aspects they will make to the natal chart during the entire life. The quarter of the chart most emphasized by transiting Pluto indicates the sphere in which the universe or society will make its most fundamental *demands* upon the individual. It also points out the area of life in which the individual can make his most significant contribution to the needs of the times. The quarters of the birth-chart accentuated by transiting Neptune indicate the spheres in which the behavior patterns of the conscious ego will be questioned or subtly dissolved through the pressure of collective events and values.

As Uranus can take an entire life or more to complete its cycle, the truly individualized use of the Uranus function is measured from the age at which the planet first reaches a natal-chart Angle. If, for example, the natal position of Uranus is in the 4th House, then the individual cycle will not begin until it reaches the Descendant by transit. In this case, the meaning of the summer quarter will be particularly important as the source of Uranian inspiration to the individual.

The Saturn and Jupiter cycles begin to have a truly individual significance after they first reach the Ascendant. The years from birth until that moment are a period in which these planets "act" as hereditary, familial or societal influences upon the growing individual. However, the age of a person when these planets reach the Ascendant for the first time is an important factor to consider for one cannot usually speak of "individual use" of either Saturn or Jupiter when the Ascendant contact takes place in early childhood. Because of this fact, the study of the generic (therefore non-individual) cycles of Saturn and Jupiter is extremely significant.* In these 30-year and 12-year cycles, the critical phases of development are marked by the transiting squares, opposition and return to the natal position.

As Jupiter and Saturn should always be studied in relation to each other, one should note where the transiting Jupiter-Saturn conjunctions, squares and oppositions fall in the birth-chart. The conjunctions are especially important keys to the basic pattern of a person's relationship to both his social and national destiny. They come at 20-year intervals, so there are usually at least three of them in a normal life span. Especially in the case of public-oriented people, one should note the transiting squares and oppositions, particularly in terms of the natal Houses involved, and furthermore where the conjunctions and oppositions of transiting Jupiter-Uranus, Jupiter-Neptune, Saturn-Uranus and Saturn-Neptune fall in the birth-chart, as well as the House positions of the critical phases in the Uranus-Neptune cycle. Finally, the astrologer should also study the eclipse and nodal cycles, and the oft-repeated retrograde cycles of the faster moving planets: Mercury, Venus and Mars. All of these are part of the cyclic unfoldment of being as related to the transits.

---

*This point is explained in detail in Chapter 6, "The Saturn Cycle."

The foundation for the interpretation of *all* these transit cycles is the age factor. The age of an individual at the time of the critical phases in the transit cycles provides a basic clue to the way in which these crises should be interpreted. By charting the critical phases of all the transit cycles according to the 7-year periods mentioned later and according to the age at which they occur, the astrologer will see a very revealing composite picture of the life as a whole. The relationships shown by such a study are of the greatest importance in understanding a present problem or crisis, and they will be completely missed if the astrologer is too lazy or event-oriented to look at more than the year or two near the moment of consultation. Above all, in humanistic astrology the individual is free to work out his own destiny. Astrology must present a category of possibilities from which a person may choose, rather than dictate inevitabilities against which he is powerless. Astrology can reveal possibilities — not certainties, and no one interpreting a birth-chart should promise anything. Humanistic astrology then becomes an exercise in making inner decisions — in selecting what one *chooses* to be out of what one *might* potentially become.

II

The Age Factor

In the humanistic approach, events are important only in the context of the *meaning* given to them by an individual. This context of meaning is directly related to and dependent on the age of that individual at the time of the event — for age is the "container" in which life's experiences are held. The exact same event occurring at different times in a life would have a totally different meaning. Take, for example, the experience of accidentally being locked in a bathroom. Such an experience might well be deeply traumatic for a 2-year-old, while an adult would probably find it either amusing or annoying.

Although most astrologers realize, at least in theory, that progressions and transits must be considered in relation to the age of the client, in the actual interpretation of a birth-chart they often ignore age and read the chart the way they were taught — i.e., by the cookbook method; they simply do not know how to employ the age factor. Most astrological texts ignore the age factor, perhaps because writers feel that it is too obvious to mention, or, more likely, because omitting it is an editorial necessity. For example, a standard text of 300 pages would run to perhaps 3000 pages or more if the "meaning" of each aspect were presented in terms of the different ages at which it might be experienced. A second and perhaps more fundamental problem lies in the breadth of an astrologer's experience. The majority of an astrologer's clients will usually be contemporaries. Thus, ninety per-cent of the clients he sees will be of a single age group — his own. How can he then be expected to have a knowledge of the life cycle broader than his own experience of life? If a student of astrology can look neither to books nor teachers, nor to the experience of his astrological practice to learn about the age factor, where then can he look? Modern depth psychology provides one source: the work of Carl Jung.*

THE LIFE CYCLE. A holistic view of life is fundamental to any discussion or interpretation of the age factor. One must see that life itself is a cycle, and that the different periods of life are merely phases in that cycle. Like the phases of the Moon, the life cycle has a waxing half and a waning half. Therefore it is an error to assume, as many people do, that the meaning of life ends with the period of youth and expansion.

---

*Cf. particularly Vol. 8, The Collected Works of C. G. Jung: *The Structure and Dynamics of the Psyche,* pp. 387-403, "The Stages of Life."

The waning half of life is as full of meaning as the waxing half, but the *meaning changes*. Astrologers must consider this difference between the problems of youth and those of old age and must recognize that they cannot be solved in the same way. Youth, the ascending wave of life, is basically extroverted, a time of growth and expansion on all levels of development — physical, mental, emotional and social. The problems of this time of life are extroverted problems — education, marriage (and divorce), children, money, social position, career and sex. The challenge is to clear away the barriers to expansion on all these levels, and this requires extroverted solutions — i.e., action in the physical/material world.

After a symbolic full moon period, the descending wave of life begins. The problems of this second half of life are introverted and necessitate a *reappraisal* of all those values esteemed during the first half. It becomes necessary to appreciate the importance of ideals *opposite* to those of youth. The challenge is to become increasingly more objective toward everything that seemed important during the first half of life. Values become less absolute. Everything human is relative because, psychologically, everything rests on an inner polarity of values. This axiom is one of the foundations of astrological symbolism as well as of Jungian depth psychology, and it should be fundamental to astrological interpretation as well. Many psychological problems which arise during the second half of life derive from incompletions and omissions during the first half. The attempt to prolong youth is a result of not having actually experienced it in its proper time. While it should be clear that the waning half of the life cycle is not the time for extroverted concerns, it should be equally obvious that the waxing half is not the time for introverted concerns. "To everything there is a season, and a time to every purpose under the heavens..."

THE GENERIC STRUCTURE OF LIFE. There are two distinct ways of approaching the age factor. The one most familiar to astrologers is to trace the planetary cycles individually, interpreting their phases in relation to the specific planetary energy. Although there is much to be gained from such a study, it must be remembered that all the planets are moving at the same time. Holistic astrology refers not only to a holistic view of the birth-chart and the individual whom it represents, but also to a holistic view of the solar system. Concentrating on the cycle of one planet alone produces a lopsided perspective.

The second approach is to study the generic structure of human life by establishing the stages of individual development which can be normally expected on the basis of age exclusively and regardless of any astrological factors. This study should actually precede the first, as it establishes the generic foundation for the individualized interpretation

Major Astrological Correspondences with the Age Factor

Age 7   Waxing square of Saturn to its natal place.

Age 12   First return of Jupiter to its natal place.

Age 14   Saturn opposition natal Saturn.

Age 19-   New nodal cycle begins.

Age 21   Waning square of Saturn to its natal place.

Age 24   2nd return of Jupiter to its natal place.

Age 27+   Progressed Moon returns to its natal place.

Age 28   Uranus trine natal Uranus; inversion of the position of the Moon's nodes.

Age 29½   Saturn returns to its natal place.

Age 30   The natal Sun-Moon aspect repeats itself in the progressions. Jupiter opposes natal Jupiter.

Age 36   2nd waxing square of Saturn to its natal place. 3rd return of Jupiter to its natal place.

Age 38-   New nodal cycle begins.

Age 42   Uranus opposition natal Uranus; Neptune in waxing square to natal Neptune; Jupiter opposition natal Jupiter.

Age 44   2nd opposition of Saturn to its natal place.

Age 47   Inversion of the position of the Moon's nodes.

Age 48   4th return of Jupiter to its natal place.

Age 51   2nd waning square of Saturn to its natal place.

Age 55   Progressed Moon returns for second time to its natal place.

Age 56   Uranus in waning trine to Uranus; beginning of 4th nodal cycle.

Age 59-60 2nd return of Saturn to its natal place; 5th return of Jupiter to its natal place; Pluto in waxing square to its natal place; the natal Sun-Moon aspect repeats itself for the second time in the progressions.

Age 63   Waning square of Uranus to its natal place.

Age 65   Inversion of the position of the Moon's nodes.

Age 66   3rd waxing square of Saturn to its natal place.

Age 72   6th return of Jupiter to its natal place.

Age 75   Beginning of 5th nodal cycle; 3rd opposition of Saturn to its natal place.

Age 80   3rd waning square of Saturn to its natal place.

Age 82-83 2nd return of progressed Moon to its natal place.

Age 84   Uranus returns to its natal place; 7th return of Jupiter to its natal place; inversion of the position of the Moon's nodes.

of progressions and transits; without this information, such interpretations can never be really helpful or vitally significant in an individual sense. It not only places the present problems of the client into a perspective, but also gives an added dimension of meaning to past experiences or events which may have led to the present crisis.

The greatest importance of this generic structure is that it exists for the psyche as well as the body, and it operates on an unconscious level in each individual however unique he may feel himself to be. This common psychic structure is what Jung calls the "Collective Unconscious" and what Rudhyar calls "the generic soul in all men, the human-ness which is the common foundation from which surge even the most exalted flights of devotion and creative imagination, the subtlest over-tones of mysticism and art".* This generic structure of human destiny can be known, and along with an understanding of the *individual* cycles of growth revealed by the progressions and transits, it is possible to attain a knowledge of Self with a depth of meaning rarely encountered. The procedure is simple; yet, as with all basically simple things, the actual understanding of what is revealed by this procedure requires careful reflection and a deep sense of psychological evaluation.

THE SEVEN-YEAR CYCLE. Rudhyar has suggested that the complete development of man, *as an individual personality* theoretically and archetypally considered, takes 84 years — a complete Uranus cycle. There are many ways to divide this cycle. The seven 12-year periods and the twelve 7-year periods will be treated at length in Chapter 5, "The Jupiter Cycle"; and Chapter 8, "The Uranus Cycle". Additionally, this eighty-four year cycle can be divided in three periods of 28 years each. These roughly correspond to the generic cycles of Saturn and will be dealt with at length in Chapter 6, "The Saturn Cycle." Each 28-year period corresponds to an essential level of development of the personality — the hereditary, the individual and the spiritual. However, as most people never reach much higher than the first or hereditary level and rarely live a truly "individual" life, Rudhyar has found it best to concentrate the analysis upon the more traditional 70-year cycle, containing ten 7-year periods. The dividing point is the thirty-fifth year. Up to that age the tide of the life-force mounts, and thereafter begins to recede. This ebbing of the life-force is a well-known fact in the realm of sports and aviation; and according to esoteric doctrines, after the 36th year there is a slow, progressive repolarization of all the nerves and vital centers in the body, and in those psychic structures which are correlated to them. At approximately this time the truly individual Self of a human being *should* begin to operate. It is an age which often coincides in a person's life with some definite step or decision — inner, outer or both — which gives an entirely new direction to the consciousness of the individual.

American Astrology Magazine, January 1942.

Prior to age 35, a human being is trying to build his life on the foundation of what his heredity, education and social environment have given him. During this period problems arise in relation to youthful illusions, the mastering of the parental images, and the overcoming of obstacles to his profession or marriage — to all those things which are a part of the expansion of life. Youth finds the solution to such problems primarily in terms of *outer* activity. Often the problems arise as a result of exaggerated expectations, under-estimation of difficulties, and unjustified optimism or pessimism. Such problems can be grouped as *contradictions between subjective assumptions and external facts.*

Another group of problems are due to inner psychic difficulties and can exist even when the social or professional activities present no problem. In many cases the disturbance of psychic equilibrium is caused by the sexual instinct, as Freud has demonstrated, while in other cases there is a feeling of inferiority due to strong sensitivity. According to Jung, young people who have had to struggle for existence are mostly spared inner problems, while those who for some reason or other have no difficulty with external adaptation, run into sexual problems or conflicts arising from a sense of inferiority. The one feature particular to the problems of the first half of life is a clinging to the childhood level of consciousness, and a resistance to the fateful forces in and around the individual which would involve him in the world. Of this feature Jung says, "Something in us wishes to remain a child, to be unconscious or, at most, conscious only of the ego; to reject everything strange, or else subject it to our will; to do nothing, or else indulge our own craving for pleasure or power."*

During each half of the 70-year cycle there are five 7-year periods. These describe the flow of the life-force and establish five levels of integration which Rudhyar has named: physiological, volitional, psychological, social and spiritual-personal. These levels correspond to the several "bodies" of esoteric teaching: physical, etheric, emotional-mental, buddhic and spiritual. According to this concept, the individual's task is to work with the forces of integration as they operate successively at each level. To become a creative and complete personality, one must try to assimilate and integrate into himself as much of the universe as he can, not only physical nourishment but also the learning and wisdom of past generations and the social substance of one's relationships — from sex to politics. If this integration is effectively accomplished, the spirit will descend into the integrated personality around the 35th birthday. The result of such a visitation of the spirit, if it takes place at all, (and at that on a deep unconscious level, unnoticed by the conscious awareness) will become clear during the second half of life. True personality

---

*Jung, C.W. Vol. 8: *The Stages of Life*, p. 393.

The 70-Year Life Cycle

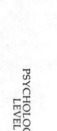

The Waxing Hemi-cycle

Phase 5, Age 28-35: Release of creative endowment of the personality. Possibility of "2nd birth" as a creative seed for the future. Negatively, progressive crystallization of personal attitude in terms of ancestral and social patterns.

Phase 4, Age 21-28: Choice of associates and of one's type of social participation. Establishment of the basic attitude towards the fruits of the personal and social-cultural past. Rebellion against family and/or society.

Phase 3, Age 14-21: Development of the emotional and mental faculties. An emotionally centered self-orientation towards associates, friends, comrades, and as well towards the culture, religion and institutions of one's society.

Phase 2, Age 7-14: Building of the conscious ego; development of the I-sense. Testing of one's personal powers in active self-expression.

Phase 1, Age 0-7: Development of the body, its organs and their psychic overtones. Basic adjustment to outside pressures, especially within the family.

The Waning Hemi-cycle

Phase 6, Age 35-42: Culmination of physical and personal endowment. Further crystallization of personal attitude & of the activities and consciousness developed between ages 28 and 35. Need to decide clearly what one has to do in life, perhaps leading to attempts at purifying the personality.

Phase 7, Age 42-49: Leading a routine life and passive submission to things as they are, or need to revise actively attitude toward intimates. Attempts at making a new start in life.

Phase 8, Age 49-56: Education of others. Assuming greater social responsibility. Negatively, mental rigidity due to incapacity to change adopted life-attitude and behavior.

Phase 9, Age 56-63: Possibility of 3rd birth in the Uranian cycle. Demonstration of the capacity to focus the spiritual quality of being inherent at birth *through* the personality. New spiritual activities or, negatively, further crystallization of mind and feeling responses.

Phase 10, Age 63-70: Conscious preparation for the after-life — or senility. Radiating wisdom or, negatively, sense of boredom, emptiness, futility. Bringing the life to some sort of seed-consummation.

INDIVIDUAL OR PERSONALITY LEVEL

SOCIAL-CULTURAL LEVEL

PSYCHOLOGICAL LEVEL

POWER LEVEL

ORGANIC LEVEL

BIRTH/DEATH

0-70

7

14

21

28

35

42

49

56

63

integration shows in an increasingly creative and luminous life, radiating vision, serene power and significance, and the capacity to lead others to greater integration and nobler living.

During the second half of life one retraces his steps from level to level, as if "reaction" moulded itself faithfully upon the pattern of "action" established by the youthful person during the 35 years of the waxing tide of vitality. There is a direct relationship, for instance, between the period extending from age 14 to 21 and the period extending from age 49 to 56. Both of these periods correspond to the psychological, emotional-mental level of development. This relationship could be called karmic in that the behavior of the youth tends to *condition* the way in which the consciousness and the social and personal reactions of the adult about to enter old age will develop. The failures and successes, the fears and the noble confrontations experienced in youth will tend to bring a harvest of corresponding value in the adult who passes through the fifties. Likewise, the tragedies of the forties are, to some extent, the repercussions of the problems met during the twenties. Rudhyar concludes:

> ...man constantly meets his past after he passes the mid-point of his life. What he does as a result of the meeting conditions in turn either his future life (if reincarnation is accepted as a fact), or his after-death state (if personal immortality in transcendental realms is believed in), or it simply contributes to the moulding of the culture and social behavior of the future generations (if one accepts only racial-cultural immortality). (*American Astrology,* Jan. 1942)

The counselling of adults must therefore have different objectives from the counselling of young people. It will no longer be a question of clearing away the obstacles that hinder expansion, production and ascent; one must instead stress everything that will help the descent and the concomitant development of wider *consciousness*. The transition from life's morning to life's afternoon means a reassessment of one's earlier values. One must come to appreciate the opposite of one's former ideals, says Jung; to perceive the error in those former convictions; and to feel how much antagonism and even hatred lay in what, until then, had passed for love. *Not* that one must throw away everything that seemed good and true, and live in complete opposition to his former tendency, but Jung insists that one must learn the lesson of relativity. One should conserve his previous values while recognizing the value of their opposites and consciously admit the *relative* validity of all opinions. This is what is meant by the development of consciousness — the keynote of the second half of life. Such a development is not easy, as Jung remarks:

> ...nature cares nothing whatsoever about a higher level of consciousness and society does not value these feats of the psyche very highly either; its prizes are always given for achievement and not for personality...We overlook the fact that the social goal is attained only at the cost of a diminution of personality. (*The Stages of Life,* p. 394)

The Waxing Hemicycle*

Age 0 to 7: The Organic Level — Development of the body, its organs and their psychic overtones. Basic adjustment to outside pressures, especially within the family.

During this period the body and the basic psychic structures of the future personality are built. The substance which will fill these structures is furnished by heredity, both genetic and cultural, by the environmental conditions of the family, and by the general social conditions prevailing at the time and place of birth. These will produce either opportunities for harmonious growth or frustrating tensions. Everything that happens at this organic level of development will leave its mark. These conditions influence not only the biological growth of the child, but also his basic instincts and the essential psychological over-tones of these instincts. As the period of maximum growth and learning, not only will a child achieve 70-74% of his physical growth potential, but at the same time he will master all the essential skills needed to live as an independent being. He learns to feed and dress himself, to walk, talk, read, write and do simple arithmetic. He also learns the specific dangers of his environment and the things necessary for survival, including negative or anti-social behavior such as lying, cheating and stealing. His basic values and beliefs are instilled in him at this time. All of these things give a child his particular characteristic attitude toward life, and many psychologists are of the opinion that the adult never really manages to overcome and transform whatever was built into his body and psyche before the age of seven.

Equally important to the child's later development is the influence of missing factors. Just as a lack of calcium during this time will inhibit the development of strong, straight bones, the lack of loving will inhibit the development of that child's ability to love. The adult who goes through life looking for a mother probably missed the experience of being nurtured at this phase. Thus, those aspects — especially conjunctions — which become exact by progression during these first 7 years of life will give the key to the basic conditioning of the child's attitude toward life.

Age 7 to 14: The Power Level — Building of the conscious ego; development of the I-sense. Testing of one's personal powers in active self-expression.

The first period ends during the seventh year, but before the seventh birthday. This change of level or phase often occurs at the time when the first permanent teeth emerge, which, according to Rudhyar, is a

---

*Many of the following ideas were formulated by Rudhyar in his articles in *American Astrology* Magazine and in his books, especially *Occult Preparations for a New Age* (Quest Books, 1975).

significant symptom of a very basic organic and spiritual crisis. As the mature, self-grown teeth replace the milk teeth, the child must then "chew" his experiences on the basis of his own ego-characteristics rather than on his mother's example. The waxing square of Saturn to its natal position is the astrological correspondence to this turning-point and reveals either an acceleration or a delay in the process of growth.

The psychic equivalent to the new set of teeth is the development of the ego as an autonomous psychic structure. Near age 7, Uranus reaches the second phase of its cycle* — the phase of substantiation or incarnation. The principle of individuality, the "I", begins to operate more forcefully within the organism as the child increasingly speaks of himself in the first person. Until the child says "I", he or she is still an expression of the influence of the parents rather than an autonomous psychic organism. This is so regardless of whether the child accepts or rebels against the image which his parents and family attempt to impress upon him. In either case, during this period his truly personal existence begins, and the child reveals an increasingly definite and individual response to life. He or she will attempt to exteriorize his inner feelings — assuming attitudes and creating situations wilfully in order to test the reactions of his body and psyche, as well as how his family and peers will react. To build his sense of "I" and his personal power, the child must make forceful gestures and take a personal stand, and then observe what happens. He must measure himself *against* the limitations imposed by parents, teachers, authority figures, and his peers.

The basic issue in this second 7-year period is *creative self-assertion* — the development of the will. To express himself harmoniously, the child must be able to assimilate fully the experience which life brings him. Whatever happens during this second period will greatly influence his capacity to reveal himself to himself, and to express outwardly what is revealed. The will may be expressed either through activities directed *against* some potential or actual adversary, or it may manifest creatively through activities which mold inert materials into an image of one's own choice. It may be seen in the competitive games of children with their opportunities for the exercise of leadership, prowess and power, the extreme example of which is gang warfare. This same force of will may, on the other hand, be expressed through the spontaneous play of the artistic faculties, especially at the age of 10½ — mid-point of this 7-year period. In creativity there exists no adversary, only materials to be used, fashioned and transformed into what one wills them to be. The potential difficulty here is that the child at this age finds his creative efforts stifled by the various social and cultural conventions and taboos of the adult

---

*Cf. Chapter 8. The phases of the Uranus cycle referred to here change every seven years; and each phase begins as transiting Uranus makes a new aspect to natal Uranus by 30° increments, hence by semi-sextile, sextile, square, trine, quincunx, etc.

world. Exquisitely perfected toys do not provide an opportunity for individual creativity to flourish, and the child misses the excitement of self-discovery in seeing the results of his own efforts at shaping and transforming raw materials. He becomes a mechanic — a technician rather than a creator. Out of this womb is born a specimen of the collective mentality instead of an individual.

Age 14 to 21: The Psychological Level — Emotional and mental development. Emotionally-centred self-orientation to associates, friends, comrades, as well as towards the culture, religion and institutions of one's society.

This 7-year period begins with the crisis of puberty. According to Jung, the eruption of sexuality corresponds to birth out of the psychic womb of the parental and family environment. A conscious differentiation from the parents should now take place. The father and mother should now be seen as adults (although in the strictest sense this term does not often apply), as human beings with the right to make mistakes, rather than as the infallible parent-figures of one's early childhood. At the beginning of this period, Saturn opposes its birth position and the sextile of Uranus to natal Uranus begins the third phase of its cycle. The opposition aspect in humanistic astrology is always a symbol of *objective awareness* through the impact of experiences in human *relationship*. In the Saturn cycle, the object of awareness is the sense of responsibility in one's intimate relationships, and this problem of relationship presents the central challenge of adolescence. Prior to the age of 14, the young person will express himself creatively and assert his will without necessarily any regard for the results of his actions or their effect on other people. His fundamental desire is simply to be himself — to discover through experimentation the possibilities latent within him. In this third phase of the life-cycle he has the chance to become more fully what he is through Saturn, while becoming different through the impact of the new type of everyday experiences he now has with Uranus.

Suddenly, at the onset of adolescence (for adolescence is something which does not happen gradually), he feels a new urge growing within him — the urge to form deep and significant relationships. Under the stimulation of biological and glandular changes, adolescent love is born and becomes the prime mover of the third phase of the life-cycle. On the biological-sexual level, and occasionally on other levels as well, the adolescent becomes subservient to a more-than-personal life-rhythm. In one way or another, he begins to feel the urge to participate in the rhythm of the larger whole of which he is an expression — the human race. Seemingly fateful forces, both within and without the individual, draw him into the world and involve him in it. Things previously alien to his experience are now of vital concern to him. The horizons widen, and the previously narrow frame of reference is shattered in the tension of opposites, leading ideally to a broader and higher range of consciousness. For the first time the young person must learn *by contrast* (the opposition aspect) who and what he is. Love becomes the great revealer. As confrontation is the nature of the opposition aspect, the beloved becomes the mirror image of the self and its needs. Initially, the loved one is an idealized figure based on the illusions of childhood and formed principally by the mass media. When the ideal image is projected onto a real human being, the experience of the difference forces one to modify those illusions. The loved one can eventually become an embodiment of the highest aspirations of the self when true conscious relationship replaces projection. Before the emerging individual can truly realize his full potential he must first envision it. Love is this vision.

The school years of this period have a purpose far greater than the simple amassing of data. This is the time one learns social responsibility. Also they are the years of higher education and, more important, *voluntary* education. Before this age the child was legally bound to remain in school. The parents were responsible for sending him to school and the teachers were responsible for keeping him there. However, after the age of 14 (or shortly thereafter) the student is free to leave; and if he remains, it is by choice. Thus accepting the responsibility for his own education, the young person becomes an active participant and takes the first step in the assumption of full, adult responsibility; and by the end of this period he may take his individual stand socially, politically and professionally.

Age 21 to 28: The Social-Cultural Level — Choice of associates and of one's type of social participation. Establishment of the basic attitude towards the fruits of the personal and social-cultural past. Rebellion against family and/or society.

This 7-year period is linked astrologically to the first waning square of Saturn and the waxing square of Uranus, which opens the fourth phase of the Uranus cycle. The latter aspect coincides with the effort to break through (waxing square) into the professional, commercial and cultural world; and to fit oneself as well as possible into the life of one's community. The Saturn aspect, on the other hand, points to the need to cut oneself off from the past (waning square) and from the attitudes which were based on the carefree life typical of the school years. Many of the ideals and aims previously held must be examined in a new light and adapted to the realities of day-to-day adult existence. This may be difficult and strenuous for many people. Youth tends to cling to its adolescent, emotional attitudes, and would like to continue to act as if life were a field for the unrestricted expression of Self according to strictly personal desires. In this fourth phase of the life-cycle, the last remaining vestiges of youth are shed.

The experiences of this age period reveal very clearly the difference between a waxing square and a waning square. The crisis described by a waxing square is extroverted and exists on the level of *activity.* It is often accompanied by a sense of elation and adventure or excitement, as the individual rushes out to meet the difficulties which life puts in his path and to work out his own destiny in an objective and concrete manner. The waxing Uranus square affects the young person in this way and directs his attention toward the *future* — to the goals he will set himself to accomplish. What lies ahead for him are new and interesting opportunities. Concurrently, the waning square of Saturn directs the attention inward toward an assessment of the *past,* pointing to those things which must be left behind, or at least modified and reconsidered. It challenges one to break with established habits and ideals, often a very difficult task. The crisis described by this waning square is introverted, demanding growth in personal maturity. Such personal needs, however, can only be fulfilled by attending to the needs of society. Thus, the principal lesson of this waning Saturn square will be to realize the necessity to act in a responsible manner in all types of relationship, whether they be interpersonal or social. The success of the Uranian effort to blaze a new path as an individual will depend on one's success in breaking away from old attachments and attitudes under the Saturn square, and the success in interpersonal as well as social relationships will depend on the strength of an individual's will to attain psychological maturity.

Astrology clarifies the point that one's personal success in later years will depend almost entirely on the way in which an individual manages these two squares between the ages of 21 and 28. The astrologer should also look to strong progressed or transit aspects to the natal chart during this period. These will show the specific opportunities or confrontations which will enable the young adult to break out of the psychic womb constituted by the parental influences of childhood, as well as by the emotional and intellectual attitudes built into the ego by a particular socio-cultural and economic environment. These attitudes and influences form the barriers to one's true experience of Self, and until one can recognize them as precisely that and not confuse them with the "I", one will not be able to assert his true individuality.

Everything experienced in life prior to the age of 28, therefore, revolves primarily around one's relationship to his family — or whatever may have substituted for it. A person must grow and discover himself — his own truth and life-purpose while living *within* a family environment. At the same time, the individual must make an effort to *grow out of* the family and separate himself psychically from its predominant influences if he is to become a true individual. As one emerges from the state of dependence upon parents and family patterns if not physically at least spiritually, the problem takes on a new and different form in his life.

After the age of 21, people generally seek to build their own families — they train themselves for a job, they marry, and they have their own children. The majority of people have experienced these things before reaching the age of 28, or at least they know the way in which they want to organize their lives. What happens after 28, until the next major turning-point in the life near age 56 to 60, will be the result of the options taken and the attitudes adopted before the age of 28. What must be clearly understood, therefore, is that whatever is done before the age of 28 will represent, psychologically, the various ways adopted in the effort to emerge from the family matrix and from the pressures of the social environment. The alternative to this is a passive adjustment — quietly accepting and following the established family and social patterns.

Age 28 to 35: Individual or Personality Level — Release of creative endowment of the personality. Possibility of a "2nd birth", as a creative germ of the future. Negatively, progressive crystallization of personal attitude in terms of ancestral and existing social patterns.

In the threefold division of the Uranus cycle, the 28th year marks the beginning of the second period with the trine of Uranus to its natal position. This opens the fifth phase of the cycle. The progressed Moon also returns to its birth position in that year, and the positions of the Moon's nodes are inverted — the transiting North node being on the natal South node, and the transiting South node on the natal North node. In the progressed lunation cycle, the Sun and Moon repeat the same aspect at age 30 that they did at birth, and transiting Saturn returns to its natal position and begins a new cycle. In addition to all this, at the age of 30 transiting Jupiter and Saturn will be in an aspect opposed, and therefore complimentary, to their natal aspect. Thus, if they were in conjunction at birth, they will be in opposition at age 30. From all this an astrologer can readily see that the period from age 27 to 30 is a most important turning-point in the lives of *all* people. A second such turning-point will occur during the period age 56 to 60, and will be discussed later. Rudhyar refers to these ages as the potential second and third births. In this phase, the individual is born out of the collective; while in the rebirth yet to come, the spiritual self is born out of the personality.

Each individual conceived is the sum-total of the collective past and, up to the 28th year, remains primarily a result of his ancestral and cultural heritage. The purpose of these first 28 years — the first complete cycle of Saturn — is to assimilate all that one can of this past. Then, and not until then, can the true creative individual emerge. Only out of an individualized synthesis of the collective influences and fruits of the past can the fully-expressed personality flow. Prior to the 28th year one is still dominated by these collective influences, and unfortunately many people continue long after that time to remain passive followers of their ancestral ways — undistinguished examples of a national or local culture and a collective mentality. At 28, however, the door is opened and one is presented with the *opportunity* to begin asserting his true individuality, manifesting his own unique destiny and making his own particular contribution to the world.

The Uranus trine — symbol of this opportunity for creative vision — is capable of making one realize *what he is here for,* however dimly this sense of relation to some ideal, goal or function may be felt. Each one of us, in the humanistic view, is potentially a completely new element which can be added to the human race — a potential answer to a new human need. The realization of that need comes around age 28 — the time of a possible "second birth" at the level of psychological and mental achievement. The 28th year is the potential beginning of life as a creative individual. From age 28 to 42 the basic issue will be the definite establishment of self as an integrated personality working in a new and particular way in one's community, and capable of producing something of value within this community. Saturn's return to its natal place marks the opportunity to give a new meaning to one's life, based on a truly individual attitude and also on the capacity to relate oneself responsibly to the greater whole of which one can be a conscious and creative part. The reversal of the Jupiter-Saturn birth aspect reveals the possibility of a more objective outlook on the traditional social, cultural and religious ways of one's times.

Theoretically, everything that has happened since birth has been leading, in the spiritually successful life, to the realization around age 28 of the individual contribution one can make to life. From then onwards, life can have an original and personal meaning, but only if one realizes more or less clearly the type of ideal, purpose or human need which he is capable of fulfilling and then concentrates his attention *consciously* on this goal. He must discover his own ways of taking an individual and independent stand in relation to the problems which he chooses to meet. Whatever one succeeds in accomplishing or producing before age 28 will be the flowering of his past — his soul past or his genetic past. It will not be an expression of his individual identity. A person may be born with special gifts; however, what matters is what he will do with them as an individual. He must make them serve some new, consciously decided purpose, or else those gifts will use him. In other words, the test is always *how to use* one's legacy from the past on all levels as a means to reveal the true spiritual identity. That is why it is important near age 28 to transform the relationship to one's past in such a way that, instead of being simply an expression of it, a person may decide how he will *use* it as a means to contribute something new — something which did not exist before he existed.

The Waning Hemicycle

Age 35 to 42: Individual or Personality Level — Culmination of physical and personal endowment. Further crystallization of personal attitude in terms of the activity and consciousness developed between ages 28 and 35. Need to decide clearly what one wants to do in life, perhaps leading to attempts at purifying the personality.

This 7-year period marks the beginning of the waning hemicycle of life. Prior to this time, the life-energies have been building and expanding; now they begin their descending wave. Each successive level from this point onward will be an introverted expression of its extroverted counterpart during the ascending wave, and the *opposite* values and ideals will come into play. The extroverted level corresponding to age 35 to 42 is the period immediately preceding it — age 28 to 35. Together these two levels form a plateau. (See diagram: "The 70-year Life Cycle") Both are Personality levels, the earlier dealing with the external manifestations and the release of creative energies; while the age 35 to 42 period deals with the personal attitudes and beliefs from which creativity springs. The latter period makes more concrete what was initiated in the previous one.

Of this plateau period between age 28 and 42, the basic requirement of life, according to Rudhyar,* is to be a self and to take one's place in the world as a self. This means being self-determined and self-sustained, aware of one's individual destiny. But before one can go on to meet this life-destiny, he must first free himself from the final vestiges of external influences, and consciously choose his own basic reaction to life. The best opportunity for such an awareness of Self will come in the 35th year, which is not only the mid-point of this plateau period, but also the mid-point of the life-cycle itself. Symbolically, the 35th year is the full moon of the life-cycle — the awareness point. Here the external confronts the internal, and the realizations which can come from a synthesis of these two factors can provide the vision of a true sense of "I". Here it becomes possible for a person to "see" why he does what he does, and then to choose either to do it or not do it. Choice, however, requires an acceptance of responsibility. As long as a person remains bound by the psychic apron-strings of some "mother image" — be it an individual person (such as a parent, marriage partner or spiritual mentor), a group or institution, or an ideology — he will have something outside himself determining his actions and assuming responsibility for them.

Feelings of guilt or inferiority provide an excellent excuse for perpetuating this kind of emotional immaturity. These feelings are fed by the memory of past failures, and by the projection of these failures into

*Cf. *Horoscope* magazine; Rudhyar's article in the November and December 1956 issues.

the future. The refusal to accept responsibility for his failures places one in the position of permanent victim — forever at the mercy of whatever he has chosen to be the "mother image" which runs his life. If, during the age 28-35 period a person has not succeeded in separating himself from the need for a psychic scapegoat, then the vision which he sees at 35 may, at least temporarily, pull the emotional rug out from under him. One may see that his life does not work and that the old scapegoats no longer serve him. So, he goes out to find new ones. Superficially, he may appear to be regrasping past opportunities; however, what he is actually doing is looking for a new "mother image" to assume responsibility for his life — a new womb to crawl into. Failing to see that it is his beliefs which must be transformed, he will go out in search of new techniques, a new ideology, a new mentor or a new marriage partner. Unfortunately, none of these will provide a solid ground-of-being from which he can meet the crises of the following 7-year period (age 42 to 49) and without which the experience of menopause can be chaotic or even tragic. This period begins approximately at the waxing square of Saturn and ends around the time of the waxing square of Neptune.

Age 42 to 49: Social-Cultural Level — Leading a routine life and passive submission to things as they are, or the need to revise actively one's attitude toward intimates. Attempts at making a new start in life.

This phase of the life-cycle corresponds to the 7-year period age 21 to 28, which is also a social level. Astrologically, both periods are marked by transits of Saturn and Uranus. In the earlier period these aspects were squares, symbolizing the extroverted nature of that time. The emerging adult moved out into the world, perhaps married, established himself socially and created his own interpersonal relationships. The aspects of Saturn and Uranus in this later period are oppositions, indicating awareness rather than action. The Uranus opposition occurs at the beginning of this 7-year period, and shortly thereafter, at approximately age 45, Saturn opposes its natal position for the second time. Thus, the primary challenge of this 7-year period is the need to find the *real* meaning and value in one's interpersonal and social relationships.

Establishing a new attitude toward one's relationships may require that certain habit patterns of many years duration be broken. The pressures of family, business and social considerations need no longer dictate the selection of one's friends. Extroverted motivations for maintaining relationships often no longer apply; therefore a personal value for those relationships must be found. A marriage held together "for the sake of the children" will dissolve when those children grow up and leave home unless a truly personal *raison d'etre* is found. Likewise, relationships originally formed because they would advance one's career or social position become meaningless with the realization that one has probably already risen as high on the social or business ladder as he will go.

The problems which arise during this 7-year period are based on a sense of loneliness which becomes increasingly difficult to bear. To compensate for this feeling of isolation one may try to escape into a dream world (soap operas, romantic novels and the like), lose himself in his work or social activities, rush off into some heroic adventure, or even run away from home to start life anew. *An undercurrent of anxiety runs through this entire period* — a general feeling of "last chance". One may find himself grabbing at love compulsively as though it were the brass ring on a merry-go-round that will never go round again. The emotional upsets that accompany "falling in love" precipitate a new kind of adolescent crisis. While the adolescent is in love with love, people in their forties seek love to absorb or blot out a sense of failure. This rush to make a new start, to find love before it is too late, can result in severe emotional turmoil and the outcome of it can be tragic.

Although the descending wave of life actually began in the previous 7-year period, it is not until age 42 to 49 that one has the conscious awareness that he is in the second half of life. As he watches his parents' generation die off and his own generation aging, suddenly one day there comes the realization that *he* is the older generation. Should a person forget for a moment the reality of his age, his grown children and the mass media will serve as a constant reminder. The natural, immediate reaction to this is denial. Many people try to prolong youth by imitating the dress, mannerisms or speech of young people, and some even reject association with those older than themselves as though aging were a contagious disease.

By the forties a person notices that his body is increasingly losing its energy and staying power, and that he can no longer depend on it as automatically as he did in the past. This causes a great deal of anxiety and results in a pre-occupation with the body — the way it looks, feels and behaves. Because in most people's belief patterns the body is so intrinsically tied to their ability to love and be loved, this pre-occupation with the body is frequently experienced on the level of relationship. A man's waning sexual potency may drive him to seek out the companionship of a younger woman as proof of his virility. The problem is entirely different for a woman. Her sex drive may be stronger in her forties than in earlier years; however, since she has always judged her sexuality in terms of her desirability, the appearance of wrinkles, sagging skin and the other external signs of age are equally traumatic. The growing awareness of physical decline points to the need for a basic change in one's attitude toward others as well as toward oneself. Try as one might, extroverted solutions no longer apply. One must realize at some time during this period that he isn't going to get stronger or richer or better — that he has climbed as high as he will climb. The exterior is starting to deteriorate, so one had better concentrate on the interior. However, this is not the *affliction* of aging, but its *reward;* as the physical vitality begins to ebb, there is a complementary development of the internal powers. The body declines, as it *must* in *all* natural organisims, while the energies of the personality concentrate themselves in the mind and the individual soul. Mental capacity can remain as strong as ever, and where the individual has achieved psychological maturity, it will become even greater.

Only in those lives in which fear and emotional distress prevent the person from changing his attitudes and cause him to rebel senselessly against the normal aging process does the mind also tire. It is, in fact, the ego which tires rather than the mind; the ego gives up when faced by the need for a basic change of outlook or when called upon to take an unfamiliar step in a new direction. Not the body but the habitual and fixed patterns of thought hanging around one's neck like a millstone pull him under. If, in his forties, a person has achieved the state of personality integration and freed himself from the unconscious demands of his beliefs, then this 7-year period can signal the time of a real illumination of the spirit, or some deep change in the positive direction of one's life.

Age 49 to 56: Psychological Level — Education of others. Assuming greater social responsibility. Negatively, mental rigidity due to incapacity to change adopted life-attitude and behaviour.

This 7-year period corresponds to the extroverted Psychological Level from age 14 to 21. Just as the growing youth who tries to carry over his childish egoism into adult life must pay for his self-centeredness with social failure, so whoever carries over into the afternoon of life the aim of money-making, social achievement, or dynastic ambition must pay for it with damage to his soul. As Jung says,

> ...aging people should know that their lives are no longer mounting and expanding, but that an inexorable inner process enforces the contraction of life. If it is dangerous for a young person to be too preoccupied with himself, for the aging person it is a duty and a necessity to devote serious attention to himself...A human being would certainly not grow to be seventy or eighty years old if this longevity had no meaning for the species. ("The Stages of Life," p. 399)

The lesson to be learned from this phase of the life-cycle is the *meaning* which can and must be gathered in from the life that has been lived thus far. This is described astrologically by the second waning square of

Saturn occurring at about age 52. Once again the person will pass through a process of severance from ancient images and ingrained habit-patterns and attitudes. While on the extroverted psychological level the individual was asked to break with familial patterns and to free himself from the traditional concepts generally imposed on him at school, at age 52 he is asked to dismiss the memories of his past failures — the psychic or organic difficulties which the crises of the forties may have brought about. He must clean the psychological slate in preparation for the time when the third Saturn cycle begins around age 59.

Here again the attachment to or identification with the parents or familial attitudes becomes prominent — however, this time in an introverted way, and on a psychic rather than physical level. During the extroverted psychological period age 14 to 21, many young people attempt to break the bonds of psychic dependence on the parents by leaving home. But rebellion does not signify freedom. The extroverted solution did not answer a problem which is basically subjective; thus, at the corresponding introverted psychological level, the problem reappears. This time one is no longer financially dependent on his parents — on the contrary, they may be financially dependent on him; and if he is living with them, it is in *his* home rather than theirs. Again one is confronted with all those attitudes and values which he may have thrown away in his youth simply because they came from his parents. Now he has the opportunity to *consciously choose* those hereditary values — to see his parents objectively, in a new perspective, and to establish an individual relationship with them. If the parents die or must be institutionalized before one can experience a truly personal relationship with them, then he may be left for the remainder of his life with a sense of incompletion. The ensuant guilt can raise a formidable barrier to the true experience of Self, and one then moves on to the third stage of life and the potential rebirth at age 60 with a permanently smudged slate.

In the 50th year Uranus enters the 8th phase of its cycle — the regenerative phase. This may bring deep occult experiences. The mental-psychological crisis of the forties now becomes a biological crisis. During this period one will see the concrete results of whatever took place in the middle forties. If the person does not succeed in constructively facing the impeding physical obstacles or the psychological obstructions arising from his failure to become an integrated personality, then he will now see a gradual crystallization of the established psychological and social attitudes and beliefs which he had not the inner will to modify. He will become "too old to change."

The person who manages to live through this 7-year period in a positive manner — because he has the spiritual courage and a strong enough sense of destiny to *go through* whatever crises or tragedies life has brought him — should now try to bring the harvest of his experiences to a seed-condition. In other words, he will be ready to assume greater social responsibility and to teach others on the basis of what he has learned and experienced. He will be ready, because in the previous 7-year period he undertook consciously and deliberately to change his relationship to society. After about thirty years of productivity, during which the tendency is usually to judge everything and everyone in terms of this productivity and its fruits, one is now ready to introduce a new quality into his relationships — the quality of wisdom. In his younger days he *received* from the past a vast legacy of knowledge, skills and comforts. Realizing this, he or she is now ready, at the end of his or her life, to *give* back to society and especially to its youth the fruits of long experience in handling and using the legacy he or she has received.

Age 56 to 63: Power Level — Possibility of a "3rd birth" in the Uranian cycle. Demonstration of the capacity to focus the spiritual quality of being inherent at birth *through* the personality. New spiritual activities or, negatively, further crystallization of mind and feeling responses.

The period from age 56 to 60 is as important as that from age 27 to 30. The 56th year coincides with the third birth in the Uranus cycle — the 9th phase. This is the second chance in every life to reorient and transform the character, as well as the nature of one's human relationships. Being able to see oneself in a new way, it becomes possible to meet others in a new way, and so to embark upon a new kind of social participation. What can happen at this time, positively speaking, is the conscious or unconscious decision to devote the evening of one's life to some form of creative fulfillment and harvest. Negatively it means letting oneself go and settling down to a crystallized and limited form of physical and mental existence — retirement. Besides the third birth in the Uranus cycle, this period sees the return of both Jupiter and Saturn to their natal placements. A fourth nodal cycle begins, which indicates the potential renewal of the pattern of destiny and personality integration. Lastly, the natal Sun-Moon aspect repeats itself in the progressions around age 59, and Saturn begins its third cycle in the life.

From all these astrological indications one sees a new trend beginning to unfold at age 56 — a trend which will reach a climax at age 59-60 with the beginning of the new Saturn cycle and which will become more clearly defined as the sixties begin. A keynote will be set here for the remaining years of the life, or at least until age 70-72, after which old age, as it is considered today, begins. "Old-age" may of course actually begin at 60 if the person does not take a positive attitude toward the change of life-direction initiated in the forties. In any case, the more the person has lived a sort of life different from the average, routine existence imposed by modern society, the more likely will the period age 56 to 70 be positive. Since the time of ancient Greece, age 60 has been considered to be the age of philosophy in the sense of a search for essential meaning and fundamental values. This should be the main interest during the afternoon and evening of life. Moreover, in the life of the creative individual, there should be an effort to harmonize one's individual outlook with the *real needs* of the collective. It will then become possible to act more wisely, more serenely and efficiently in all relationships. The creative individual will use these latter years to bring the spiritual or socio-cultural fruits of his experience and reflection to his community. For this he may receive honor and relative fame, and perhaps a relative degree of social security. If, however, the community does not appreciate the value of this harvest, then these latter years can be lonely ones.

Dane Rudhyar once observed that a creative person usually does not manage to make his mark upon his time before he is 60. The works performed by that creative person after age 28 (the time of the beginning of true individual creativity) become impressed upon the consciousness (and even the unconscious) of the generation *born at the time these works were performed or produced.* This impress is the foundation of the social and cultural immortality of the truly creative mind. When the generation born at the time of such a mind's creations reaches maturity — age 28 — then it will be in a position to understand and appreciate their value. The creator will then be about sixty years of age. Thus, it should be during this period of life that one should realize the importance of trying to make some permanent, and in some cases immortal, contribution to the life of his community, great or small. He must concentrate on the spiritual future, both of himself and of humanity.

A spiritual repolarization can occur at this time of life. Essentially, this necessitates a review of everything one has assimilated during his life — deciding what to keep and eventually to pass on to future generations, and what to discard. The individual must discover the best way in which what he has become can fulfill some basic collective need of the times. It is never too early to begin the task of discarding what is non-essential, and then to go about strengthening, clarifying and, if need be, recording for the coming generations the harvest of one's experience. One should do this during this 9th phase of life, because at age 60 one will be best fitted to do the job. What should count is not so much the time spent on the task, but the *quality* of the achievement.

Age 63 to 70: Body or Organic Level — Conscious preparation for the "after-life", or senility. Radiating wisdom or, negatively, sense of boredom, emptiness, futility. Bringing the life to some sort of seed-consummation.

Sixty-three is a particularly crucial age. At this time Uranus comes to the waning square to its natal position, and Saturn is then nearing the waxing square in its third cycle.* The waxing square of Saturn around age 66-67 can mean a new, great adventure into spiritual realms. If, on the other hand, the person has nothing positive to offer society or he is not open to new realms of consciousness, then the process of body crystallization and lowering of vitality takes on added power. The latter alternative will occur particularly if the waning Uranus square at 63 has meant the gradual severance of the creative self from the body and established routine existence. This severance may be due to a feeling of hopelessness at the way in which society and the power of tradition keep frustrating any creative effort of the Self. It may also be the end result of the outer personality's failure to meet the crisis of the forties and to deal with its results during the fifties in a constructive way.

As ever, the positive role is played by *the spirit within*. When the everyday personal life can no longer contribute anything of value to the spirit, then the spirit gradually or suddenly withdraws. The body and the mind are then left to disintegrate, or, for a while, to crystallize. One grows old out of a lack of interest in life — out of a sense of failure to gather any harvest of value from personal experience. This is a Uranian death: a letting go of some unbearable situation largely under a Neptunian sense of defeat. Saturnian death, on the other hand, is the slow result of a progressive crystallization of the bodily and psychic structures which have become increasingly rigid and contain ever less spiritual content. This means death in automatism, meaninglessness or senility. The reason the time of death so often does not seem to register clearly in the birth-chart is that the actual time of disintegration of the body is not *spiritually* the most significant moment. Many people are inwardly "dead" whose bodies are still organically alive, and some are indeed "live" whose bodies no longer function. Here, says Rudhyar, we touch the mystery of what *really* constitutes a man's true identity.

BEYOND THE SEVENTY-YEAR LIFE-CYCLE. The sense of responsibility toward one's own and humanity's spiritual future which may have redirected the life from age 60 onwards, can lead to a "third puberty" near the age 73-74 when Saturn comes to its third opposition to its natal place. If the end of life is being dedicated to the attempt at becoming a seed for the future in terms of what the individual has accomplished during his life, then a new rhythm of life-contacts can now be established (73-74) between the individual and society, and between

---

*The 63rd year is also the age of consummation of the important 7-year and 9-year rhythms of the life-cycle: 7 x 9 = 63. The spiritual-individual rhythm (7) and the physical-collective rhythm (9) can be fully harmonized in the individual at this time; thereafter the life will be stirred to its depth by a new impulse. The number 9 — and therefore all 9-year periods — refers in humanistic astrology to the gradual working out of the spiritual and ancestral karma. Therefore, at age 63, the way in which the individual destiny and the collective destiny meet is a determining factor for the future.

the conscious ego and the spirit within, depending on where the attention is concentrated. If the body has stood the strain of this new type of relationship from age 70 onwards, then the fruits of this new relationship will lead to a further change of magnetism at age 77. This age corresponds to 7 times 11 — 11 being the number of the Sun and of the circulation of solar energy throughout the solar system. Then, at 84, a "fourth birth" occurs. This, according to Rudhyar, takes the individual altogether into a new realm of destiny — to a disintegration of the personality or (relative) immortality.

The Individual Years

Each year within any given 7-year period* has its individual meaning and is an expression of the period within which it falls. The starting point for a given year is the birthday of the person considered, and it extends to the next birthday. The occurrence of a major transit or progression must be considered not only in the context of the overall period within which it occurs, but also in terms of the specific year.

The First Year. The type of development which will characterize any 7-year period begins as a new impulse which is based on what has happened in the *last year* of the preceding 7-year period. This impulse is usually not immediately clear, even though some definite occurrence may set the stage for it. Very often, this year is peculiarly elusive and uncertain in character, or filled with emotional confusion. The primary development is internal and below the level of personal consciousness. Life seems neither one thing nor another. Yet, in some cases, there is great impulsiveness, experimentation and emotional intensity which may include a sense of freedom and of new beginnings.

The Second Year. In this year the new impulse and the new destiny may give a new direction to the life and change the foundation of the person's feelings. On the other hand, what happens may reveal a great deal of resistance to the new trend in the form of fears, memories, and social inertia. What was developed in the preceding 7-year period may oppose the new direction one wants to follow, or else the new trend has to push through the old ideas step by step. Psychological conflicts and financial or social problems may arise at this time. Important decisions may have to be made.

The Third Year. The new trend takes on a more definite form. One usually has some idea of what life now offers. This should be a year of definite exteriorization and action, even though one may feel very lonely; the new ideals appear unrealizable, and one's abilities seem most

---

*Cf. *American Astrology*, Rudhyar's article on "The Seven Year Cycle", April 1942. Also Rudhyar's book *Occult Preparations for a New Age*, C.6, p. 86 ff.

The Seven Year Cycle

The 1st year begins at birth,
    then age 7, 14, 21, 28, 35, 42, 49, 56, 63, 70, 77, 84.
The 2nd year begins at age ...... 1,8,15,22,29,36,43,50,57,64,71,78,85.
The 3rd year begins at age .... 2,9,16,23,30,37,44,51,58,65,72,79,86.
The 4th year begins at age ...... 3,10,17,24,31,38,45,52,59,66,73,80,87.
The 5th year begins at age ...... 4,11,18,25,32,39,46,53,60,67,74,81,88.
The 6th year begins at age ...... 5,12,19,26,33,40,47,54,61,68,75,82,89.
The 7th year begins at age ...... 6,13,20,27,34,41,48,55,62,69,76,83,90.

The first half of the cycle (3½ years) manifests an *involutionary* trend with an accent on ACTIVITY and the effort to INCORPORATE the new impulse born in the 1st year, to find adequate means to ACTUALIZE it.

The second half of the cycle (3½ years to 7 years) marks an *evolutionary* trend with an accent on growth of CONSCIOUSNESS. There should be an attempt to express individual VALUES and MEANINGS through ideas or through group activity.

SPIRITUAL LEVEL

1st YEAR

The new impulse is felt; feeling one's way toward a new condition of being. Experimentation.

7th YEAR

Seed period. Culmination of whole 7-year trend, either in fulfilment or in defeat. Inner preparation for new cycle to follow; or sense of inadequacy in face of family or social pressures.

MENTAL LEVEL

2nd YEAR

Resistance of past, in the form of memories, complexes, fears, social inertia. But the new impulse arouses the depths of the nature.

6th YEAR

What is implied in the 7-year period now bears fruit. Sacrifice of past to a future to which one dedicates oneself. Evaluation of one's success or failure.

PHYSICAL LEVEL

3rd YEAR

Effort to exteriorize impulse in definite form. Deep sense that one has to go on, in spite of feelings of loneliness, despondency, or lack of technical means for realization.

5th YEAR

Flower stage of 7-year period, within the limits of what has been realized or visualized during the 3rd year. Positively, creative activity and expansion of consciousness. Negatively, destruction of hopes; "matter" wins over "spirit."

4th YEAR: Critical turning-point at 3½ years.

Struggle to give concrete form to impulse. Overcoming of the pull of the past; or fruitless return to the past. Achievement of means for concrete realization of new impulse; or beginning of trend leading to later failure or disintegration. Time for concrete personal or social choices.

inadequate. This lack of technique and of adequate means is often acute, yet there is a deep sense that one has to go on, even if motivated only by emotion or irrational enthusiasm or devotion.

The Fourth Year. The new trend should now be incorporated into definite activities. New possibilities are revealed, and new issues are met — both social and personal. This must be a year of struggle, of conflict, and often of hard work, yet also of spiritual fecundation — otherwise it will be a fruitless resignation to old patterns. A choice, either conscious or unconscious, personal or social, is usually made, or seemingly forced upon the person by circumstances. It may come at the exact mid-point of the 7-year period (three and one half years, which is the cyclic turning-point), but more generally it occurs throughout this fourth year.

The Fifth Year. This is often the year of greatest self-expression, when the keynote of the entire 7-year period may reveal itself with the greatest personal intensity — a year of flowering and of *conscious* development within the limits of what has been realized or visualized during the third year. A contact with the highest reaches of one's nature attainable in that 7-year period is usually made now. One may find a "teacher", a guide or helper — or one may function as a leader himself. Negatively, destruction of hopes, "matter" or "human nature" wins over spirit.

The Sixth Year. This may be a year of fruition and culmination, yet with the need for some kind of sacrifice, perhaps the giving up of some cherished ideals and personal contacts. One must cultivate compassion and understanding to encounter the deep and often tragic experiences, the dissatisfactions, and the restless sense of frustration which may arise — even in the midst of apparent success and happiness. One should try to evaluate one's degree of success or failure and be ready, ideally, to dedicate one's efforts to the attainment of some future new state.

The Seventh Year. The seed year. The entire period is being concluded, and the *need* for some new life-values and a new phase of destiny or character development is felt — sometimes with a poignant intensity. This should be a period of consummation and illumination, a high-point in consciousness. In many cases, however, the negative factors predominate; the *need* and hope for a new phase of life is stronger than the joyous fulfillment of the old phase. And yet, the fulfillment of the old will actually *create* the new. Where there has been frustration instead of fulfillment, or a sense of inadequacy in the face of family or social pressures, the need and hope for the new "cries out to heaven" for another opportunity to start afresh. In either case, this seventh year contains in seed form the substance of the subsequent 7-year cycle, the promise of a new beginning, and one should prepare confidently for it.

Applying the Age Factor

This is a very general pattern which the astrologer must apply according to the age, life-conditions and social or personal problems of the individual. When the astrologer takes these generic cyclic patterns as a background for his interpretation of the individual progressions and transits, his interpretation will have a deeper and more intimate meaning. The age factor will not reveal the success or failure (both of which are value-judgements) of a venture, or whether an event will end happily or unfortunately; rather, it will indicate the part the event will play in the *total life-development* of a person. The astrological configurations — natal, progressed and transiting — at the time will help to determine whether the positive or negative meaning of the year and the 7-year period will enter most into consideration.

We may take marriage as an example. Rudhyar stresses that in attempting to discover the meaning of a marriage, or any strong partnership psychologically similar to marriage, one must not think only of outer happiness or apparent success in the eyes of society. Many an outwardly successful marriage has meant spiritual death to at least one of the partners. What counts here is the purpose which that marriage will play in the life-destiny of that individual. In this, the age factor can reveal as much as any other astrological factor as to the deeper significance of the union. The 7-year period between age 21 to 28 is the time during which everyone normally develops the *social* phase of his character and destiny. Since marriage is basically a social impulse, most people who marry do so generally between the ages of 21 to 28, or make some decision then which will lead to marriage later. Next, the astrologer should note during which year of this 7-year period the marriage, or the decision to marry took place. If it occurred during the second year, one might presume that the partnership is likely to be somewhat confused, and the social issues at stake may bring conflict of some sort. The partnership will help greatly to make concrete the keynote of the 7-year period, yet resistance and psychological confusion can be expected.

If marriage, or any union to be considered the psychological equivalent of marriage, takes place either before or after the "social level" — age 21 to 28 — this fact in itself will give a particular meaning to the union. A marriage taking place before the age of 21 would stress the "psychological factors" in the relationship rather than the "social" and may be based on a purely emotional or instinctual-sexual impulse which may or may not last. At that age a person may be looking for emotional security and a parent-figure rather than a partner. The same may be true of a marriage which takes place during the introverted psychological level — age 49 to 56. At that time, however, the person may be looking either for a parent-figure, or for someone to whom he can be a parent-figure. In both cases, however, the primary motivation is emotional security.

Marriage after the age of 28 is likely to have a very "personal" meaning. A more mature personality unites with another to satisfy mutually personal, spiritual needs — needs which are *individually* formed, rather than the results of collective agreement. From age 35 to 42, which is the introverted personality level, there will also be an expansion of consciousness through human relationship as a motivating force in the union. A marriage taking place during the introverted social period — age 42 to 49 — may be based on the need to ensure social security; the person may be looking for an escort or a hostess rather than a soul-mate. It may also be a psychological reaction to the frustrations of work, or to personal losses experienced during the first half of life (the basic keynote of the period 42 to 49).

What is suggested here in relation to marriage or other close pair-bonded relationships also applies to the choice of one's life-work. The usual time such a decision is made is during the age 14 to 21 period — the extroverted psychological level. At this time of life, a person is most influenced by peer-group pressure so that a choice of career at this time is likely to be based on the emotional security of peer approval — i.e., that it will provide him with a good income and thereby social standing in the community rather than being the expression of his personal creativity.

The selection of a career made at another time in the life would have a very different meaning. Take, for example, four individuals all of whom chose to become doctors. None of them made that decision at the usual time (age 14 to 21). The first decided to become a doctor when he was five years old. In this case he was merely exteriorizing the values of his family — his father and grandfather were also doctors. Thus, for him, medicine was an expression of a family tradition, and his life-work was decided by the pressures of that tradition rather than by a consciously made choice. The second person did not decide to enter medicine until his 22nd year. At that time he was a psychologist working with schizophrenic children, and he realized that he could do more for those children if he had a medical degree. His decision to enter medicine, therefore, was made on the basis of the contribution he could make to society. Scorning the more lucrative and glamorous branches of medicine which appeal to one seeking the approval of his peers, he entered the field of genetic research — a specialization which reflects the social level (age 21 to 28).

In the third example, the individual did not decide to become a doctor until she was twenty-eight years old. Earlier she had abandoned a career in mathematics in order to marry, and although she was devoted to her family, felt that the role of wife-mother was personally stifling. Her choice of a medical career was an expression of her individual creativity. The fourth example did not choose to become a doctor until he was thirty-nine. He felt that this was his last chance to fulfill the dream of a lifetime. More than a change of career was involved here; there was also a change in personal attitude and life-style. By that time his children were approaching college age and he was well-established in another career. Entering medical school necessitated the liquidation of all his worldly goods and uprooting his family. It created many financial hardships for the entire family; however, since the decision was made with their total approval and support, when he finally received his degree, the wife and children shared in his sense of personal accomplishment.

In this same way, all important decisions or turning-points in the life can be measured in terms of the age factor, thereby providing an additional dimension and a more personal *meaning* above and beyond the event itself. In addition to marriage and career, all major illnesses, changes of residence, divorce, loss of a parent, creative or social achievements, birth of children and religious conversions may be examined in terms of the age at which the individual experienced them. This generic cycle gives a framework which will be universally valid even though each individual introduces particular modifications of the pattern it establishes. At the same time, the more significant the individual destiny in a spiritual sense, the closer the individual cycles will follow this generic pattern. This, according to Rudhyar, is the great paradox. As he said in *The Astrology of Personality*,

> The supremely individuated personality reveals the most perfectly in its outline of character, consciousness and destiny the form of generic Man. The most individual becomes the most universal, just because of being the most individual. He becomes a "solar Hero" — an Exemplar or Avatar, whose deeds and whose personality are universally significant. (1st edition, 1936, p. 239)

III

The Sun-Moon Cycles

When earliest Man first looked upward toward the heavens, he measured his life by the transits of the Sun and Moon. Then, even as they do today, these two "Lights" represented the two basic factors in human experience: *light and life.* It is highly significant that, when viewed from Earth, the solar and lunar discs appear to be nearly the same size; for although the Moon is approximately 400 times smaller than the Sun, it is 400 times closer to the Earth. This illusion of equality, which explains the phenomena of solar and lunar eclipses, will be dealt with at length later in this chapter. When Rudhyar first noticed this illusion of human perspective in 1939, he interpreted it as meaning, symbolically, that the factors which the Sun and Moon represent occupy the same space in Man's conscious awareness. In other words, there is an even balance between Man's higher solar-nature and his lower lunar-nature — the light-radiating Self and the light-reflecting psychic nature of Man are equal in both meaning and size in Man's total being.

In humanistic terms, the Sun symbolizes not only the central core of this solar system and the well-spring of all life within it, but also the life-purpose of everything sustained by it. Only the Sun radiates its own light, while the other planets reflect this light and are sustained by it, just as their positions in the solar system are maintained by the Sun. By extension, therefore, the Sun symbolizes the power of Self — the purpose and direction of an individual's existence. Traditionally, the Moon governs a person's instinctual reactions and behavior as well as his feelings. Since these feelings and responses change constantly, just as the phases of the Moon are constantly changing, the Moon is attributed only a minor significance by event-oriented astrologers. The notable exception to this is the relative importance given to New and Full Moons, and especially eclipses which are said to "cause" events — particularly when they contact the birth-chart in some way. The constantly-changing phases of the Moon are a uniquely geocentric phenomena. They can be seen only from the Earth, and therefore, they relate specifically to the realm of human consciousness. The Moon does not actually change, except in its relationship to the Sun. Therefore, on a symbolic level, what changes is the *manner* in which the solar life-energy is being translated to the Earth and by extension to all life-forms on Earth.

This chapter will deal principally with the cycles of the Moon's nodes and the eclipse cycles. These are not, in fact, separate cycles, but rather are facets of the same solar-lunar transit cycle; although they will be treated separately, they should be regarded together. Additionally, the individual cycles of the transiting Sun and Moon will also be described; for although these transits are generally considered too fast moving and therefore too superficial to be of significance in terms of predicting events, they do have a specific meaning in the humanistic approach to astrology.

The Cycles of the Moon's Nodes

Nodes are not planetary bodies, but points in space which describe the intersection of two orbits. They have no mass, and therefore there is no logical way they can be considered mechanistically as exerting "influence" which determines activity on Earth. Yet in spite of this the nodes, and especially the Moon's nodes, have been used for centuries in Hindu astrology and are considered important in every contemporary system including the Uranian and Cosmobiology systems. The notable exception to this is the "Church of Light" method, which totally ignores the nodes. This fact suggests that the concept of "influences" has not been taken literally in much astrological thinking, or else, that astrologers have not understood the fundamental principles on which traditional astrology was founded. In terms of the current scientific world-view, astrology can be explained most logically and reasonably as the science of cycles — the art of interpreting abstract cyclic relation-ships. As a science of cycles, astrology uses celestial bodies as focal centers of living relationships NOT because they exert physical or metaphysical "influences", but rather because they constitute a very complete series of points of reference. The earth observer can use them to plot the many cycles of change in all life-relationships in terms of space-time values. Thus, modern astrology can be, in the words of Marc Jones, a science of the relationship of all things to all other things in the space-time continuum.

As astronomical data form the basis of any truly scientific astrology, the astrologer must inquire into the astronomical nature of the nodes if he would use them as astrological symbols. The elements to be considered in an analysis of the Moon's nodes are 1) the Ecliptic, the apparent path of the Sun around the Earth, which is actually the orbit of the Earth around the Sun; and 2) the orbit of the Moon which, as a satellite of the Earth, revolves around the Earth. The planes of these two orbits, the Earth's and the Moon's, intersect each other at an angle of 5 degrees 8 minutes and 40 seconds. This line of intersection is the axis formed by the Moon's nodes. Every month the Moon comes to its North node position, cuts the plane of the Ecliptic, and thereby changes its latitude from South to North. When the monthly transit of the Moon reaches its South node, its latitude changes from North to South in relation to the Ecliptic. Therefore, when the Moon is conjunct either of its nodes, it has no latitude. In the traditionally accepted interpretation of the Moon's nodes, the Ecliptic — the factor of zodiacal longitude — is considered to be the stable, permanent factor, and the plane of the Moon's orbit is seen as sliding backward along the Ecliptic. Therefore, the movement of the nodes through the zodiac is retrograde. As the Ecliptic (geocentrically considered) reveals the relationship of the Earth to the Sun, and the Moon's orbit reveals the relationship of the Earth to the Moon, and since the nodal axis is the link between the planes of these two orbits, the nodes may be said to symbolize the relationship of the Earth to the two "Lights" — the Sun and Moon.

In astrological symbolism, the northward crossing of the Ecliptic is a movement toward the positive and creative factor of the Spirit, and the southward crossing is a motion away from Spirit and toward the material realm. The North node, therefore, carries a traditional meaning of positiveness and spirit — a point of divine protection or providence, or of success through the use of the spiritual will. At the North node the Moon is interpreted as orienting herself definitely toward the Sun, becoming thereafter the reflector and distributor of solar power, will and purpose. At the South node the Moon symbolically turns her back on the pull of the Sun; as a result it falls under the control of the energies of matter and Man's personal nature. This alternating orientation first toward spirit and then toward matter is the key to the meaning of the nodal cycle. When the Moon is moving in North latitude — from the North node to the South node — that is a time for positive activity under the interior guidance of the Spirit, and for building adequate structures for creative action consecrated to material needs. As the Moon moves in South latitude from the South node to the North node, it signifies a time for either assimilating and then releasing what was prepared during the former period of activity, or for repudiating what one has not been able to assimilate or use constructively. Both these trends are good and necessary, and all cycles must necessarily include them, for polarity is the universal law governing manifestation on Earth.

Thus, the nodal axis of the Moon refers to the twofold process of integration and disintegration through which the solar or spiritual and the lunar or personal natures of an individual's total being are continuously linked and then separated. The North node and the period of the lunar cycle during which the Moon has North latitude are symbols of the times in one's life when his psychic or lunar nature is oriented toward, and is a transmitter of, the power of creative spirit. The South node and the period of the lunar cycle during which the Moon has South latitude symbolize the times of assimilation of spiritual and vital forces generated during the northern half of the cycle. This process should lead to a release of these forces, or negatively, to their waste and disintegration.

At the North node, life asks an individual to exert himself in a particular direction indicated by the node's Sign and House position. It points to qualities, faculties and accomplishments which are new, which therefore will demand a conscious and sustained effort and which determine the direction of one's future. If one concentrates his energies in this direction, he will build both his spiritual power and his capacity to live in a significant manner. At the South node, according to Sign and House, one has the indications of what is already built into the personality at birth. Those qualities, faculties and accomplishments do not present any difficulties in their manifestations. They may be so ingrained that they are expressed without any conscious awareness. Many traditional astrological texts describe the South node as a symbol of one's self-undoing — the line of least resistance. In order to resist something one must first become consiously aware of it. Just as water flows downhill, the tendency in all of nature is to take the easiest path. That direction, however, is not the path of personal growth. As long as an individual persists in following the path described by his South node, he is denying the possibility of growth. That way will lead him to becoming a slave to the inertia of habitual behavior, and to depend on his natural gifts and abilities rather than developing new ones.

This does not mean to imply that one should not use his natural gifts — those faculties which he has inherited at birth (or which were due to some positive effort in a past life if one believes in reincarnation). What it does mean is that an individual should use such gifts and faculties in order to foster the *new* development demanded at the North node. Very often, life creates circumstances which do not allow a person to use his South node faculties automatically — circumstances which oblige him to concentrate on North node types of development. Astrologers must avoid the tendency to give an entirely negative meaning to the South node in a birth-chart. The element of Karma, of bondage to the past, in the South node need not work itself out through negative events. The South node in a natal chart is a symbol of habit — of customary behavior and the easy release of power based upon past or inherited achievement. This may lead to inertia, automatic and spiritless action, and self-undoing; or it may indicate perfect instinctual performance and the release of genius through congenital gifts or spontaneously acquired technique.

Additionally, astrologers must never forget that the nodes form *an axis* and that their meanings are complementary. This nodal axis links two opposite Houses (and Signs) and establishes a focal relationship between two areas of experience, the meanings of which must be integrated. The North and South nodes are the polar aspects of a single process — the intake and release of spiritual power in relation to rhythms established in one's past (family or soul heredity). It is a lunar process of adaptation to life, and in any adaptation, personal and collective past experiences play an important part. Furthermore, the nodes have a retrograde movement. Such a movement, both in progressions and transits, refers to a return to source — to a review of past behavior. For this reason the nodal axis is often referred to as the axis of Fate or Destiny, because whatever it touches in the natal chart may be strongly conditioned by the past — by one's personal or racial karma.

Although the birth position of the nodal axis is a basic factor throughout the life, the retrograde cycle of the transiting nodes has a very real significance — especially on the psychological level. The length of this cycle is approximately 18.6 years, and thus every 19th year the bi-polar activity of personal destiny will receive a new impetus.* At the ages of 19, 38, 57, and 76 an individual has the opportunity to be reborn — to see his destiny in a new light. At those times something can — but not necessarily will — happen which may be likened to a spiritual descent of power or, negatively, to a precipitation of karma. Whatever occurs will mature the personality, either through a change in the substance and quality of one's consciousness, or through some deeply disturbing psychological crisis. The outward manifestation or event linked to such changes may occur much later, however, since the phases of growth and disintegration take place gradually.

The year prior to each of these four nodal returns is a sort of 12th House phase of the nodal cycle — a time in which one should attempt to sum up the meaning and activity of that entire cycle and prepare for the next. The age of 18, for example, is a time to sum up the experiences of one's youth so that an individual may develop an objective foundation for the new departure into adulthood at 19. In this context it is interesting to note that in many countries the voting age is being lowered from 21 to 18. At the end of the second nodal cycle at age 37-38, one should try to assess the degree of success (or failure) in his attempts to realize his ideal life-purpose through concrete activities. This evaluation, coming shortly after the beginning of the waning hemi-cycle of life (See Chapter II — The Age Factor) should set the tone for the second half of life. When the third nodal cycle ends at age 56-57, each person should assess the degree

---

*See diagram on Moon's Nodal Cycle in this chapter.

The Three-year and Nine-year Subdivisions
of the Moon's Nodal Cycle

As the nodal cycle lasts about 18.6 years, there is a slight discrepancy in the ages given below. Experience has shown that 19 rather than 18 is significant. The other ages mentioned are in relation to the three phases of the nine-year cycle: thesis, antithesis and synthesis. Every 19th year the transiting North node comes back to its natal position. Nine years later, there is an inversion of the nodal positions: the transiting North node comes to the natal South node position and the transiting South node comes to the natal North node position. Each nine-year period or half nodal cycle is divided into three periods of three years which are related to each other in the manner of a thesis (first three years), antithesis (second three years) and synthesis (third three years).

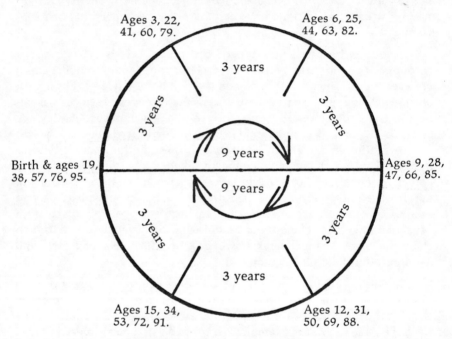

of personality fulfillment he has achieved, and the measure to which his creative work as a social individual has been successful. Since this nodal return occurs shortly before the end of the second Saturn cycle, it is a time to evaluate the productive years of one's life. According to the Age Factor, it is the second year of the Power Level — the time of a change in the spiritual direction, as well as the foundation of one's personal feelings. The fourth nodal return occurs at age 75-76. At that time there should be an assessment of the personality's spiritual realizations, and of the success of one's efforts to conclude his life in a significant manner, leaving a seed to nourish future generations.

The mid-point of the transiting nodal cycle occurs every ninth year. At those times there is an inversion of the natal nodal axis — the transiting North node falling on the natal south node, and vice versa. Thus, each 9th year is polar to the next, as the North node is polar to the South node. Since the number "nine," and therefore the 9-year period, refers in humanistic astrology to the gradual working out of one's spiritual and ancestral past or karma, the mid-point periods of the nodal transit cycle present an opportunity to begin clearing up the results of his past mistakes or omissions. It also signals a time when an individual can bring out of the depths of his personality those elements which will assist him in becoming a seed for the future. *External events and changes in one's life are more likely related to the mid-points of the nodal cycle than to the nodal returns.*

This 9-year cycle may also be divided into three periods of three years each, signifying generally Thesis, Antithesis, Synthesis. The first period establishes a quality of activity regarding one's relationships, the second period describes a reaction to that activity, and the third period is an attempt to synthesize the past and the present. Since the transiting nodes move at an average of 3 minutes a day (retrograde), these 3-year periods correspond to sextile-trine aspects of the nodes to their natal positions. In each case, whether leading to the inversion or the return, the 9th year is a seed year — a time of potential fulfillment. This 9-year cycle may also be individualized. Instead of counting the years from birth, one should begin this cycle from the time when the North node reaches the Ascendant for the first time in the life. This transit will occur at some time during the first 18.6 years of life and should be related to the Age Factor.

THE NODAL TRANSIT OF THE BIRTH-CHART. The nodal axis distributes the polar force of personal destiny throughout the life, making its placement in the hemispheres and quadrants of the birth-chart highly significant. As the nodal axis moves on, the positive energy of the personality-building forces of destiny is liberated into the hemisphere and quadrant through which the North node is passing. Power is being *generated* there. On the other hand, the hemisphere and quadrant containing the transiting South node receives the negative energy, that is, the energy built on past habits and used on the basis of previous efforts. Power is therefore being *released* there.

Because the movement of the nodal axis is retrograde, the astrologer must number the Houses differently. This is an important technical point. If, for example, one takes the coincidence of the nodal axis with the birth horizon as the starting-point — the North node conjunct the Ascendant and the South node conjunct the Descendant — then the North node will move up through the 12th, 11th and 10th Houses, reaching the Descendant via the 9th, 8th and 7th Houses nine years later. Therefore, when the North node is found in the natal 12th House, it is in *its own 1st House* and will refer to the beginning of a new phase of personality-integration. When it is found in the natal 9th House, the North node will be in its own 4th House, indicating a period of personal focalization. Here the individual destiny will come to a concrete focus and the person will have the opportunity to become conscious of the power at his disposal. As this occurs, the South node will be transiting the natal 3rd House, which corresponds to the nodal 10th House. The power generated in the personality and in the home (North node in the nodal 4th House), should be *released* through one's public or professional life, and matters of a 10th House nature will come to the fore. Experience has shown that sometimes the transiting North node's House position will seem especially important and evident, while in other cases, the transiting South node's House will appear to fit more definitely what is happening. But if the astrologer will delve deeply enough into the psychological implications of the moment, he will probably find that both nodes contribute to the general meaning of the period. In any case, exactness in relation to outer events is not to be expected. What is important is the meaning of the House *phase.*

Apart from the individual House meanings of the nodal transit is the general hemispheric meaning which changes every nine years. Thus, when the North node is passing through the hemisphere above the birth horizon, it is transiting through its own first six Houses. During this period, therefore, the personality is being developed through inner compulsion, and the outer life is left to the play of negative-passive forces. One will continue to behave in an habitual manner powered by the momentum furnished by his previous efforts. When the North node reaches the Descendant and goes below the birth horizon, the outer life will demand of a person that he exert himself in a positive manner, while the inner life will become more habitual or passive in character. Here the terms "inner" and "outer" do not refer particularly to the events in one's life, but to the development of the personality through a concentration on introverted or extroverted activity — on subjective or objective values.

Any interpretation of the nodal transit cycle must be defined, as previously stated, by its retrograde movement. This cycle, like the retrograde periods of the planets, must be seen as referring to something which operates against, or in a direction opposed to the normal flow of life's activities and one's instinctual behavior. It will refer to whatever can interfere with or check an individual's normal, spontaneous, instinctual activity. The greatest interferer is the will of the conscious ego, conditioned as it is by all of one's past personal experiences as well as the social, ethical and moral standards of the community in which one lives. For this reason, the nodal transit cycle indicates confrontations with the results of one's own past, and also the past of one's society. This concept may be easily verified by noting the times when the North node by transit conjoins a natal planet. This contact tends to bring confrontations related to one's past use of that planetary function, to past frustrations or repressions, or to the desire to repeat fulfilling experiences. It can affect either one's inner or outer life, dominating his conscious behaviour or influencing his subconscious state. Whatever is generated at this North node contact *may* potentially be released approximately nine years later when the South node conjoins that same planet. The results of this release will then work themselves out during the following nine years leading up to the new North node contact. Of course, not everyone will be conscious of significant experiences when the North node transits natal planets, especially since these contacts do not generally relate to external events. In such cases, the meaning of the House opposite the one through which the North node is passing may give the astrologer valuable data concerning a person's changing attitude toward both his past and also toward his attempts to build his future. The times when the nodal axis coincides with the natal horizon and meridian are usually of particular importance.

THE TRANSITING NODES THROUGH THE HOUSES. Because the contacts between the transiting nodal axis and natal planets are of a subjective nature and cannot be counted on to coincide with external events, it is far more important for the astrologer to concentrate his analysis on the progressive accentuation of the Houses. In terms of this cycle, *the position of the transiting North node will show the field of experience in which power may be gained through self-exertion and concentration.* There should be a conscious attempt to develop new faculties or some new facet of the personality *through* the life-experiences symbolized by the House containing the transiting North node. The power which may be theoretically gained in terms of the North node's House position will be released in the field of experience in which the transiting South node is found. Here one should not try to exert himself in terms of the South node House, but rather to allow things to happen according to established habits built on his previous efforts while the North node transited that House nine years earlier. Moreover, as I have said, since we are dealing with an axis, *both* nodes will generally contribute to the overall meaning of their transit of two given opposite Houses.

North node in the nodal 1st House — South node in the nodal 7th House (natal 12th and 6th Houses). As the transiting North node crosses the Ascendant and moves into the natal 12th House, a new nodal cycle of 18.6 years begins. The age at which this transit occurs should always be related to the Age Factor (see Chapter II), as it will establish the tone for the entire cycle. At whatever age a nodal cycle begins, that period of life may correspond to some new departure in one's destiny. It will, of course, depend on the success or failure of the preceding 18-year cycle; and in some cases, the confrontation with one's true destiny can provoke a spiritual crisis. The external results of such a crisis will manifest much later when the South node crosses the Ascendant. During this period, progress through personal self-exertion will be seen in terms of 1st House matters, while the 7th House will indicate the line of least resistance. In 7th House matters one will tend to act according to established habits. Therefore, one should seek to build up his personality and to progress as an individual — to act according to his own personal truth in everything he does. The negative tendency will be to allow one's life to be governed by his habitual associates, or by an intemperate yearning for love and thereby to lose one's identity in a partner. By doing this, one refuses to grow as an individual. The compulsions of the past, either real or imagined, come through one's close associations. Those habitual patterns of meeting one's social obligations bind one to the past. The future calls through the decision to take a more individual stand — to accentuate those things which make one different from the norm, and to develop a deeper sense of Self-awareness.

North node in the nodal 2nd House — south node in the nodal 8th House (natal 11th and 5th Houses). This polarity stresses one's personal resources and the adequate management of those resources. The time has come to use one's powers in a new way, and to evaluate more deeply the influence of personal and collective habits on the way in which one tries to carry out his individual vision. The line of least resistance may be that of relying too much on the resources of others — and of one's close associates in particular. One should not depend on an automatic acceptance by others or by society at large of what one has to offer. Rather, one should develop those physical, psychological or mental abilities for which there is a present demand. Only in this way will an individual be able to act in a socially meaningful and effective manner.

North node in the nodal 3rd House — South node in the nodal 9th House (natal 10th and 4th Houses). This nodal emphasis demands that one exert himself in building his intellectual capacity in order that he will be better able to deal in a more practical and effective manner with the concrete problems of his environment. At this time one should seek to give an individual slant to the habitual way in which things and experiences are interpreted, and to become more self-reliant in his adjustment to the circumstances of everyday life. If one chooses to remain in a world of abstract principles or meta-physical ideals, then he is following the line of least resistance. One must not only act according to his own personal philosophy rather than the generally accepted principles of society, but he must also bring those ideals down to earth and make a practical reality out of his dreams. Theory is not enough.

North node in the nodal 4th House — South node in the nodal 10th House (natal 9th and 3rd Houses). At this point, destiny demands that an individual reinforce the foundations of his personal power — that he exert himself in the development of his home life, rather than seeking to strengthen his ground of being in the external world. Power will now be generated in the home and in one's personal feelings; that power will deepen one's creative capacity and enable him to release his energies in a more individual and spiritual manner in his dealings with the public. His established habit-patterns may cause him to neglect the development of his roots, his home and his inner being in favor of total absorption in routine professional activities. This is the time to develop both the personality and its creative capacity, and to act in terms of one's personal needs and subjective feeling-values. If this is not done now, one's professional life will suffer later, for without those new capacities, one will have nothing to offer in terms of the new and changing demands of the public.

North node in the nodal 5th House — South node in the nodal 11th House (natal 8th and 2nd Houses). The present path toward self-integration demands one's personal efforts in terms of creative self-expression. One must act out the new capacities developed during the transit of the 4th nodal House and put them to the test, even to the extent of dramatizing oneself and one's achievements. The line of least resistance lies in a dependency on the approval of a group. In losing oneself in the social ideals of a group, one will lose his own creative initiative. The easy escape from personal creativity is to take up a cause. Both habitual friendships and social activities can dampen the enthusiasm of the self-expression demanded here. There may also be a tendency to dream great heroic dreams; such idealism will make for failure in one's creative efforts. At this time one should rely on his own judgement rather than on the agreement of his friends; and if he does attach himself to a group or organization, he should lead it. In that way his creativity will find a channel through which to express itself. The major obstacle at this time will come from feelings of emotional frustration due to past failures, and these must necessarily be put aside.

North node in the 6th nodal House — South node in the 12th nodal House (natal 7th and 1st Houses). These two Houses represent, respectively, the end-phase of the hemi-cycle of new individual development, and the end-phase of the hemi-cycle of extroverted social activity. The progressive emphasis at this time is on the working out of new techniques of living. Whether these be expressed through one's personal devotion to an ideal, a cause, or an individual; or whether they find an outlet in one's sense of personal reponsibility, the accent will be on the desire to be of service. During this time the path of greatest ease will be to crawl inside oneself — to withdraw either physically, emotionally or spiritually from the external world. In some cases, the unfinished business of the closing 9-year period of social activity will compel one to review his behavior and to seek new ways of adapting his individual creativity to the needs of society; however, this must be done with the ultimate objective of service to humanity rather than service to one's ego needs. A crisis of transformation may precipitate health problems, especially if this time is used for brooding introspection rather than participation and service.

North node in the nodal 7th House — South node in the nodal 1st House (natal 6th and 12th Houses). This nodal transit marks the beginning of a 9-year period of extroverted activity indicated by all 7th House transits. One must begin to exert himself in the area of building relationships. One's powers of co-operation will be put to the test, and an individual will learn more about himself at this time through the experience of his inter-personal relationships than through meditative introspection. The negative tendency will be to project oneself and one's desires onto other people, and to be filled with pride and overly concerned with one's personal achievements and qualities. One must go out into the world, meeting people openly and freely, rather than losing oneself in purely ego-centered considerations. The path of least resistance lies in one's own mirror.

North node in the nodal 8th House — South node in the nodal 2nd House (natal 5th and 11th Houses). This polarity stresses the necessity to build up the resources of one's inter-personal relationships, to stress those values which can be shared positively with others. At this time one should strive to attain mastery over both his personal resources and his everyday circumstances through partnership activities and the co-mingling of efforts. This may occur in business, group activity or occult work, or through one-to-one relationships. Development of one's personal values as well as one's tangible assets will come through some sort of joint effort, or through the experiences of intimate relationship. Following the line of least resistance, one may squander his personal resources, or he may attempt to force his own values onto the partner. A possibility for self-regeneration exists; however it must be achieved through partnership, through a sensitivity to the needs of others, rather than an ego-oriented concentration on those things which are of strictly personal value.

North Node in the nodal 9th House — South node in the nodal 3rd House (natal 4th and 10th Houses). This opposition stresses the need to transcend the petty problems of day-to-day existence through an expansion of the mind. The assimilation of alien ideas, whether they come through long journeys and contacts with strangers, or through some philosophical or religious study, can assist one in getting out of the rut of daily routine both in his behavior and thought and can provide new meaning for one's everyday reality. During this transit one should seek new ways to integrate the near and the far — the known and the unknown. The path of least resistance at this time will be a temptation to scatter oneself, rather than focusing one's goals and ideals in a specific direction. Nevertheless, one must realize now that a religious or scientific dogma is no valid substitute for the *human* understanding which can come from relationships fully and freely experienced.

North node in the nodal 10th House — South node in the nodal 4th House (natal 3rd and 9th Houses). The nodal axis here emphasizes the opposition between one's profession and his home — the public and private sides of his life. In this instance, the public sector is the proper channel for self-integration and the field in which one should exert himself fully. One may want to give one's time mainly to private considerations, especially within the home itself, and to withdraw from one's social and professional obligations. This can only lead to self-undoing and a disintegration of one's public image or reputation. A person must not be too swayed by his emotions; rather than retiring, he must make an effort to extrovert his energies — to develop his social or professional capacity in order to fill a role of public significance in the community. This transit period is particularly important within the complete nodal cycle. Since it reveals, theoretically, the concrete results of everything which one has attempted to do since the North node crossed the Ascendant 14 to 15 years earlier, and especially since the North node transited the 4th and 7th (nodal) Houses. One must not forget that these results can be either positive or negative.

North node in the 11th nodal House — South node in the 5th nodal House (natal 2nd and 8th Houses). The point of power which will lead to an expression of Self is generated here in the House of ideals, humanitarianism and social-mystical creativity. The challenge is to become in some way an agent for that spiritual, social or cultural purpose, and to work toward changing existing social conditions. The position of the South node indicates that the path of greatest ease lies in following one's personal desires and dramatizing one's personality — to go on an ego trip, acting from purely self-centered motives. One must integrate those personal creative capacities with the needs of society, and thereby lead a transpersonal life. In order to do this, one may have to make greater efforts to discover his true friends and to work with them for truly individualized ideals.

North node in the nodal 12th House — South node in the nodal 6th House (natal 1st and 7th Houses). This is the end-phase of the nodal cycle with the positive, progressive accent on the fulfillment of one's collective and social responsibilities. The individual will must be curbed. In some cases, the karma of the past, the unfinished business, or the social results of one's actions during the previous nine years, may precipitate a crisis on personal as well as social levels. Through meditation and introspection one should extract the meaning and true value of all he has done, felt and thought since the beginning of the nodal cycle. Such meaning and value must be found not only in terms of one's personal Self, but also in terms of what one has tried to contribute to others and to the world. Then, on the basis of one's understanding of this value (even if it be of a negative character), one will be ready to orient himself toward the new cycle in clear consciousness of what he should or should not do. The path of least resistance at this time is described by the South node in the nodal 6th House. Unless one can shake off the acquired habit of personal devotion to an ideal or personal control of "inferiors", he will not be able to fulfill the destiny of that social task or responsibility which transcends his individual will and policy.

The Eclipse Cycles

An eclipse is the total or partial obscuring of one heavenly body by another. Although it may apply to any planet, visible or not, the term generally refers to the two "Lights", the Sun and Moon. This phenomenon is possible because, when viewed from the Earth, the solar and lunar discs appear to be nearly the same size. Thus, when the disc of the Moon covers the disc of the Sun, the eclipse of the latter is total; and the corona of the Sun, which spreads outside the solar disc, is made visible. In a Lunar eclipse, the Earth passes between the Sun and Moon, casting its shadow on the lunar disc. Eclipses are not isolated events, but special moments in the Moon's nodal cycles. They occur when a New Moon or a Full Moon takes place on or near the zodiacal degree at which the North and/or South node of the Moon is found. As previously discussed, the Moon's nodes are points in space at which the planes of the apparent path of the Sun and the path of the Moon intersect. They represent a synthesis of the solar and lunar factors within human consciousness; an eclipse, therefore, symbolizes an obscuring of one of those factors. It is a symbolic war between the "Solar Angel" and the "Lunar Lords" governing the past of mankind. Because in Man's awareness they appear to be of equal size, the opponents are evenly matched.

Solar eclipses occur when a New Moon falls within about 18 degrees of zodiacal longitude on either side of the North or South node. Thus each node is at the center of a 36 degree zodiacal region within which solar eclipses may occur every year. Since the Sun takes nearly 37 days to pass through these regions, while the Moon takes only 29½ days to pass from one New Moon to the next, it follows that there must be a solar eclipse at *each node every year.* The maximum number of solar eclipses possible in a single year is five, and this occurs approximately every three centuries. The last time this phenomenon occurred was in 1935. Only a few eclipses are total, however; most of them are partial and some are annular (when the periphery of the Sun's disc shines like a ring of light around its obscure core.)

Because the shadow of the Moon is only about 90 miles wide, total solar eclipses are visible only within a small section of the Earth's surface. An eclipse is only "total", therefore, for those regions located within such a 90-mile-wide path on the Earth's surface. Elsewhere it can only be partial — or altogether unseen, because at a solar eclipse or at any New Moon, the Moon passes between the Sun and the Earth. The Moon's nodes move at the rate of about 3 minutes a day, with a complete nodal cycle being 18.6 years duration. Since the motion of the nodes through the zodiac is retrograde, their zodiacal longitude is constantly decreasing. Therefore, the Sun comes to the North and South nodes of the Moon at an earlier date every year. The interval between two successive annual conjunctions of the Sun and the North node of the Moon is approximately 346 2/3 days. This interval is called an "eclipse year", and is *on an average* about three weeks shorter than the complete solar year. Thus there was a South node solar eclipse in May 1975, April 1976, April 1977 and April 1978, each year occurring about 12 days earlier than the preceding year. In those same years there were also North node eclipses in November, October and September. There also exists what is known as the "Metonic" cycle — named for the Greek astronomer Meton who purportedly discovered it in the 5th century B.C. This cycle is 19 years long and contains 235 lunation cycles. It measures the recurrence of an eclipse at approximately the same degree of the zodiac and on the same day, whether or not that eclipse is visible at any specific location.

Actually, there are New Moons which occur on the same day and at the same zodiacal degree every 19 years; however, only a few of them are eclipses. This is because the nodal cycle is shorter than 19 years. In terms of person-centered astrology, the nodal cycle of 18.6 years is most useful for determining the approximate regions of the zodiac in which eclipses *can* fall each year. For example, if a person has a planet or planets near 5 degrees Aquarius and an eclipse falls on or near that degree at the end of January during the first year of his life, then every 18.6 years thereafter there will be an eclipse near 5 degrees Aquarius conjuncting his natal configuration. Furthermore, either six months before or after that January eclipse, there will be another eclipse in opposition to the natal Aquarius point. This opposition eclipse will also repeat itself every 18.6 years.

All of this goes to show that *there is a sort of eclipse season every 9 to 10 years touching the same natal planet or planets* once the first eclipse contact has been made. The results of such eclipse contacts will depend, in the first place, on the number of eclipses recurring within a two-year period upon an important zone in the birth-chart. At certain times there can be as many as seven eclipses, five solar and two lunar (as in 1935, which was an exceptional year); at other times there may be only two solar and no lunar eclipses (as in 1951). What should be stressed is not the occurrence of one particular eclipse upon one particular natal planet, but rather the existence of recurring eclipse seasons. Thus, the transit cycle of the nodes themselves (near which eclipses will inevitably occur) is probably more significant than the eclipses *in individual birth-charts*. Total eclipses and their geographical paths of totality are most significant when related to physical phenomena such as weather, earthquakes and so-called mundane events. Their importance has, however, been grossly exaggerated for individuals.

The significance of the transiting nodal cycle through the Houses has already been discussed. Since eclipses occur near the nodes, they simply emphasize those Houses. Such an emphasis may be spectacular; however, what it usually indicates is that the individual *may* find himself in some way dramatically related to events affecting either his geographical region or the collectivity of which he is a part. There are many instances in which the individual is not at all affected by such happenings — especially those cases where he does not feel related to the greater whole. In many cases where eclipses seem to relate to specific happenings in a person's life, the effect is felt some six months earlier than the time of the eclipse contact with the natal chart. This means that the effect came about either when the transiting Sun conjoined the opposite node to the one involved in the eclipse, or when the transiting node conjoined the planet before the eclipse did.

Although solar eclipses, when total, are visible only within a 90-mile-wide path on the Earth's surface, lunar eclipses are visible to the entire hemisphere which is turned toward the Moon at the time. Lunar eclipses occur when a Full Moon (the Earth positioned between the Sun and the Moon) takes place within a region of approximately 12½ degrees on either side of the North or South node. Since the Sun — and consequently the Earth's shadow — takes at most 26 days to pass through these regions of which each node is the center, there is a period of 26 days twice a year during which a lunar eclipse is possible, although not inevitable. There are, therefore, two eclipse seasons every year, when the Sun is near the North and the South nodes. During these times there may be a solar or a lunar eclipse, or both. A North node eclipse season occurs when the Sun is near the North node, and a South node eclipse season when the Sun is near the South node. As North and South nodes have different — although complementary — meanings, it follows the North node eclipses have to be interpreted differently from south node eclipses.

If a solar eclipse occurs near the North node of the Moon, it will partake of the meaning of the northward motion of the Moon; while if it occurs near the South node, it will take on the meaning of the southward motion. In general, when a planet or the Moon is at its North node, it has an especially strong projective power and extroverted meaning; whereas, when at its South node, it has a more receptive and introverted meaning. For this reason, during a North node solar eclipse, the Moon is a positive factor, while the Sun is relatively more passive. On the other hand, during a South node solar eclipse, the Moon being receptive, the solar power is the strong positive pole. Here we may recall the illusion of the equal size of the Sun and Moon when seen from the Earth, for in eclipses the astrologer deals with a relationship between two equal factors which exchange polarities. Furthermore, as Rudhyar points out in his book *Person-Centered Astrology,** eclipses relate the Moon most significantly not only to the Earth, but also to the Sun. As the Moon represents the past and the Sun the present, the past will tend to obscure the present in a solar eclipse, while the present will tend to wipe out the past in a lunar eclipse. A North node eclipse begins something which comes to a conclusion at the following South node eclipse. When eclipse occurrences are measured according to the 18.6 year nodal cycle, the astrologer is always measuring eclipses of the same polarity. A North node eclipse is followed 18.6 years later by another North node eclipse. The same is true for south node eclipses. A North node eclipse on a natal point, however, will be followed by a south node eclipse on that same natal point about nine years later. This creates an individual eclipse cycle relating specifically to that natal position on which the eclipses fall.

THE NORTH NODE SOLAR ECLIPSE. Since the Moon is conjunct her North node, she is the positive factor in this kind of eclipse. New Lunar faculties or powers are to be built into the personality, and a new type of adjustment to circumstances is demanded. The obstruction of the Sun by the lunar disc, which takes place in all total eclipses whether of the North or South node variety, becomes the dominant factor in North node eclipses. The Moon absorbs as much as it can of the solar power normally directed toward the Earth and, depending symbolically on the degree of totality of the eclipse, quantitatively reflects nothing. Lunar factors, therefore, will dominate the consciousness, accentuating the ego needs, expediency, opportunism, selfishness, and the emotional needs born of the past. The compulsion of habits and automatic behavior is strong, for the solar-spiritual vision is, for the time being, eclipsed.

If a lunar eclipse follows a North node solar eclipse, the Moon will then be conjunct her South node and the Sun will be the positive factor. The lunar emphasis gives way, and a reactionary effect due to a reinstatement of the solar will and purpose is possible. The compulsion of the

---

*Published by CSA Press, 1976, pp. 288-289.

past, the strong egocentricity, and the karmic forces aroused during the North node solar eclipse may slowly recede into the background, or be effectively neutralized or fulfilled. During a lunar eclipse, as the Earth passes between the Sun and the Moon, the Moon is symbolically cut off from the light of the Sun. There is a temporary obscuration of man's psychic nature, his feelings and his personal psychological capacity to adapt to circumstances. Karmic forces, or inhibited or repressed psychic or emotional energies can overwhelm the consciousness momentarily, as one faces his "dweller on the threshold" — the fruits of his psychological complexes.

Unless the lunar eclipse touches important points in the birth-chart, specifically the Horizon or Meridian axes or some important planetary opposition, its occurrence may not be evident. However, if the eclipse does touch an important axis or opposition, the pole which is affected by the eclipsed Moon can be stimulated in a disintegrative way. One's habitual use of the planetary function or his habitual pattern of meeting the experiences of the House whose cusp is touched by the eclipsed Moon, tends to break down. The results will differ in each case, depending on the psychological strength of the individual. In the best of instances, this confrontation can lead to a liberation from past weakness- es — to positive fulfillment of karma and a dissipation of the "dweller on the threshold." In any case, however, the experience tends to be a bit frightening.

THE SOUTH NODE SOLAR ECLIPSE. Since the Moon is conjunct its South node, she is the passive factor in such an eclipse. The Moon is receptive to the Sun and is stimulated to release what has been assimi- lated and built up in the past, especially in the area of one's personal feelings and emotions. An intensification of solar will and purpose stirs the ego and the feelings, and pushes one to act forcefully according to "one's lights." If "one's lights" — one's sense of individual destiny — make it possible, then the person may be stimulated to take a strong personal stand in relation to some present social trend, or to some spectacular event in his geographical area. This will be especially true if he lives in a location touched by the path of the eclipse.

When a lunar eclipse follows a South node solar eclipse, the Moon will then be conjunct her North node and will be the positive factor. Here a reaction- ary effect to what was started at the solar eclipse can be expected. Ele- ments out of the past, habitual egocentric behavior especially related to the display of one's moods and feelings, and the everyday automatisms can reaffirm their force in conditioning an individual's actions and may even cause one to react negatively to what was set in motion at the solar eclipse. The often apparent negative and destructive effect of a solar eclipse may be said to come from the lunar eclipse which follows and which challenges the spectacular opportunity to take a new and positive stand offered by the South node solar eclipse. It is therefore important to note whether or not a solar eclipse is followed by a lunar eclipse. Many times the lunar eclipse precedes the solar eclipse during a given eclipse season. The astrologer must take these possibilities into consideration in his interpretation of the situation.

If the solar eclipse is followed by a lunar eclipse, we have a complete lunation cycle which stands out as a whole. Whatever extraordinary activity is started at the New Moon eclipse will be fatefully and spectacularly fulfilled or repudiated at the following eclipsed Full Moon. The whole lunar month will be a period of concentrated vital activity. The nature of that activity will, however, depend on whether the initiating solar eclipse is a North node or a South node eclipse. If, on the other hand, *a solar eclipse is preceded by a lunar eclipse,* then the Full Moon will serve to break down some past condition within one's personal nature or in his circumstances, leaving that person free to emphasize new elements in his life and make a new start at the time of the subsequent solar eclipse. In this instance, the Full Moon results will not be so spectacular — especially if the solar eclipse is of the South node variety. Then there will not be a negative lunar reaction capable of upsetting the powerful new trend set up at the eclipsed New Moon.

Here again, however, much will depend on the nodal polarity of the eclipses. *If a North node lunar eclipse is followed by a South node solar eclipse,* one may be confronted during the two week interval which separates them with a resurgence of repressed psychic energies. The results of one's previous patterns of adapting to circumstances may suddenly seem too automatic and deadening for one's continued growth. One's awareness of these personal limitations will perhaps push him to make a dramatic move at the following South node solar eclipse. Everything will depend on the way in which one meets the lunar eclipse confrontation — whether this confrontation will make him stronger, or merely end in an emotional storm.

If a South node lunar eclipse is followed by a North node solar eclipse, one is faced by a dilemma opposing the spiritual will, purpose and vision to the demands of one's conscious ego and automatic habit patterns. Theoretically, the Sun is the stronger, and therefore it should be possible to look at one's past and one's conditioning in an objective manner. A person can then take steps at the following solar eclipse to free himself from the compulsions of his lunar nature. A new adjustment to circumstances is demanded, requiring basic changes in one's habit patterns. At *a North node solar eclipse,* however, the Moon is the stronger, so freeing oneself from the power of the ego becomes difficult. The ego will take the intiative and decide what has to be done in order to build itself up in what it feels to be a better and more powerful way. Lunar factors will dominate the consciousness, and so freedom from their pull will be more difficult in this case than in the instance of a North node lunar eclipse followed by a South node solar eclipse.

In all these cases, the importance of the eclipse experiences will, of course, depend on whether or not the eclipses tie in specifically with the natal chart. If important planets or planetary oppositions or the Angles of the chart are implicated, these will be over-stimulated and a person may be knocked off balance. Eclipses are always challenges to change one's established manner of behavior, feeling and thought and are often accompanied by emotional upheavals which are an individual *reaction* to the challenge. One should try to get behind these surface reactions and to find out what change is asked of him. Then he must put his will at the service of the Self to bring about a spiritual rebirth.

FEAR VS. THE HUMANISTIC APPROACH TO ECLIPSES. From the humanistic point of view, it is not psychologically healthy to view eclipses in the traditional manner as isolated, awesome events. Astrologers, as well as their clients, can easily be overcome by the ancient superstitious fear of eclipses which is still alive in the collective unconscious. Far from being isolated phenomena, eclipses are essentially strong moments of emphasis in the nodal cycle of the Moon. All astrological factors, eclipses included, derive their essential meaning from the various cycles of which they are characteristic features or crucial phases. Those who wish to use astrology humanistically must understand at the outset that the given *cycle* is the source of basic meaning, not the particular point or planet, or its position or aspect considered as an isolated fact. For this reason, it would be psychologically safer when counselling not even to mention the word "eclipse." If an eclipse is about to fall on an important point in a birth-chart, the astrologer should not say, for example, "There will be an eclipse falling on your birthday," but rather, "You are coming to an important phase in the 19-year nodal cycle in your life." The humanistic astrologer is not trying to predict events; he is trying to assist that person to understand himself or herself better, and to feel through astrological cycles the rhythmic development of an overall life-purpose and life-meaning.

Eclipses simply measure intense confrontations with all those things in human nature which hinder spiritual progress by keeping one in a rut, albeit a comfortable and happy rut. They are opportunities to use the past and the present — all that one has previously acquired, as well as where he stands at a given moment — in order to build a more creative future. Since they always challenge an individual to discard all limiting influences and to start something new, they may be stressful times. Whether or not there will be destructive results will depend on the strength of one's inner nature and his capacity to maintain his personal integrity while remaining open to necessary changes in the *expression* of his personality. Lunar eclipses may be more difficult to face constructively than solar eclipses; however, they are also challenges to attempt a new adjustment to life — to give a new quality to one's relationship to his environment. But an astrologer must always remember that eclipses which do not touch important points in the natal chart are not likely to produce strong confrontations for the individual, even though in terms of world events or natural phenomena they may be spectacular.

Solar and Lunar Cycles

The Metonic cycle of 19 years which measures the recurrence of New Moons at approximately the same degree of the zodiac is very close to the nodal cycle of 18.6 years. It is therefore worthwhile to record the contacts of the New Moons each month with the natal chart, bearing in mind that each contact will be repeated 19 years later. These New Moons will measure the opportunities to make a new start in the use of whatever element they touch in the birth-chart. Additionally, each new beginning must be related to the previous similar contact 19 years before, as it will be conditioned by what one did at that time. The eclipse contacts are simply particularly outstanding moments in the general New Moon cycle of contacts with the birth-chart.

THE SOLAR CYCLE. The yearly cycle of the Sun can be followed by establishing a birthday chart or a solar revolution (solar return) chart. These are well-established techniques and give pertinent data concerning the year for which they are drawn up. The meaning, however, must be read in terms of what the Sun means in an individual natal chart. Theoretically, charts can be drawn up for the cyclic return of any planet to its natal place, and the solar return is obviously the most important. Such solar charts will show how the outer environmental conditions will help or hinder one in his yearly attempts to renew his solar life-purpose.

Plotting out the passage of the Sun through the four quadrants of the birth-chart is also valuable. Whenever the transiting Sun crosses an Angle of the chart each year, it is the time to accentuate the use of the psychological function related to that Angle and quadrant.* The Ascendant and the 1st quadrant indicate an emphasis on the intuition and all one's attempts to reach a deeper self-awareness. As the Sun crosses the Nadir and transits the 2nd quadrant, the feelings and all one's attempts to express the deeper aspects of one's nature are accentuated. As it crosses the Descendant and moves up through the 3rd quadrant, the Sun will stimulate both one's capacity for sensation and his attempts to develop his perception, esthetic or otherwise, through deeper contacts with people and the outer world of objects. When the Sun reaches the

---

*See diagram of the four quadrants in Chapter I.

Midheaven and transits the 4th quadrant, one's thinking capacity and his attempts to establish himself more significantly in the social scheme will come to the fore.

THE LUNAR CYCLE. An astrologer may treat the transiting lunar cycle each month in the same way as the annual solar cycle through the quadrants of the birth-chart; however, the indications are generally too weak to be noticed unless other more important transits accentuate the same trend. It may be more significant to mark the days each month when the transiting Moon goes through the Sign in which it was posited at birth.

The Moon has already been defined as representing the repeated, nearly automatic way in which people adjust themselves to the challenges and impacts of the environment in their everyday lives. The Moon shows the most expedient way, the compromises one is ready to make in order to take advantage of the situations which confront him, or to maintain the happiness and comfort of his body and emotions. Certain ways of behaving become so automatic that they are, in reality, quite compulsive. Because a person feels he is made a certain way, or because he adjusts to life according to his mother's example (or because he has tried to repudiate her example), the Self often identifies itself with one's instincts and feeling urges. A person will often passively follow or give in to circumstances which fit in with his instincts, feelings or the mood of the moment, and he will often rebel automatically against whatever seems contrary to those habit patterns. Repeated past actions and feeling attitudes, therefore, tend to dominate one's present behavior without his conscious awareness, even though they may at the same time hinder his attempts to meet the present situation in a new and creative way.

Each month the Moon returns to its natal position and re-accentuates its natal characteristics. Therefore, if one is trying to free himself from his compulsive habit patterns, the days when the transiting Moon passes through its natal Sign furnish the opportunity *(provided one is conscious of the fact)* to free himself from such compulsive behavior. Instead of reacting month after month in more or less the same way to everyday life situations — a repetition which makes the body and the emotions ever more fixed — one can become aware that the "I" is *not* identical with one's habitual reaction patterns. Because one is conscious of it and has decided to do something about it, he can use the accentuation of the natal Moon habit pattern by the transiting Moon to detach himself and to see what has compelled him to respond in a certain way to everyday life circumstances. This does not mean that a person must constantly struggle to suppress his lunar nature or to try to dominate it forcefully. Like it or not, the lunar aspect is part of the whole individual. But if one acts constantly in accordance with his lunar nature, he will not be conscious of his *solar* will, purpose and destiny. The Moon is an *instrument* of solar destiny or at least it should be, although most often it points to elements out of the past which must be overcome or transmuted before a person can really live according to that solar promise.

CARDINAL MOON. An individual's habit patterns can be dominating on three levels: activity, feeling and thought, and they have their astrological correspondence in the Cardinal, Fixed and Mutable Signs. If the natal Moon is in a Cardinal Sign, one tends to *act* repeatedly in a particular way in response to the everyday challenges of life. Cardinal Signs seek to release their energies in a direct fashion in relation to *circumstances*. They are the doers in life, reacting to concrete situations and problems without much regard for the people involved.

Moon in Aries. An individual with this natal Moon placement will act from a feeling of insecurity. The reaction to the mundane challenges of life is personal and generally according to the emotions or moods at that moment. The reactions change constantly, and consequently others may feel that the Aries Moon person cannot be counted on. The major life-emphasis is on being first, and they try to act in ways that make them stand out as individuals. Tranquility is an anathema, so to perpetuate a sense of aliveness, they seek challenging situations and continual excitement.

Moon in Cancer. The individual will limit the scope of his activities to some definite sphere, and within those established limits there will be a full and rich expression of the emotions. Situations and people are judged idiosyncratically, according to his personal experience. He will therefore have difficulty in facing up to situations which present him with elements beyond the limitations of that experience. Childhood experiences, and particularly the relationship to the mother, can establish habit patterns for a lifetime. A strong memory in regard to emotional wounds can lead to brooding and moodiness. The Cancer Moon can also be very patronizing and partisan in both his actions and his reactions.

Moon in Libra. A strong desire for social acceptance leads to extreme sensitivity to other people's opinions of him. The cultural values and ideals, and the standards of etiquette by which he judges others are the same criterion by which he is certain that society is judging him. Because he feels that he is being judged by the company he keeps, he becomes very class-conscious, even opportunistic in his choice of friends and associates. Above all, a person with a Libra Moon wants everything to be "nice". He abhors crudity and has difficulty confronting the harsher realities of life. For this reason he will attempt to surround himself with beautiful things (and people) and may even project his ideals upon them.

Moon in Capricorn. An individual with this placement will constantly seek to justify himself in the eyes of society, constantly striving to earn their approval and to show that he is worthy of being loved. The root cause of this insecurity lies in his childhood feelings of being unloved or unwanted. As an antidote to those feelings of emotional insecurity, he will seek some concrete form of social power, and he may use the prestige of his position or the attachment of those who look up to him for his own personal ends. This person has a strong sense of his own manifest destiny and may sacrifice anything or anyone to achieve that goal, for the ends seem to justify the means. He will work hard and can act superbly in the face of crisis. Above all, the Capricorn Moon person wants to feel needed and will do all in his power to make others feel that what he does is necessary to them.

FIXED MOON. When the natal Moon is in a Fixed Sign, the habit patterns are established primarily on emotional levels. There is a fixed desire to feel again and again what has been experienced in the past — to relive the experiences which brought intense happiness, emotional satisfaction or even pain and suffering. These people seek self-justification and are moved by the consequences of what happens around and to them. Their primary interest is in the effective use of power, and they will concentrate their energies in a specific direction and toward some definite purpose. People with fixed Moon can be dominated by ethical either/or judgements — right/wrong, good/bad, true/false; it is difficult for them to see the grey area which lies between such polarities. An inherent inflexibility in their lunar nature causes them to try to adapt their environment and the people in it to suit their needs, rather than adapting themselves to the demands of their surroundings.

Moon in Taurus. With this natal Moon placement a person will seek coherency and consistency in all things. He is pragmatically oriented, and his feelings are conditioned to appreciate both things and people according to realistic, tangible values rather than abstract concepts. Change is extremely difficult for him, especially sudden change. For this reason he may rely strongly on traditional cultural attitudes and customs. The Taurus Moon person is more sensuous than sensual and can gain a great deal of emotional satisfaction from the physical world around him, often to the extent of becoming totally absorbed in his own comfort. He is affectionate and will demonstrate his affections rather than repress them; therefore, in a society in which men are supposed to shake hands rather than kiss and hug, this type of behavior may be mistaken for effeminate.

Moon in Leo. This individual will often display a strong personal magnetism, which may be seen by some as arrogance and self-conceit. Of all things, he most values his reputation and will do whatever necessary to be admired. The Leo Moon person will be charming and persuasive. He loves to entertain and can be compulsively generous. His vanity is easily wounded and he does not take criticism easily, nor does he tolerate people who put obstacles in his way. Superficially he may appear more flexible than people with Moon in the other fixed Signs, but he isn't. He is emotionally self-determined and has a strong sense of responsibility both to himself and to those who have given him their admiration. He loves to go "1st class" and may do without rather than having to economize.

Moon in Scorpio. One with this natal Moon Sign displays a strong control over his emotions. Although he seeks intense emotional experiences, especially in the area of inter-personal relationships, and can become very jealous and possessive regarding a loved one, he will rarely *display* the depth of his feelings. This is especially true if the person has been hurt in some way by that relationship, or feels that he has been betrayed by someone. He actually prides himself on the fact that no one knows the seething mass of torment deep inside him. He is more sensual than sensuous, and may become pre-occupied with sex, seeking some form of completion through the partner or a self-loss in the act itself. He will not only remember every wrong done to him, but may spend years plotting revenge. He often gives in to emotional fears, especially regarding the loss of a loved one. The power of the inner compulsions under which he acts are incomprehensible to others, as are the depth and intensity of his feelings.

Moon in Aquarius. The personal feelings are strongly colored by a highly developed social consciousness with this position. There is also an emotional dependence on the values and ideals of some group or organization. This is often, however, more a camouflage for a basic underlying fear of emotional involvement on a one-to-one basis than a desire to belong to a greater and more inclusive whole. If he becomes a compulsive joiner it will be to find safety in numbers, because essentially he prefers to work alone. Emotions are examined intellectually rather than experienced on a feeling level. He would rather observe life than participate in it, and therefore his basic approach will be impersonal. Because he thinks of himself as unique, he will be more likely to follow some fad or fringe movement rather than a traditional, orthodox group. Rebellion for its own sake is for him a virtue, and he may occasionally do or say something bizarre just to see the effect it will have on other people.

MUTABLE MOON. When the natal Moon is in a Mutable Sign an individual's habit patterns are established mainly on mental levels. The tendency is to adjust one's experience in terms of some theory or belief system and then to express oneself according to the adopted style.

Mutable Moon Sign people love word association games. They invent concept upon concept as to what *is*, and then wonder why such and such a thing happened. They work out intricate formulas and plans in an attempt to repeat pleasant experiences and avoid hurtful ones. They tend to be more personally involved in the concept than in the reality; and more than the Cardinal and Fixed Moon Signs, their actions and reactions to life are governed by their belief systems.

Moon in Gemini. The personal adjustments to life are conditioned by the desire to be knowledgeable in many diverse fields of interest, and to be admired by others for his know-how. The danger here is superficiality and lack of consistency in thought. The personal feeling-judgements are often mistaken for logic and rationality. Everything is interesting, but that interest, whether it be in things or people, is rarely sustained. He is a good propagandist but rarely will be deeply committed to the idea which he puts forward with momentary enthusiasm. Above all else, the Gemini Moon person thrives on mental stimulation. He can become so preoccupied with manipulating words, ideas and symbols that the reality to which they refer often escapes him. He does not like to be pinned down. Stability is an anathema to him, and he will seek variety at the expense of security. To him the difference between a rut and a grave is only a matter of degree.

Moon in Virgo. An individual with this natal Moon position will follow strict patterns of behavior established for logical or moral reasons in his personal adjustment to life. He is often rigid and prudish both in thought and behavior and will value detail, neatness and technique. Usually the Virgo Moon person has an innate fear or distrust of his emotions and may be unwilling to allow them a free expression. He prefers, rather, to adapt to life according to intellectual systems or psychological theories. He has an extraordinarily developed sense of duty and is highly conscientious. Above all he will seek order in his life, and prefers doing things according to an established plan. When taken to extremes, this can result in behavior which is old maidish and critical. This person can also raise worrying to an art form.

Moon in Sagittarius. The personal adjustments to life are conditioned by a strong desire for freedom, both physical and mental. He thrives on a feeling of wide-open spaces, and when he feels fenced in he will run away. He is generally open and friendly with people but not always capable of reacting to their particular differences and needs. He does not like having to deal with the petty details involved in his long-range plans. He is a good talker, and since he enjoys stimulating people intellectually and feeling the mental effect he has on them, he also makes a good teacher. Above all, a person born with the natal Moon in Sagittarius needs to feel that there is a purpose in life. He needs some form of belief system, although not necessarily an organized or traditional one. There is a tendency to gamble — if not with his material possessions, then with his health, his career or his social position. Because he cannot lie, he is often gullible.

Moon in Pisces. An individual with this natal Moon placement will often condition his life in terms of his personal hopes for a better future — for some ideal condition or transcendent state. He is extremely sensitive to the collective mood and is very susceptible to it. He may be hyper-sensitive on many levels, from psychic to allergic. Although he is always ready to sacrifice himself to others, he is often deeply (and not necessarily silently) resentful of his own condition, in which case he becomes the sighing woe-filled martyr. Since there is a strong tendency to live vicariously, as well as the ability to reflect the moods and feelings of others, he may find an outlet for this in acting. Essentially he does not like concrete reality, and some form of escapism, such as drugs or alcohol, can become a danger. The tendency to dwell too much in a dream world can greatly hinder his ability to act effectively in the face of concrete reality, as can his tendency to empathize rather than to sympathize with the problems of others.

These are some of the possibilities which may be accentuated by the transiting Moon passing through the natal Moon Sign every 28 days. Because such tendencies will be reinforced, they will enter more easily into one's conscious awareness, which is the prime requisite for any change to take place.

IV

The Personal Planets
Mercury, Venus & Mars

The transit cycles of these three fast-moving planets are generally ignored by most astrologers because, due to their speed, their aspects are supposed to correlate only to the superficial trivia of day-to-day existence. Although this attitude is entirely comprehensible in terms of an event-oriented approach to astrology, the person-centered astrologer finds these cycles to be especially significant in the understanding of an individual's inner life. As with all the planets, their essential meaning is derived from the astronomical data — especially in their relation to the Earth, which in humanistic astrology represents the human being. Most significant are the retrograde periods of these planets. This phenomenon of retrogradation is, in fact, an optical illusion. The planets do not *actually* move backwards; only from the vantage point of Earth is this observed. Thus, in the humanistic approach, the cycles of Mercury, Venus and Mars are intrinsically related to *both* the Earth and the Sun. When a person looks from the Earth (the human point-of-view) toward the center of the solar system (the life-giving Sun), he sees two planets between himself and the Sun: Venus and Mercury. These are called "interior" planets and refer to man's inner life of feelings (Venus) and thought (Mercury). When he looks outward toward the furthest reaches of his solar system, the first planet seen is Mars. For this reason, Mars refers to the power of initiative — the way a person starts things and exteriorizes his energy.

THE INVOLUTIONARY AND EVOLUTIONARY TIDE. In his book *The Practice of Astrology**, Dane Rudhyar speaks of a tide in the circulation of energies within the solar system. Accordingly, all planets have a two-fold meaning, first in terms of their progressive exteriorization of solar energy from the Sun outward to Saturn, and secondly in terms of the progressive evolutionary return tide from Saturn back to the Sun, which signifies a growth in consciousness. The energy symbolized by the Sun is a primal, undifferentiated solar potential sweeping out into the universe and modified progressively by each planet it touches. Mercury is the first differentiator of the solar life-force, Venus the second. Thus, these two inner planets define the essence of all concrete manifestation — the electro-magnetic field. Mercury provides the electricity and Venus the magnetism.

---

*Published by Servire, 1968, Holland and now available from Shambhala Publications.

Mercury-electricity is the type of electricity which scientists have now found to be the dynamic core of organic life — the potential in all living organisms that makes cellular inter-changes possible. Flowing through the nervous system, this energy makes muscular activity possible and conveys sensory impressions to the brain, providing a physiological foundation for thought processes. Mercury symbolizes both the rhythm of this bi-polar, oscillatory, alternating current, and the special character of the electric potential which it makes available to the organism out of the vast reservoir of impersonal solar life-force. In the birth-chart, Mercury represents not only the nervous system itself, but more profoundly the quality of the organic electrical potential which animates it. The cycles of Mercury measure the changes of polarity in the distribution of this electrical potential; its position in relation to the Sun at birth will establish the type of electrical polarization in both the nervous system of the individual and also in the etheric body which is the energy counterpart of the physical organism. This will be discussed in detail later in this chapter when I refer to the Sun-Mercury cycle.

Venus, the second differentiator of the solar life-force, then attracts this electric potential and gives it an archetypal form — creating an electro-magnetic field. Just as a magnet induces iron filings to assume a definite, though invisible, pre-existing pattern, Venus-magnetism can be described as the power to give form. Involutionary Venus is therefore the symbol of all seed-patterns — that which gives all matter its unique magnetic and cohesive strength. Thus Venus refers to what is often called the "Higher Self" — the latent spiritual archetype toward which the living and growing human personality may conform if one lives true to his solar impulse, i.e., his reason and purpose for being. It is not the spiritual essence as such, but rather the potential inherent in all matter to be what it truly is.

The next step in this involutionary tide is Mars, symbolizing the power of initiative. Before the essential solar-purpose of a man's destiny can be released into effective action through Mars, it must first be polarized by the electrical and nervous function of his organism (Mercury) and then be given a particular form by the Venus magnetic field. Thus Mars represents the impulse to act according to one's *particular* character with its particular needs. This is what differentiates Mars energy from solar energy. The Sun in the birth-chart indicates the *direction* of the source of one's spiritual potential. Through the Mercury-Venus electro-magnetic field this solar potential takes on an individual character and quality, becoming organic power for individual use and according to an individual purpose. Then, according to the particular function and character of the individual, Mars is the means of release of this power in outward action and initiative. This means that Mars' action is conditioned by the quality and quantity of Mercury's electrical potential (necessary for Martian muscular activity), and by the particular character, needs and values which establish a person's uniqueness of being — his archetypal form described by Venus.

The Venus-Mars Cycle

Astronomically, Venus and Mars form a complementary pair on either side of the Earth. Being the closest planets to the Earth, they refer symbolically to the most intimate factors in the human personality — the most immediate and spontaneous expressions of human nature. There is a deep, reciprocal action between these two planets which constantly measures an individual's most intimate and direct responses to whatever or whomever he meets in life. The individual finds his self-motivation through these planets and thereby takes up his personal standard. The sense of "I" and the feeling of being different from others, along with the instinctive knowledge of what is good, valuable and fulfilling for that "I", are linked to the Venus function. Mars represents the desire and ability to act out this feeling in a purely spontaneous manner. When Venus decides that someone or something may be of value, then Mars will go out to conquer or to meet that person or thing; and if Venus finds it dangerous or detestable, then Mars will either fight against it or run from it.

Venus and Mars, therefore, refer to whatever makes a person act in a natural and spontaneous manner *without reference* to any outside social conditions (which come under the symbolism of Jupiter and Saturn — the social planets). They correspond to purely *personal* exigencies: Venus determining one's particular character and needs, and Mars governing the impulse to act according to this particular character with its particular requirements. These may be conditioned by instinct, by one's heredity and environment (as is the case of a person who is not yet psychologically individualized and therefore acts according to the collective norm), or they may be truly individually and spiritually oriented. As the results of this Martian expression lead to the experiences of pleasure or pain, satisfaction or disappointment, greater confidence and faith or despondency and fear, Venus will build up through these experiences a personal sense of values. The feeling of what is good or bad is established at the Venus-Mars level of experience; and, from these essential feeling-judgements, one acts. Venus, however, not only establishes the individual character and needs of a person but also decides whether or not a particular life-experience really corresponds to one's organic and psychological needs. Thus, the Venus feeling-judgements are made not only on the basis of experience, but also *a priori* — before the fact and independent of experience.

As a person individualizes himself and establishes his personal reality — his sense of — "I am I", the Venus seed-pattern will progressively grow from the biological level to the mental-emotional level, and ultimately to the spiritual level according to the spiritual archetype toward which he strives. Each of us acts at certain times on an instinctual level and at other times in terms of individualized and personal characteristics and needs. Rarely do we act as an individualized form of Spirit. Nonetheless, whatever the level of functioning, Venus will indicate the basic character of being, and the strength and quality of the Venus feeling-judgements will depend on the *value* placed on the person, situation or internal organic condition.

In addition to the personal values of Venus, which are a purely subjective sensation, one must not forget the considerations of society. The importance given to the prevailing social, cultural, religious and moral traditions of the community into which one is born and in which one lives cannot be discounted. Venus values are constantly conditioned by collective agreement. People and things will be judged good or bad, hateful or desirable, not purely on the basis of one's individual character and needs, but also by the collective norm. They may also be defined by the value which an individual places on the moral or religious ideals of behavior, feeling and thought inherent in the philosophy to which he subscribes. All the conflicts extant in the world today — the either/or ethical judgements — are based on Venus values being opposed one to another. In any interpretation this fact must be taken into account.

In traditional astrological interpretations, Venus generally refers to the emotional life — and most specifically love. In the strictest psychological sense, however, this is not true. Venus symbolizes feelings because one's feelings are based on the value which an individual places on things and people. If one "loves" or experiences "emotion", it means his basic concepts of good or bad have been stirred, and therefore he will go out to seek that which he has judged as desirable. E-motion means just that — to "go out" — and is the expression of Mars rather than Venus. Actually, emotions are the *projection* of feelings — they follow feelings just as Mars follows Venus. The love to which Venus refers must be viewed in a far larger context than that of personal feelings. It is an expression of the universal law of attraction and repulsion and as such is quite unrelated to the emotions. Venus in a birth-chart shows the *quality* of one's capacity to love — the value placed on love, rather than the individual expression of love. Venus shows the way in which one will meet love, if and when love comes his way. This individual way of meeting love will depend on those values which stir the feelings and make one attach the label "desirable" or "undesirable" to a person, idea or situation; therefore, it may be conditioned as well by negative factors within the self.

At the level of life symbolized by Venus and Mars, a person only experiences feelings and passes "emotional" judgements. Anything dealing with the thinking processes — concepts or intellectual judgements — comes under Mercury. Venus and Mars refer to the expression of an individual's essential character of being and its basic feelings and values. Those essential elements of human nature are often distorted or frustrated by the conscious ego. The conscious ego does not reveal in any clear way the primary character of an individual — it simply shows the structure of consciousness which has been built up progressively *as a result* of the experiences of that primary character in its contacts with the outer world, and especially through the behavior, feelings and thoughts of others. The conscious ego is a manifestation of Saturn and the Moon, which describe the established way of adjusting one's inherent Venusian character to life. The relationship of Saturn and the Moon to the Venus-Mars pair in the birth-chart will show the degree to which the expression (Mars) of the inner spiritual being (Venus) will tend to be distorted or confused by parental or familial pressures, or by the social patterns of behavior and thought prevalent in one's environment.

THE VENUS-MARS NATAL PHASE. In the cyclic conception of astrology endorsed by the humanistic approach, the conjunctions of Mars and Venus begin cycles of relationship between these two planets. These cycles refer to the development and expression of the most intimate and personal aspects of one's character, to one's most spontaneous responses to life (whenever Saturn and the Moon permit), and to the confrontations, challenges and opportunities which life offers. We are all born during a particular phase of this Mars-Venus cycle, and that gives a specific coloration to our intimate feelings and emotions. Even when there is no aspect between these two planets at birth, there will be a phase relationship between them. This phase relationship — whether waxing or waning; moving toward a waxing sextile, square, trine or opposition; or moving from the opposition toward a waning trine, square, sextile or conjunction — the phase will always accurately portray the way in which Venus and Mars will function within the personality. The source — whether karmic or ancestral — of the natal feeling and emotional tendency will be found in the Mars-Venus conjunction which occurred prior to birth. If this conjunction took place before the time of conception — which will be the case when Mars and Venus are in a waning phase at birth — then special attention should be paid to the opposition of these two planets prior to birth.

In any case, the aspects between Mars and Venus during the waxing half of their cycle — from conjunction to opposition — will have quite a different meaning from those aspects formed during the waning half of their cycle. During the waxing phase, Venus is the servant of Mars. The accent will be on the desire to express oneself, and to go out into experience on the basis of instinctive or subjective values. Here the value of an experience will be revealed *after* the act. For this reason, a waxing square between Venus and Mars — regardless of their Sign and House positions — often relates to the fact that the result of the experiences in the personal, intimate sphere of these two planets is not what one had hoped for at the time of initiating it. Conversely, aspects during the waning half of the cycle have their source in the opposition between Mars and Venus. The opposition of these two planets is, positively, a symbol of emotional objectivity; however, negatively it can also reveal a condition of emotional deadlock, indecision or conflict between the desire and the will to act. It may reveal an incapacity to mobilize sufficient energy to go after what one wants intensely. A waning square may create a crisis in consciousness brought about by a conflict between desires and established values. It is an aspect of emotional involvement — of experiences aiming at breaking the comfortable inertia of one's happiness or self-complacency. One is led to revise the values on which he has based his behavior, and to reconsider his conscious motives in the emotional sphere of his life.

VENUS LUCIFER AND VENUS HESPERUS.* Viewed from the Earth, Venus will never be more than 48 zodiacal degrees from the Sun; thus it will never be *visible* high in the heavens, but only near the horizon. Venus will either rise before the Sun and appear in the early morning sky near the eastern horizon, or it will rise after the Sun and be seen in the evening sky near the western horizon. In both instances, its hour of glory is brief; for the morning star disappears with the dawn, and the evening star shortly follows the Sun beneath the horizon of our conscious awareness. To the *morning star* Rudhyar has given the name: *Venus Lucifer,* connoting an emotional life geared toward the future. Here one is filled with an air of expectation, and often cannot wait for the consummation of his desires. There is an adolescent emotional attitude — impulsive and over-sensitive. Sometimes there may be difficulty in expressing one's feelings, or the person may cover up his real feelings and appear outwardly cold. In its best manifestations, however, Venus Lucifer is emotionally communicative, creative and filled with enthusiasm for new things; and additionally, there may also be a prophetic sense.

Rising after the Sun, Venus appears as the *evening star.* Rudhyar has named this astronomical phenomenon *Venus Hesperus,* and correlates it with a more "cultured" emotional life which is colored by ethical or moral precepts. The person feels *after* the act. These feelings and emotions tend

---

*Cf. Rudhyar's *Astrological Study of Psychological Complexes,* Shambhala Publications, Chapter II.

to be conditioned by past experiences and also by what society dictates that one should feel under the given circumstances. The tendency will be to judge the value of one's experiences according to accepted moral or esthetic standards. Here one is constantly making efforts to be "objective" in emotional matters. This tendency, or that of subjecting one's feelings and emotions to what the community considers to be ethically or morally right or wrong behavior, can hinder any truly spontaneous expression of one's particular character and needs. If one's experiences have been disappointing in the past, then the tendency to feel after the act can also inhibit the emotional life through fear. Thus, Venus Hesperus often gives indications similar to what can be expected from a weak or blocked Mars function, for Mars is the *function of expression* of Venus values and feelings.

VENUS RETROGRADE. A second important consideration in establishing the kind of Venus values which an individual will try to exteriorize through Mars is whether the planet was direct or retrograde at birth. When Venus is retrograde and therefore appears to move in a direction which is counter to that of the soli-lunar life-force, this means that the person's sense of value and feeling-judgements will be different from what is collectively considered as being "normal". This "difference" makes a person potentially capable of becoming more objective toward the habitual or assumed values and judgements of the community. He may act in his emotional life counter to accepted moral or ethical principles. In a general way, Venus retrograde asks a person to detach himself from the natural and compulsive desires and instincts which sway most people. It also demands a release from the habitual pressures exerted on the individual by the cultural, moral and religious standards prevalent in society.

This will be a life problem if Venus is retrograde at birth. The person with such a Venus may find himself obliged, as a result of personal-emotional conflicts, to develop a more introspective and perhaps even a mystical attitude toward life. There may also be sexual problems — either circumstances forbid a normal sexual life for one reason or another, or the person willingly foregoes the sexual aspect of life in order to fulfill some higher spiritual purpose. If the astrologer is confronted with a Venus retrograde problem, he should try to help his client realize that what is objectively a question of emotional or sexual frustration may have a positive spiritual value in terms of the essential life purpose. It seems that spirit develops in a direction which runs counter to the natural instincts. Venus retrograde is a symbol of such a counter movement. For this reason, this person must learn to work with the spirit within him and to accept the fact that so-called normal, instinctual fulfillment is not for him. He must transcend this urge and try to become creative on higher levels. Since Venus is retrograde, his Self (not necessarily his ego) is *potentially free* from the usually compulsive demands of the life-instincts (survival of the species); therefore, he stands a better chance than "normal" people to live according to his own truth. He may develop his personal capacities and detach his sense of value from those cultural, social and religious considerations which hold sway over unindividualized people. Of course, when a person tries to live in such a spiritually free way, he will certainly have difficulties in his contacts with so-called "normal" life-situations. Venus retrograde can signify problems in terms of normal social and outer *effectiveness*. However, the life-purpose of a person with such a Venus does not aim at such effectiveness in terms of already established values but rather at an inner change which could lead the individual to become a force in attempts at reorienting those established values.

MARS RETROGRADE. As is the case with all the planets beyond the orbit of the Earth, Mars is retrograde around the time of its opposition to the Sun. At that time Mars is closest to the Earth and fully illumined by the Sun, just as the Moon when it is Full. For this reason, the opposition phase in the Sun-Mars cycle is a symbol of *objectivity in action* — Mars retrograde is not a weak Mars. On the contrary, because the planet makes a loop and approaches ever closer to the Earth, its reddish light becoming increasingly more intense as it approaches its opposition to the Sun, its presence is imposed ever more insistently on human consciousness. When Mars is retrograde, the task before the humanistic astrologer is to try to see, in the fullest and clearest possible way, the meaning of the individual Mars function and the best way to use it. The Martian energy, normally outgoing, when retrograde is turned inward and subtly reoriented in a new direction. It may also be dammed up or frustrated in some way. Since Mars is the impulse to act — the external manifestation of Venus values — then a retrograde Mars is the principle significator of a deviated or frustrated capacity to express outwardly those values which Venus suggests. No one can say whether Mars retrograde will be regenerative or self-destructive in any given case. Both possibilities are always present. Generally speaking, however, the individual born with Mars retrograde should be advised by the astrologer to direct his emotional energies inward, and to be prepared to control them. He must use them in a way which is different than what is considered "normal".

In examining the lives of people born with Mars retrograde, one finds that their main concern has been to live according to some moral, religious, spiritual or other ideal of perfection. Superficially, this may appear to be a motley assortment, containing both saints and showpeople, martyrs and musicians, prophets and princes. It includes those who have suffered martyrdom for their faith such as Martin Luther King, Jr. and those who have received only fame and recognition such as Lord Byron and Mozart. Prophets such as Nostradamus and pioneers such as Annie Besant (birth control) and Sigmund Freud also had Mars retrograde in their natal charts, as did Beethoven, Alan Leo, Louisa Mae Alcott and Annie Oakley. A binding factor among this group was their resistance to the normal expression of their instincts — sexual or otherwise — either for some imposed reason such as O. Henry and Toulouse-Lautrec, or freely such as Thomas Mann. Although this group does include famous murderers and revolutionaries such as Pancho Villa and Leon Trotsky, one notices relatively few people involved in highly competitive occupations such as politics, sports and chess players.

When Mars is found retrograde at birth, the astrologer must immediately look to see whether the planet is in the first half of the retrograde period, when it has not yet reached its opposition to the Sun, or whether the opposition aspect has already taken place. If the opposition has not been reached, then the Mars problem may become clearer at the time when, by secondary progression, Mars comes to the opposition. There can then be a *conscious* experience of the problem and its possible solution. When, however, this opposition has already taken place before birth, the Mars problem will be a karmic factor existing in the unconscious mind, or it will refer to hereditary or social limitations on the individual's destiny.

THE TRANSITING MARS-VENUS CYCLE. As with all cyclic manifestations, the meaning of the Mars-Venus cycle is derived first from the astronomical data. The most significant feature here is the accent on the number five. Although the conjunctions of Venus and Mars occur about every two years, a cycle of *five* conjunctions can be detected in which nearly every fifth conjunction is one with Venus retrograde. Venus is retrograde at other times, of course, but not while in conjunction with Mars. This accent on the number 5, which is also revealed in the Sun-Venus cycle, is interesting in the light of Venus' basic symbol — the five-pointed star or Pentagram, which is also the symbol of creative man. Thus, the Venus-Mars cycle is intimately related to the creative potential within each individual. The conjunctions of Mars to retrograde Venus occur not only approximately every 77 months, but also every 32 years they recur in the same zodiacal signs (with approximately 7 degrees and 20 minutes average lag). Every *fifth* conjunction of Mars-Venus is therefore usually a conjunction with Venus retrograde; and *five* times, at 32 year intervals, this Mars-Venus retrograde conjunction occurs in the same sign. Furthermore, the numbers 32 (years) and 77 (months) both add up numerologically to *five*. Thus, in every respect, the conjunctions of Mars to Venus retrograde occur according to a five-fold rhythm, suggesting that they are particularly related to the Venus function. These fifth conjunctions — the only ones with Venus retrograde — come at the center of an approximate 9-month period during which there are three Mars-Venus conjunctions. Rudhyar considers them to be basic turning-points in the Mars-Venus relationship; since they fall in the middle of a 9-month period, the entire period will be of special significance to everything which deals with man's emotional life.

At the time of the Venus retrograde conjunction there is an opportunity to change one's Venus values and give a deeper spiritual significance to one's individual actions. A person should then try to move more freely and effectively, in terms of his true character and needs, toward whatever appears valuable and desirable. It would be worthwhile to check the times in the past when Mars conjoined Venus retrograde to see in what way they coincided with attempts at personal metamorphosis, at trying to establish a deeper and truer relationship between one's true Self and the set patterns of behavior of the conscious ego. One can use these periods to become more objective toward his intimate personal nature, so as to realize how far and in what way his behavior is conditioned by exterior and alien elements.

Mars-Venus Retrograde Conjunctions

1914	November 22	Sagittarius 8
1921	April 7	Taurus 10
1927	August 30	Virgo 23
1934	January 25	Aquarius 22
1940	June 7	Cancer 14
1946	November 7	Sagittarius 1
1953	March 22	Taurus 1
1959	August 14	Virgo 16
1966	January 9	Aquarius 14
1972	April 21	Gemini 17 — *Danny*
1978	October 22	Scorpio 23
1983	September 19	Leo 24 (Venus St. D. two days previous)

As always in the humanistic approach, one must relate this information to the natal chart in order to derive an individual meaning. The personal significance of these conjunctions will be colored by the natal House in which they fall.

In the 1st House this conjunction is likely to indicate a personal involvement in the general climate of change affecting the orientation of consciousness and attitudes in the collective. One will throw himself with intense emotional enthusiasm into activities aiming at a transformation of his personal feeling-judgements — perhaps flying in the face of the prevailing social and cultural trends. Since the emotions are strongly aroused, it may be necessary to avoid rashness and angry impulses and to hold oneself as steady as possible. A person can accomplish a great deal if he maintains the proper attitude at this time — especially by transmuting the lower impulses through some form of artistic or creative activity.

When this conjunction falls *in the 2nd House*, a person may have to reconsider the value-judgements for which he is ready to expend his energies and resources. One should ask himself if it is really worthwhile to spend so much time and effort on the furtherance of whatever has been attracting his attention. It may be necessary at this time to break free from the influence of one's cultural or ancestral past if that has been the primary determinant of his values, or to give those feeling-values a new, and more personalized meaning. The tendency to spend too much of one's resources and personal energies may be very strong and should be controlled. This could conceivably lead to a problem of self-control and purity of motive, or to a loss of either material possessions or values. In other cases, danger may arise by allowing oneself to act on the basis of irrational impulses.

Falling *in the 3rd House*, this conjunction can indicate a desire to reorient the way one expresses his personal feelings. This can precipitate disturbances in the everyday contacts with one's immediate environment, and especially within the family. One may verbalize one's feelings, or wish to put them on paper. Here one must remember that revolutionary feelings can lead to repercussions, and those things which one said or wrote in the heat of anger may be used against him later on. Emotional agitation can also lead to accidents. A person should not try to impose his newly endorsed values too forcefully on others. Although the mind may be stirred to seek independence from its many past illusions and traditional entanglements and to express its views with passion, the Mars-Venus retrograde conjunction in the 3rd House aims essentially at building the capacity to give a more beautiful, harmonious and significant meaning to one's everyday experiences.

In the 4th House this conjunction will signal a trend toward change in one's personal feeling-judgements, and those values will be felt rather than analyzed. The necessity to hold traditional ideas in a personally significant manner will be experienced rather than conceptualized, and one will try to reinterpret them and so release their vital meaning on an emotional level. There may be intense devotionalism — a fervent search for inner stability. The personal relationship to one's family and home may undergo a drastic change. At this time a person should try not to be too selfish or too preoccupied with his own particular problems. There will be a constant challenge throughout this period to act at all times from the deepest harmony of one's own nature.

The desire to express new feelings and new personal or cultural values can be very strong when this conjunction falls *in the 5th House.* During this period, the emotions tend to be arrogant and selfish. One can easily take on an aggressive attitude which, in the long run, can lead to difficult situations. Here one should watch the welfare of his children, or those whose education is in his care. The desire for new experiences of love, happiness and beauty may impel one to exteriorize his romantic dreams, or to fulfill a sensuous lust. The challenge, therefore, is to act with faith and strength of character as one tests his capacity to express his own significant values and symbols against the established attitudes and opinions of society. The reaction of loved ones and society at large will provide a mirror, revealing oneself to oneself as one really *is,* whether this be through intense happiness or great frustration.

When this conjunction falls *in the 6th House,* the strong emotional arousal can precipitate emotional and physiological disturbances. There is a challenge to overcome one's personal weakness and selfishness through work and service, which may necessitate a change in the basic values in his employer-employee or "master-disciple" relationships. In some cases, mixing love with work can provoke a crisis. A sense of a higher spiritual value, of a larger, more-than-personal reality, can provide the impulse to work for new and better life-conditions in spite of any pain or suffering which might be entailed.

Falling *in the 7th House,* this conjunction will indicate the tendency to become emotionally involved in changes which will significantly affect one's intimate relationships, especially marriage. There will be an urge to give new values and a new meaning to these relationships, or else to seek a new relationship. The quality and level of experiences in some intimate relationship may no longer satisfy, and one will feel the need to transcend them. One may realize that he must bring something of greater value to his relationships, or that he himself must become a symbol of some new value to others with whom he is in intimate personal contact. It will be necessary to control possessiveness and selfishness in love.

When this conjunction falls *in the 8th House,* the emotional outlook toward business enterprises or the fruits of one's interpersonal relationships will undergo a basic change. Here new values are being imposed from without, or else one will try personally to introduce those values into the relationships or groups in whose activities he partici- pates. One may need to control his emotions in order to avoid anger and violent methods when dealing with partnership matters, or matters of business organization. This does not mean, however, that one should not take the initiative in driving others to accept new goals in relation to marriage, business or group activities.

In the 9th House this conjunction will challenge the individual to involve himself emotionally in some new way in some philosophical, religious, or perhaps legal endeavor, while at the same time maintaining his basic sense of perspective. New developments affecting one internally on the feeling level may lead to a significant journey, or involve contacts with strangers or perhaps foreigners. At this time a person should seek to develop his creative imagination, and expand it according to the new point of view on which he has pinned his new faith. He should try to illuminate his personal and emotional life through a deeper understanding of social or spiritual values, thus enabling him to find a more personally significant place within the larger scheme of activity. There may be the desire to fire the imagination of others, or to force one's newfound emotional outlook upon them.

There is a vast amount of emotional energy being released for use in one's professional work when this conjunction falls *in the 10th House,* provided that one is ready to introduce new values or change his habitual way of participating in the "work of the world". It may be necessary to use greater caution, however, for if one's initiative is too self-centered, it may result in emotional entanglements affecting one's public standing or which cannot be kept from the public eye. Much may center around the behavior of a woman of social or professional influence who obliges one to change his public image, or these new values may result in a change in one's professional goals.

When this conjunction falls *in the 11th House,* a generalized desire for reform in social ideals and purposes will stimulate an individual to become personally involved in such reform. In some cases, there may be emotional disturbances caused by friends or advisers, or in relation to social organizations. In other cases, one may be challenged to replace physical passion and romantic love with friendship of a creative or spiritual nature. There is a general tendency to question habitual ideals of living, and to replace a selfish enjoyment of the fruits of one's public or professional activities with some form of social work or humanitarian activity. This may prompt an active participation in what one now feels to be more worthwhile cultural or spiritual goals.

Falling *in the 12th House,* one finds that the present trend to question the value of social institutions and precedents may provoke peculiar emotional tensions of which the individual is not fully aware but which, nevertheless, are disturbing to him on a subconscious level. There may be an intense urge to reorient oneself in relation to collective values; however, this may manifest in a personally uncontrolled manner. There is a danger here of becoming a passive instrument of the collective social passions of the time, or of the pull of one's own seemingly overpowering unconscious instincts. The capacity to transmute the feeling-values and make a new start in one's intimate personal life will depend on the meaning which a person can now give to his own past and to the accomplishments of his society.

The Sun-Venus Cycle

Viewed from the Earth (geocentrically) Venus will never be more than 48 degrees of zodiacal longitude from the Sun, and therefore the usual cyclic phase-relationship based on 360 degrees which exists between the Sun and Moon and the outer planets does not apply to this cycle. Venus does not move from conjunction to opposition and back to conjunction. Instead it moves from the conjunction to the semi-square (actually 48° ahead of the Sun), then retrogrades back to the conjunction and moves again to the semi-square (48° behind the Sun) where it again changes direction and proceeds forward to the conjunction. Heliocentrically (viewed from the Sun), this constitutes a complete orbit of Venus around the Sun, and describes a complete Sun-Venus cycle. The Sun-Venus conjunction, when Venus is direct in motion, is called the "superior" conjunction. Venus is at or near her greatest distance from the Earth at this time; and the Sun is seen between the Earth and Venus, just as the Earth is between the Sun and Moon at the time of the Full Moon. This is the "Full Moon" phase of the Sun-Venus cycle. Venus retrograde conjoining the Sun is called an "inferior" conjunction. At this time Venus is as close to the Earth as she can be, and shines with her greatest brilliance. Because Venus is seen between the Sun and the Earth at the "inferior" conjunction (just as the Moon is at the New Moon), this is the "New Moon" phase of the Sun-Venus cycle.

In an 8-year period, Venus will make ten conjunctions to the Sun: 5 direct (superior) and 5 retrograde (inferior) — thus completing five Sun-Venus cycles. These cycles refer to the development of one's sense of values, based on the feeling-judgements of Venus. Unlike the Mars-Venus cycle, however, they relate the feeling-values of Venus to the spiritual potential of the Sun rather than to Mars action. The evolution of personal likes and dislikes which attract or repel are associated in this cycle with the experience of Self, quite apart from the considerations of society (Jupiter and Saturn) or the thrust to exteriorize them (Mars). Although theoretically the scale of Venus-values can be based on personal experience — separate and distinct from the social, religious and cultural strictures of one's environment, in actuality these collective standards can and do have a far greater influence on one's behavior and one's seemingly personal responses than the individual will be consciously aware of. Even the rebellion of youth *against* such strictures is conditioned by the standards of the peer-group — the microcosm in which one operates. The effort *not* to conform is, therefore, as binding and deterministic as blind conformity itself. All such conditioning is a form of bondage — especially when it functions beneath the level of conscious awareness — and is the greatest barrier to a real development of those fundamental values on which a truly individualized person bases his feeling-judgements.

When transiting Venus is retrograde, the individual is presented with a special opportunity to become more objective toward all those values on which he has based his personal identity. As Venus moves in a direction counter to the normal flow of the solar life-force, one can divorce himself from the powerful currents of biological and social drives which run his life. At such times, the individual consciousness has a better chance to detach itself from and to contemplate objectively, both the compulsive and instinctive desires, as well as the pressures of the cultural, religious and moral standards of society. There is a better chance to face one's motives objectively — to evaluate the cost of one's desires and all previously assumed values. The inferior conjunctions of Venus with the Sun can reveal a *new* set of values — new standards of behavior on which one may base his own truly personalized feeling-judgements. Without them an individual's psychological and spiritual development cannot take place. These conjunctions are crucial moments in the retrograde periods, and potentially they are moments of revelation. Such an increased illumination or intuitive discovery of Self may, however, take place totally on an unconscious level, without the individual *knowing* that he has done anything extraordinary to change his life-experience.

The existence of Venus retrograde does not, however, guarantee such an illumination. Like all astrological indications, it is a possibility rather than the certainty of something concrete occurring. Before any new personal values can be found, a person must first be willing to establish a new standard for his feelings and actions — the yardstick of personal truth — and that requires *conscious attention*. This may appear paradoxical. How can a change which often takes place on a subconscious level require conscious attention? There is, however, no essential contradiction. Conscious attention does not mean a wilful effort to change one's values and establish new standards, but rather an effort to focus one's attention on the reality of what is. A person must be willing to see his values as they *are*, whether they be individual or determined by the external considerations of his family or society. He must also be able to see that some of his feeling-judgements are founded in the truth of his individual experience, while others are merely the reflection of the prevailing social norm. He must consciously ask himself: "Is this true for ME?"

In humanistic terms, the Venus retrograde period is not measured from the day the planet goes retrograde until the day it turns direct, as one might suppose from traditional astrology. Rather, it is described astronomically by the apparent loop which Venus makes in the heavens in terms of its relative distance from the Earth. This loop actually begins when Venus (direct) first reaches that zodiacal degree on which it will later conjoin the Sun. At that time, Venus begins approaching ever closer to the Earth until the time of its inferior conjunction, when it is at its closest to the Earth. Then, leaving the solar embrace, it moves away from the Earth until it reaches its normal distance, when it will once again return to the conjunction degree by direct motion. For example: Venus conjoined the Sun while retrograde (the inferior conjunction) on April 6, 1977 in 17° Aries. The first time Venus reached the conjunction degree was on February 22, which was also the time when it began its loop earthward. On May 19-20 it returned to 17° Aries by direct motion. Thus, the Venus retrograde period began to become active on February 22 and lasted until May 19-20. These dates do not correspond to the stations which Venus made on March 16 and April 27, which describe the period during which it was actually retrograde in motion.

The new cycle begins with the inferior conjunction. That period of time between February 22 (the first time it reached the conjunction degree) and the inferior conjunction on April 6 is the 12th House phase of the old cycle. During this time the old cycle comes to a fulfillment, and one is confronted with the results, both positive and negative, of his attempts to express his Venus-values in a personally meaningful way. If, during the previous cycle, one's behavior has created problems, then these problems may become acute during this period. It will be at the time of the inferior conjunction that one can theoretically find a solution to such problems. The symbol of the degree* of the conjunction will provide a significant key to this solution, which will serve at the same time as the seed-idea for the new Venus cycle. The basic adjustments in consciousness necessary in order to inaugurate a new Venus cycle may come during the period between the inferior conjunction and the third transit of Venus over the conjunction degree (i.e. April 6 to May 19-20). One must wait until the following superior conjunction, however, to see the *objective results* of the new trend set in motion on April 6, for the superior conjunction represents the 'Full Moon' phase of the Sun-Venus cycle. Although the indications furnished by the inferior conjunction's degree symbol and the House position of the conjunction are the basic factors to consider in an individual interpretation of this cycle, the significance of any natal planet or Angle which Venus may contact during its retrograde period must not be neglected. The natal planet or Angle will somehow be related to the need to establish a new set of values in terms of one's psychological and spiritual development.

---

*The Sabian symbols interpreted in Rudhyar's *An Astrological Mandala* (Random House, 1973) seem the best to use in this context.

If, on the other hand, the astrologer is attempting to interpret the Venus retrograde period in general terms as it will affect people everywhere, then he should note all the major aspects, particularly the conjunctions, which Venus retrograde may make during this period. In this example, Venus retrograde came to the conjunction with Mercury on March 29, 1977, prior to its conjunction with the Sun. Following the inferior conjunction it made an opposition to Pluto on April 12, and a trine to Saturn on April 18. The conjunction with Mercury was part of the old cycle, and must be seen as a conditioning factor or a pre-condition of the new Venus trend. It points to the necessity to communicate, as well as an emphasis on the general quality of Mercury communication. The opposition (awareness) to Pluto (the masses) points to a potential for regeneration — the reformulation of values and the elimination of wornout or obsolete standards. This will be followed shortly by the trine (a harmonious blending or synthesis) to Saturn (security and responsibility). It is interesting to note that during this time there was much discussion (Mercury) regarding strategic arms limitation. From a growing awareness on the part of the general public of the great destructive power of nuclear weapons (Pluto), the talks aimed at blending national security with a responsibility to the human race (Saturn).

In an individual interpretation of the Sun-Venus cycle, the wheel of Houses forms the basic frame of reference, as it does for all *personal* experiences. The House position of the inferior Sun-Venus conjunction will show the field of personal experience in which there can be either Venus problems and the need to review one's basic values, or Venus fulfillment.

In the 1st House. There is a strong indication of emotional fulfillment in the personal life — perhaps the culmination of something started along the lines of romantic self-expression. On the other hand, a need may exist to sublimate the sex drive into artistic or creative activity of some sort. The sense of the beautiful and the transcendent can be greatly stimulated at this time, since one possesses more creative inspiration than usual which may be channeled into actual creative activity or into an appreciation of the arts. The person emanates a magnetic glow which will make him most attractive and can indicate social success. Negatively, however, one can dissipate this creative energy through his social activities or pleasure-seeking adventures.

In the 2nd House. Here one should take advantage of the constructive conditions prevailing in relation to finances and general resources, and thus plan ahead. The accumulation of wealth seems certain, and possessions can bring much joy. One may find himself with an abundance of inherited creative gifts ready to be used. The main question now is: For what purpose is one going to use those gifts and resources? It may be worthwhile at this time to question assumed values and purposes in the use of possessions.

In the 3rd House. An emotional situation in the environment is reaching fulfillment, and a female neighbor or relative may be the focal point. New intellectual values can stimulate the feelings and make it possible to create more harmonious conditions in the everyday life. One should share the best of what he has with those around him and seek to discover new meanings in all relationships and habitual experiences. There will be a need throughout this cycle to communicate those new-found values to others. Emotional self-indulgence should be avoided.

In the 4th House. Definite and harmonious results related to one's efforts in matters of real estate or in the home life. Something is coming to fruition which should bring great happiness and a sense of fulfillment. Actions should stem from the deepest harmony of one's own nature. If an individual does not feel at peace with himself — secure and happy in the home — it will be because new values and emotional realizations encourage him to establish his personal life on a foundation of wider significance. One should not hesitate to introvert his energies with the aim of giving a new and deeper meaning to his basic feelings and feeling-judgements.

In the 5th House. The emotional implications of this situation are very strong. Here, the person's desire for love, happiness and beauty are urging him to exteriorize his romantic dreams or to fulfill his sensuous desires. There is the possibility that some emotional complex may complicate matters, making it impossible to act with emotional freedom. The love-image which one projects onto another may be rejected. There may be a test of purity of motive, and a need to express more significant or more spiritual feeling-values than one has done before this time. One must now learn to be more sincere than ever before.

In the 6th House. Significant and harmonious things can happen in one's everyday work. At this time organization is easy, and one can release his creative powers through his job. Certain basic values seem to have to be changed, and what one is doing has to be given a new meaning in the light of higher spiritual values or larger realities. In some cases, emotional conflicts can be transfigured by using them as an inspiration for creative activity of some sort.

In the 7th House. An intensification of the emotional life is reaching a climax here, and some close relationship is being fulfilled which warms the heart. In some cases, this can be an indication of marriage, while in other cases there may be a tendency toward undue emotional indulgence in one's inter-personal relationships. What happens may make it necessary to change the value and meaning one has given to close relationships, since instinctual experience may no longer satisfy. Love must take on a new quality.

In the 8th House. This is the time to bring to fruition all matters which have recently come out of one's business associations. One may need to reorganize one's affairs in a more efficient manner or in terms of larger values, or to make the value of what one offers more convincing. For some people, this can be a time for self-renewal — for a personal re-orientation towards more meaningful social or religious ideals.

In the 9th House. One may experience a great emotional uplift at this time through a realized significance of the great principles on which one has pinned his faith. Long journeys for pleasure, or perhaps for a honeymoon are favorable. In any case, one should not be afraid to seek wider horizons — to expand his consciousness through accepting what had previously seemed to be alien ideas. Now is the time to imagine things anew, and to seek a constructive meaning for the experiences and fruits of one's relationships. Such a significance will enable one to fit more harmoniously into the social scheme.

In the 10th House. There is a strong urge for emotional fulfillment through public recognition. Positive efforts are now bringing a rich harvest, and there is the possibility of public acknowledgement of one's past creative activity. What happens now could lead to more significant participation in the work of the world, provided that one is open to change and growth of the values he espouses. An individual can build his professional career through efficient management, and perhaps also due to the help of a woman of social or professional influence.

In the 11th House. Friendships and group activities can give great emotional satisfaction at this time. This means, however, that friendship of a creative and spiritual nature should take the place of passionate, romantic love. The things which one has worked for or longed for can now come to pass, and much may have to do with a woman, or with artistic or cultural factors which are taking on a new importance in one's life. Ideals of social reform may stir one emotionally, and one can now have the power to crystallize public or group opinion or feelings along some new line of endeavor.

In the 12th House. Very profitable social occurrences appear as the culmination of one's efforts to reach a greater awareness of the hidden factors in one's life — especially on the level of one's most basic and fundamental feelings. A strong emotional glow pervades the inner life, and it is possible now to concentrate one's emotional power out of the depths of the subconscious for some future objective use along new lines of endeavor. At this time one must orient oneself in a new way toward the collective values of society. Some people may even succeed in creating new symbols or new cultural forms to take the place of those generally accepted. Others may simply lose themselves in an introverted dream world.

The Sun-Mars Cycle

Mars is the first planet outside of the Earth's orbit. Its cycle begins with the conjunction to the Sun and culminates at the opposition. The Sun-Mars opposition falls in the middle of Mars' retrograde period and is the most important moment of the cycle. The power which is released instinctively and without conscious awareness at the time of the conjunction can, at the opposition, be understood objectively and consciously in terms of the solar purpose determining its use. This will sound less abstract when one realizes how often the instinctive, emotional release of psychic energy or libido through Mars is blind and without aim. Mars energy is almost always confused and egocentric, thus often leading to problems. For this reason, Mars is traditionally deemed a "malefic" planet. Of course, Mars is not the cause of the problems — it is the individual *use* of one's Martian energy which leads to trouble. The confused and self-centered activity begun at the Sun-Mars conjunction is always deeply conditioned by the past frustrations, inadequacies or failures of the ego in past Mars cycles. This is bound to produce varying degrees of tension which will mount during the waxing half of the cycle from the conjunction to the opposition. The waxing square is a particularly stressful moment. After this square, Mars continues to move along; however, the pressure of all that has not gone well builds up, symbolically slowing down Mars' motion until it seems to stop.

At the time of Mars' closest proximity to the Earth (the opposition to the Sun), the Mars problem must be solved one way or another. If solved rightly at the moment of the opposition, any difficulties have not been in vain. Knowledge and wisdom can grow out of the close confrontation with Mars. The ego may have been frightened by that confrontation; however, it has grown wiser and more mature because of it. During the remaining half of the cycle what has been learned should be incorporated into the consciousness and demonstrated effectively through one's individual actions. If, however, the Mars approach to Earth has caused destructive fear, sudden anguish or a passionate reaction in the shape of violence, or if there has been an attempt to escape from the resulting confrontation, then the remainder of that Mars cycle will merely add more confusion, more egocentricity, more violence and more tragedy to the heavy load of past inadequacies which the ego already carries, and which may have made it miss the opportunity offered while Mars was retrograde. Everything, therefore, depends upon what the ego — the individual in his waking consciousness — will be able to do when Mars power comes very close to the individual and challenges him to a wise, clear, objective, realistic and *considerate* appreciation and understanding of its nature and of its correct and effective use.

The past obviously cannot be undone; yet, by looking at one's past action (or inaction) at the time of the Mars opposition in the light of a new understanding and a new determination to do right, one can make of it the foundation for a transformed attitude toward life. Past misfortunes or lost opportunities can be viewed in a new light and from a new perspective at the time of the opposition. What may have been a deep psychological wound or an overpowering sense of remorse can be seen to have been, in reality, a necessary experience in terms of one's spiritual training. In this sense one may *change the meaning* of his past experiences. Whenever an individual can fit whatever happens to him into the larger framework of his complete life-span, realizing that it is but a step toward the realization of his total life-purpose, then he will be able to transform the meaning of his life. As a result of this new perspective, one will be in a position to give a new direction, a new motive and a constructive purpose to his future Martian actions. This is not, of course, an easy thing to achieve; something within seems to resist one's efforts toward such transformation. The ego seems not to want to eradicate the memory of the painful experiences, and one may become prey to self-pity. Therefore, it will take real courage to transform the past hurt or the failure to act, and to give it the meaning of a constructive step in spiritual growth. However, at these times of Mars' opposition to the Sun, life seems to lend a hand and to make the process of self-analysis and self-transformation easier. Moreover, when one experiences this opposition with a fully conscious knowledge of what it implies, he will certainly encounter an opportunity to repair a mistake, to do right by someone he may have wronged, to forgive someone who has wronged him, or to do something which he failed to do in the previous months or years.

When the energies are being used spontaneously in the attempt to satisfy one's personal desires while Mars is direct in motion, there does not seem to be time to do much in the way of transforming, refining or purifying them. When Mars is retrograde, however, one becomes uncertain about the best way to express himself. The feelings and desires appear confused and conflicting. This time, then, affords the best opportunity to change one's use of Martian energy. Only when one doubts or fails or finds obstacles in his path does he stop to question himself. One *can* stop and ask himself questions then; however, this does not mean that he will. Most of the time people rather wish that something would happen to make them change. One hopes that others will put things right or change in regard to oneself. Pride and self-esteem stand in the way and will not permit one to take that first step toward a conciliation. Thus, matters have a way of becoming worse when they might have become better if one had taken the constructive initiative. As a result, the opportunities offered by Mars retrograde periods are often missed; and, instead of showing a way of self-transformation, Mars forces a crisis.*

If the opportunity offered by Mars retrograde is given under stress, then one must realize that it was because he has misused, deviated or perverted the Martian energy in his own life. A person can only blame himself. Mars is a personal planet and acts in terms of the particular quality of one's individual ego. Nonetheless, blame, remorse or regret are of no positive value. The Martian opportunity for the redressing of wrongs and changing one's personal attitude toward society and the task of spiritual living is there to be *used*. There is no point in lamenting upon how hard life makes it all. "Why did this happen to *me?*" is a fruitless question. One must recognize that his troubles began in the first place because he tried to dictate to life — because he acted in an immature way, or missed an opportunity to grow in psychological and spiritual maturity when he had come to the natural and proper time for such growth.

The four critical points — conjunction, waxing and waning squares and opposition — demand one's conscious attention in every Mars cycle. Not every transit cycle of Mars will reveal itself as equally significant to everyone; however, there will always come a time when a Mars retrograde period will bring to light the results of one's Martian outpouring of energy and will challenge the individual to purify his motives and re-orient his activities. When applying the Mars cycle to a specific individual life, the astrologer must consider the natal or solar House in which the Sun-Mars conjunctions fall every two years, and most especially, the House through which Mars retrogrades at the time of its opposition to the Sun. These Houses will indicate the fields of experience in which the individual will most likely have to introduce changes into his behavior because of problems or crises produced by his past actions. Any natal planets in these Houses will be implicated in the Mars problem or challenge.

SUN-CONJUNCTION-MARS. **In the 1st House,** the climax of the Martian factor in one's life will bring a great deal of forcefulness and initiative to the personality. If that energy is not properly controlled, it can also bring disturbances. Mars is releasing new power for sheer self-expression, and for deliberate use if the personality is consciously oriented. One must be careful not to let his enthusiasm lead him out of his depths. One attains the ability to mobilize one's energies for quick

---

*The events in the Near East during the Mars retrograde period from October 30, 1977 to April 26, 1978 are a good example of this.

and decisive action, but also the tendency to stick too narrowly to one's personal approach to life and its problems, forgetting that other people have opinions as well, and that they may be right. While strong personalities may succeed spectacularly in pushing themselves to the fore, weaker natures risk being overcome by the intensity of their emotions and impulses.

In the 2nd House, this conjunction can put a strain on the finances and one may be obliged to spend more than he originally intended. It will be necessary to maintain a strong control over one's resources and not give away too much of oneself — financially, psychologically or physically. Nothing should be done on the basis of irrational impulses; and if one takes risks, they should be calculated risks.

In the 3rd House, the momentum of events may lead one to go further than he really intended to go. The possibility exists for a change of environment, although this may indicate a psychological change rather than a physical or geographical move. One should control his moods and be wary of traffic accidents. There is also a strong possibility of quarrels with relatives or neighbors. The mind can be sharper than usual, which will be a good thing since the challenges of everyday existence may now necessitate a maximum of intellectual agility as well as the capacity to make rapid decisions and to act quickly.

In the 4th House, the conjunction may indicate the time to make a definite move. This should be undertaken without forcing issues in any way. In the home one should be as positive as possible, avoiding fights and keeping one's temper in check at all times. On the other hand, the strong personality can now attempt to probe more deeply into his own psychological nature, piercing through his ego conditioning so as to be better able to release the qualities of his essential being.

In the 5th House, emotional impulses reach a climax and can precipitate trouble. One can lose himself in the passion of a love affair. As the conjunction stimulates creative expression on one level or another, a person will be able to act with more faith and greater force than usual. One should, however, watch out for the risks entailed in following impetuously the call of his personal desires or instincts.

In the 6th House, a great deal of heat may be generated where one works, and one may suffer from the impatience or the irritation of his superiors, or from some man who has much to do with his position. If previous Martian expression has brought trouble, this is an excellent time to transform oneself through discipline, work and service to others. One can be driven now by ruthless ambition or burning zeal to better the conditions of his life. In some cases, previous health difficulties can come to a culmination. Foods causing undue fermentation should be avoided.

In the 7th House, one may want to rush eagerly into some new close association or partnership. The feelings are strongly stimulated in relation to the marriage or business partner, and there is an element of stress in relationships which must be watched. One should be as considerate of others as possible. The impetuous motion toward social experiences and relationships can be an escape from self if it is not a gift of self in the form of devotion to a person or cause.

In the 8th House, there will be an element of danger or of rash impulse in relation to one's business life, or to the property or wealth inherited or coming to one through the action of the marriage partner or some close associate. Partners may tend toward over-expenditure and risky financial ventures. One should not act from motives which are too personal when taking the initiative in group endeavors, although one's courage and faith can serve as an example and stimulate others to action.

In the 9th House, these will be a strong impulse to embark on expansive moves, to travel far, and perhaps to be a sort of evangelist. This search for larger fields goes forward with faith and courage. Whether it be a search for material wealth and power or for spiritual truth it will be a personal search — for oneself and not for others. It may not be wise to plan too far ahead at this time.

In the 10th House, one may meet a crisis in the development of one's career or of one's public ambition. There may be a need for caution and gentleness in any forceful initiative one feels obliged to take. The possibility of having to overcome antagonism and obstacles is present at this time and will be even more pronounced if one's own ambitions are purely egocentric. One will tend to drive oneself, and others, ruthlessly to reach the goal which one has set himself. A mature personality, conscious of the role he must play within the greater whole, will now mobilize his personal energy, his will and his faith in order to further the public purpose to which he is personally dedicated.

In the 11th House, the relationship to friends and social organizations becomes important. There is a need at this time for calm judgement and impersonal action. If one is a reformer, he may find a great opportunity for action; yet there is also a danger in this and cooperation must be stressed. The social or cultural attitudes tend to be aggressive, even if they are also pioneering, and often lead one to conflicts with friends, associates and advisers. There should be an urge to work out certain ideals by experimenting with them or by acting them out in some concrete behavior. One's inclination towards forceful criticism may lead to lost tempers in intellectual controversies over social problems.

In the 12th House, the inner life will be very active and might lead one to give way to unconscious fantasies or impulses which can carry him down the garden path. On material levels, there is a possibility of danger from hidden enemies and business competitors. Social passions or forceful instincts can overwhelm the conscious behavior. This can, in certain circumstances, be a good time for spiritualistic investigations and practices. Psychologically, however, the past will have to be faced in one way or another, and old skeletons in the closet may rattle with considerable intensity.

SUN-OPPOSITION-MARS RETROGRADE. Although this phase marks the culmination of the Sun-Mars cycle, it must always be seen within the context of the conjunction — the beginning of the cycle where the seed was originally planted. This holds especially true for the House position, for although the House placement of Mars retrograde will indicate the area of life experience where the crisis is most likely to manifest, the House in which the conjunction fell will reveal how that crisis originated. For example if Mars retrograde falls in the 7th House there is likely to be some sort of conflict or confrontation involving partnership — either marriage or business. This does not, however, reveal the root-cause of this conflict. For this, the astrologer must look to the House in which the conjunction occurred. If it fell in the 2nd House, then the crisis may have stemmed from an unwise expenditure of one's personal resources. In the 8th House it may indicate a rash outlay of the partner's money, especially for personally selfish reasons. If the conjunction fell in the 3rd House, the cause of the crisis may stem from something said or written in the heat of anger, and may involve a neighbor or a relative. The opposition is an aspect indicating the potential for objective awareness. In the following cases, although the emphasis will be on the Martian energy, one must not forget that it forms a polarity with the Sun, and the solar life-purpose may provide a greater understanding of and perhaps a spiritual insight into his Mars energies. The Houses involved also express this polarity. The conflict or crisis will arise in the retrograde Mars' House and therefore will probably receive the most attention. It is, however, the polarity of that House — the House in which the Sun falls — wherein the greatest potential for self-enlightenment is possible.

Sun in the 1st House — Mars retrograde in the 7th House. The problem here is defined by the use of the power born of interpersonal relationships. The crisis may be precipitated not so much by one's actions, as by the failure to act. One may project one's own Mars energy onto the partner, expecting him or her to take the initiative and to fight one's battles — whether physical or spiritual. The conflicts which ensue, be they marital or with the business partner, often come as the result of one's failure to pull his own share of the load. Because the first angry words may, in fact, come from the partner, one may not see that he himself has created this situation and is responsible for it. Instead of giving way to the impulse to project his emotional needs onto others, one should look to the 1st House placement of the Sun in this opposition and become aware of the strong energy flowing through his own being. This energy is his to direct, and the responsibility for fulfilling his solar-purpose cannot be designated to another.

Sun in the 7th House — Mars retrograde in the 1st House. At this time one feels himself filled with emotional fervor and power — perhaps more than he can use constructively. Throughout this period, therefore, one must carefully remain in control of himself and be conscious not to force himself or his desires with too much insistence onto his marriage partner or close associates. The tendency to act out one's selfish desires will be strong at this time, and from this conflicts can arise. The lesson of Mars retrograde in the 1st House is that of learning control of all one's personal desires and impulses. He must differentiate between positive action and rash, impetuous behavior. One should look to the 7th House placement of the Sun in this opposition and become aware that he is not alone — that his actions do indeed affect others. He must learn to cultivate compassion and become sensitive to the needs of others. In that way he will be able to act out his own individuality without harming someone else, and to courageously proclaim his own deepest truth without deafening those closest to him.

Sun in the 2nd House — Mars retrograde in the 8th House. Large demands may be made on one's reserves of power and on both one's internal and external resources at this time. One must learn to show discrimination in their use. One may become dependent on the resources of others and may squander them or treat them carelessly if he has not learned to value them as he does his own. This is especially true of the fruits of one's relationships, principally sexual, and one may become so concerned with his own satisfaction that he totally disregards the physical and emotional needs of the partner. In this case, physical love becomes largely an escape from self, and the resultant feeling of loneliness is generally blamed on some supposed inadequacy on the part of the partner, rather than on one's own selfishness. The position of the Sun in the 2nd House points to a need to become aware not only of one's personal resources, but of his individual and truly personal values. He must learn that his real wealth lies within himself, rather than in what he takes from others.

Sun in the 8th House — Mars retrograde in the 2nd House. There are plenty of resources at one's disposal during this time, and the challenge lies in how one may best use them. The problem may be simply one of learning wise and prudent management — not to squander those resources rashly in the heat of the moment. This may, however, involve more than a simple bookkeeping task, since the tendency here is to become totally absorbed in one's own values to the exclusion of the wants and needs of the partner. Life itself may become an impassioned quest for more and greater wealth. One must be able to step back and view this objectively and to discover where his own real security lies. The 8th House position of the Sun shows that the only things which will truly belong to anyone are those which he has shared with another. One's real wealth lies in the harvest of his relationships, fulfilled for the mutual benefit of all concerned.

Sun in the 3rd House — Mars retrograde in the 9th House. The passion of one's new-found faith can become oppressive to others if a person uses this time to stand on a soap box and harangue anyone who will listen. The lesson to be learned here is that the true value of one's great thoughts and expansive dreams must be found in the actions which they inspire one to *do* — right where one is *now* — and not in the number of people one succeeds in converting to his point of view. Nothing will be solved by running off to distant realms, either geographically or mentally, when the immediate demands of life within one's environment begin to press in and require attention. Long journeys or metaphysical pursuits tend at this time to be merely an escape from mundane reality and the real needs of the present moment. The 3rd House position of the Sun points to the need to be able to act according to one's own truth freely and without the need for others' agreement.

Sun in the 9th House — Mars retrograde in the 3rd House. The intellect appears full of vigor and fire at this time; and, while one may find himself irritated by conditions affecting near relatives or neighbors, nevertheless the condition can be turned to one's personal advantage if he does not lose patience. There may be some risk of an automobile accident if one vents his temper through fast driving, so it may be wiser to scream and yell than to drive 90 mph. During this period, dilemmas may arise which oppose the near and the far, wisdom and intellect, long-range plans and everyday necessities. One should not become too hypnotized by the near and the intellectually practical, however, and an effort should be made to concentrate the present restlessness and scattered activity of the mind on a goal or a philosophy. There is no point in behaving like a squirrel in a cage, or in postponing decisions which must be made now. The answers to one's present problems are to be found in the 9th House — in philosophy, religion — the sense of the greater reality and of the divine. One should still the restless promptings of the intellect and seek instead to listen to the inner voice — seek understanding rather than technical know-how. The desire to dominate others intellectually should give way to the effort to understand the meaning of one's life-purpose.

Sun in the 4th House — Mars retrograde in the 10th House. This period may bring a great sense of personal power and perhaps a call to public activity in which the individual will have to take the initiative. Such a development may cause some emotional conflict in the home, especially if one seeks to avoid his public duty and crawl into the shelter of his domestic security. If, however, one assumes responsibility for the energies now operating in his nature, he can achieve a great deal both in the professional sphere and in terms of his personal growth. One must discover whether one's public activities are founded on a personal ground-of-being, which is expressed by the 4th House position of the Sun, or are merely the expression of an empty ego-centered ambition. At this time the home and the family can take on a new and personalized meaning. Instead of seeing one's hereditary traditions as chains which bind him to a life of servitude to an outworn past, one may recognize that they are in fact his roots — the foundation on which he can build a life of meaningful public service.

Sun in the 10th House — Mars retrograde in the 4th House. The tendency toward extremes of temperament must be curbed here, and one should be careful not to give in to the rising heat of momentary emotions. This energy can be used, instead, to transform one's ambitions and to forward his professional standing. Much can happen in one's home life affecting the foundations, both physical and spiritual, on which his life is being built. Self-centeredness causes problems, and life now demands that one seek to grow not for oneself alone, but for society — for the world. A person should not build only to become a greater and more powerful ego, but rather to play a more significant role in terms of the actual needs of society. To do this he may have to depersonalize his desires and detach the true experience of Self from his emotions.

Sun in the 5th House — Mars retrograde in the 11th House. When a person channels his Mars' energy into the groups and organizations to which he belongs, heated discussions with one's friends and advisors are bound to ensue. As long as they do not turn into self-indulgent and immature temper tantrums, they can serve to get the creative juices flowing. Great achievements and realizations are possible at this time, provided one is in full control of his creative energies and knows how to direct them without dissipating the energy released. Violent arguments are pointless, and emotional indignation and anger serve no purpose. This is an excellent time to learn this lesson. Because the Mars energy here focuses on groups and friendships, one may find it necessary to probe the deeper meaning of these facets of his life — to question the personal value of his strongest ideals and loyalties. There is a danger here of becoming fanatically attached to an organization and forfeiting one's own power to that of the group. The 5th House position of the Sun in this opposition shows that the greatest gift one can give to any Cause is his true self and that a person must learn to realize his ideals through his own creative force, rather than passing them off onto the group. This is the time when an individual can become a creator in whatever field lie his most effective and real abilities.

Sun in the 11th House — Mars retrograde in the 5th House. One must realize now that the fundamental conflicts of life are usually not solved, but rather transcended. What must be overcome here is the tendency to squander one's energies and resources through taking ill-advised risks. At this time one may become too egocentric in his mode of self-expression, and he may try to project his desires onto other people. Mars in the 5th House certainly demands that one be creative; however, it does not demand that one sacrifice all (most specifically his friends and loved ones) to his "art". Creativity must be put in its true perspective — it involves more than simply projecting one's ego out into the world. The 11th House position of the Sun challenges one to dedicate his creative efforts to some greater cause or purpose which transcends the level of ego desires. The pull of this opposition must be integrated through a calm and steady determination to demonstrate in some concrete form the value born of one's sense of purpose. Impatience and the desire to achieve quick results will be the greatest barrier to creative fulfillment at this time.

Sun in the 6th House — Mars retrograde in the 12th House. At this time a person may be endowed with a far greater energy potential than he previously believed possible. This is an excellent time to accomplish a lot of work, especially completing all those projects and tasks which one started some time ago and are still unfinished. A few angry words can bring hidden enemies crawling like bugs out of the woodwork, and one will be forced to deal with them. His greatest enemy at this time, however, will be his own hidden fears and anxieties, which can have a detrimental effect on the health. In the area of work it is now important to reflect on the true relation between what one is doing and the demands of society. The conscious limitations imposed on one's activities by the restrictions of his heredity and environment, as well as the memory of the past from which he springs as a spiritual being (karma), produce problems to which one can only respond through a willingness to undergo some sort of personal metamorphosis. The 6th House position of the Sun indicates a necessity to learn that one's happiness can be found only in the present moment, and that true growth can come in the midst of one's daily activities. Throughout this time, as one confronts the dark side of his own nature — the violent instincts and irrational impulses which one has kept hidden not only from the world, but from himself as well — one must realize that this is not his true Self, but simply the manifestation of his secret fears.

Sun in the 12th House — Mars retrograde in the 6th House. One must work carefully and with patience at this time; for haste or rash behavior can lead to accidents on the job. This is especially true if one works with or near any type of machinery. Emotional self-control and kindness are necessary in all one's working relationships. The essential challenge of this time is symbolized by the 12th House placement of the Sun, which calls for personal dedication and service to humanity. This goal can be easily lost in the drive to increase one's efficiency and productivity. It must be remembered that these are not an end in themselves — they n.ay be the path, but they are not the destination. The purpose of life is not to produce, but to serve; work is not the final goal, but rather the means by which an individual may participate.

The Mercury Cycle

Mercury is the planet closest to the Sun, and when viewed from the Earth it appears to behave toward the Sun in much the same way that the Moon responds to the Earth's orbit. The Moon weaves in and out of the Earth's orbit during every 28-day lunation cycle, and Mercury moves back and forth, toward the Sun and then toward the Earth three times a year. Thus, both Mercury and the Moon are distributive agencies of the solar life-force. Traditionally, both the Moon and Mercury are said to symbolize the mind — Mercury having to do specifically with the nervous system, the intellect and the verbal expression of ideas, while the Moon relates to the memory. Like Venus, the other inner planet, Mercury always remains zodiacally close to the Sun. Because they will never be separated by more than 28°, Mercury is never visible at the midheaven. It will either rise just before the Sun and disappear from view with the dawn, or it will twinkle in the evening sky close to the western horizon and then follow the Sun beneath the line of our vision. Thus, Mercury will be either a morning star or an evening star.

MERCURY-PROMETHEUS AND MERCURY-EPIMETHEUS.* To the astronomical phenomenon of Mercury appearing as either the morning or evening star, Dane Rudhyar has given the names, respectively, "Mercury-Prometheus" and "Mercury-Epimetheus" after the Greek Titans. These two demigods were brothers, and their names translate as: *Prometheus* — "forethought" and *Epimetheus* — "afterthought". In the legends of Greek mythology, Prometheus is known for stealing "fire" (symbolizing the power of reason) from the gods and giving it to man. His brother, Epimetheus, is principally known as the husband of Pandora. Thus, Mercury-Prometheus represents the progressive, forward-looking mentality, while Mercury-Epimetheus symbolizes the

---

*See Rudhyar's *An Astrological Study of Psychological Complexes* (Shambhala Publications, 1976), Chapter 8.

conservative mentality which bases its judgements on precedent. In Jung's view, Prometheus is the introvert and Epimetheus the extrovert. The former represents a mentality which sacrifices everything connected with the present in order to create in anticipation of the distant future, while the latter symbolizes an approach to life based on traditionally "right ideas" — the worldly wisdom which manifests through public opinion. Prometheus cares nothing about public approval, while Epimetheus strives always to remain in harmony with the general expectations. The Promethean mind deals principally in ideals and abstractions and is little concerned with the details of daily life. His orientation is strictly toward the future. The Epimethean mind, on the other hand, represents the contemporary "nothing but" intellectual attitude, limited by its slavish adherence to the collective norm.

It is a mistake, however, to assume that Mercury-Prometheus is in some way better or more desirable than Mercury-Epimetheus. They represent two different types of mentality — each having its strengths and short-comings. The Mercury-Prometheus type of person can spend so much of life in the future that he fails to see what is in the present moment. There is thus the possibility of losing a spontaneous approach to life's experiences. Epimetheus, with its gift of 20-20 hindsight, may have difficulties because of a tendency to act first and think about it later. There is also the potential for one to dwell on past experiences, thinking of what one *should* have done rather than about what one is going to do next.

MERCURY RETROGRADE. In many traditional astrological texts a natal Mercury retrograde is interpreted as referring to a weak, dull or lazy mind. This is far from being the truth. Symbolically, a retrograde Mercury indicates a mind which operates in a realm which opposes the instinctual nature and the normal flow of the life-force. Thus, for such a person, the greatest spiritual growth can come from experiences precipitated by the contrasting pull of rational, mental values on the one hand, and instinctual feeling-judgements on the other. The results of such a contrast can be many and varied, but, as in the case of retrograde Mars and Venus, the tendency is toward introversion — that is to say, the Self is more interested in the development of personal consciousness than in other people, events or the material world in general. Inner, mental growth will be more important for that person than outer success. For this reason Mercury retrograde *can* be a negative influence for a person wishing to lead a *normally* successful life.

Even though the natal condition of Mercury gives a basic tendency to the mentality, in most lives there are several changes of polarity in the mental life. These can be measured by the secondary progressions of Mercury, both direct and converse. Marc Jones published an article in

American Astrology magazine during the second World War entitled "Mercury Magic", in which he illustrated the importance of the changes in Mercury's polarity during a life-span. Briefly, he said that the year which corresponds by secondary progression (either direct or converse) to a change in Mercury's polarity is always an outstanding year in an individual's life. He used this information as a means to gain the confidence of a "client", since he could simply look at the ephemeris before erecting a chart and note the years in that life when Mercury changed direction. Since such a correspondence is usually correct, the client, even if sceptical on arrival, felt that he had come to a good astrologer and would pay closer attention to what the astrologer said subsequently. Apart from this use of Mercury's progressed stations, definite shifts in the *conscious mental attitude* usually coincide with changes in Mercury's polarity, as do changes in the electrical and nervous potential of the organism. The main difference between the indications furnished by direct and converse secondary progressions is that all backward motions symbolize, in humanistic astrology, a return to source. Converse progressions therefore refer to factors rooted in an ancient racial or spiritual past which come to the surface of the consciousness under the pressure of karmic forces. There is usually something fateful and uncontrollable related to whatever is measured by the converse progression. This is especially true in relation to Mercury, Venus and Mars, and to the converse New and Full Moons.

As with Venus, Mercury's transit cycle begins at the time of Mercury's inferior conjunction with the Sun in the middle of its retrograde period. When Mercury reaches its inferior conjunction and is therefore at its closest point to the Earth in its cycle, it is positioned between the Sun and the Earth. Symbolically, this is as if Mercury were focusing that solar energy especially strongly upon us. At this moment it changes from its Epimethean-retrograde phase to Promethean-retrograde phase. The conjunction thus indicates a reversal of polarity in the electro-magnetic fields of all living organisms, and therefore the need for readjustment in all Mercury matters and functions. For this reason, the inferior conjunction and the whole retrograde period of Mercury can refer to important changes both in world affairs and in the lives of individuals as well. It can also reveal the new mental values which are necessary to one's personal development. This introduction of the "new" may at first necessitate a critical purification process, especially during the period lasting from the time Mercury is stationary retrograde up to the inferior conjunction with the Sun. Whatever form the new opportunities for growth may take, the key to what happens will be found in the degree and Sign of the inferior conjunction. In this connection, the use of the symbol for the degree, especially from the Sabian series, will be most enlightening to the psychologically and spiritually oriented astrologer.

When Mercury is retrograde, the general tendency will be toward mental introversion. This means that people everywhere will be preoccupied with their own personal affairs and will have less energy at their disposal for objective activity and inter-personal relationships. It is wiser, therefore, not to force issues or rush ahead with new plans at such times, since other people will not be inclined toward interest in someone else's projects. When Mercury is retrograde, one should watch and wait, trying to understand as objectively as possible what is happening in the field of his own thinking and in the lives of other people and the world in general. There will be no point in trying to forge ahead on an old momentum which is about to exhaust itself, as Mercury is in its Epimethean-retrograde phase. Moreover, it is too early to count on the power of the new Mercury tide which is still in its early and insecure phase of growth during the Promethean-retrograde phase immediately following the inferior conjunction.

The humanistic approach, therefore, suggests that one *use consciously* the retrograde periods of Mercury in the attempt to reorganize and purify the mind, and to free one's thinking from the usually compulsive demands of the natural instincts. Of course, if one tries to do this, he will obviously not be able to give his full attention to the so-called normal extroverted activities. He must be ready to temporarily sacrifice his extroverted effectiveness to the effort of self-improvement. At this time one should seek new goals, develop new techniques, and do all he can to change the *quality* of his thinking.

The retrograde period of Mercury is divided into two parts. The first part, from the moment of change of direction up to the inferior conjunction, is a sort of 12th House period in terms of the ending Sun-Mercury cycle. It should be treated as such and used as a summing-up period during which one assesses his successes and failures. Then one will be able to decide what new factors should be introduced, and what mistakes should be corrected. If the old cycle poses problems at this station, then one can expect a possible solution to present itself at the time of the inferior conjunction. He may then use the last half of the retrograde period to work it out. The new trends set in motion can then reach fulfillment at the time of the following superior conjunction between the Sun and Mercury, which is the symbolic "Full Moon phase" of the cycle. The natal House through which transiting Mercury retrogrades will be the field of experience to which one should give special attention. It will *focus* the Mercury challenge to improve the quality of one's thinking, and to seek new standards and new ideals for living. Any natal planet touched by Mercury while retrograde will also be involved in the process.

In closing this chapter on the three personal planets, it must be said that the most important retrograde periods are naturally those when the planet retrogrades over an Angle of the birth-chart, and particularly over the Ascendant. Such transits generally refer to a need for regeneration or reconsideration of one's attitude. This will occur in a climate of mental and nervous stress in the case of Mercury, and of psychological-emotional stress in the case of Mars and Venus. Such retrograde periods should not be used for truly new departures; however, they will give one the opportunity, even if it is under pressure and with the risk of making matters worse, to put things right that have been wrongly or inadequately started in one's personal life.

V

The Jupiter Cycle

In the traditional approach to astrology, Jupiter is known as "the great benefic", the planet of all opportunities — personal wealth, social prominence, professional prestige and even high political office. When the astrological symbolism is related to psychology, this planet actually has a much wider significance, for all forms of inflated self-esteem, over-confidence and exaggerated self-importance also belong to Jupiter. Astronomically Jupiter is the largest planet visible in the heavens, having a mass which is 2½ times that of all other planets combined. Its volume, too, is greater than the sum-total of all the other planets. Thus, the Jupiterian urge, both within an individual and within society as well, is an expression of the philosophy that "more is better". Unlimited expansion, however, is not intrinsically good. Although traditional astrology often attributes the rulership of the disease "cancer" to the Sign Cancer, on the biological level it is a cellular manifestation of the Jupiter principle of unrestricted growth. The evils of unlimited expansion can also be seen on the social level as economic inflation and urban sprawl. Thus, the lesson of Jupiter on all levels of reality is the importance of limitations. Too much of anything, no matter how good or desirable, becomes an evil in itself. The consumption of too much food will lead to flatulence, sloth and obesity; too much liquor will result in a hangover. A balloon can hold only so much air before it bursts.

On all levels of reality — psychological, physical and social — Jupiterian expansion can only take place within defined limits. Those limits are symbolized by Saturn; Jupiter and Saturn therefore form a complementary pair. An astrologer can never really understand how Jupiter will work in an individual birth-chart without taking Saturn into consideration. Together these two planets will show how a person will manage to maintain (Saturn) and expand (Jupiter) the characteristic features of his personality within a specific geographical environment, and particular social, cultural and religious standards. Jupiter dominating Saturn in a natal chart is a strong indication that the person is prone to take in more than he can specifically use. Absorption outruns assimilation, and at the level on which this occurs — physical, psychic or mental — indigestion will result. The Jupiterian urge toward expansion is not of itself discriminating, and without the moderating hand of Saturn it will lack both direction and purpose. It would continue to take in "nourishment" on all levels of being until that individual or society eventually choked on its own abundance. What is absorbed must be assimilated if it is to have any value. If Jupiter is to participate in the fulfillment of an individual's solar purpose, then its urge toward expansion must be channeled. This is stated symbolically by the Sagittarian archer who aims his arrow upward and thus gives a specific direction to the Jupiter energy.

Jupiter and Saturn are the social planets, symbolizing the hereditary and environmental factors which provide both the potential for individual growth and the limitations on such growth. They describe the particular framework established by the social, cultural and economic conditions in which an individual lives, and their energies can never be separated from this framework. The striving for personal and social fulfillment always takes place within the values of one's society. Within the humanistic approach, the Jupiterian urge toward growth can lead an individual to fulfill the potential of his birth circumstances, namely, the family and society into which he was born. Social maladjustments, therefore, can be understood astrologically by studying the natal positions and aspects of Jupiter and Saturn, and also the phase relationship of their transit cycles, both at the time when the difficulty first appeared and also at the time when a solution is being sought. These will show specifically how an individual relates to the social current of the times.

THE JUPITER FUNCTION IN JUNGIAN PSYCHOLOGY. Jung relates the Jupiter function to the *persona,* which is the compromise between the individual and society — between the demands of one's social environment and the necessities of one's inner constitution. It is a mask created by the social role one plays, and with which the conscious sense of "I" often identifies itself. Through the persona, an individual appears to be what he essentially is not. He builds an artificial social facade behind which to hide his feelings of inadequacy or personal inferiority. Its essential purpose is to hide that person whom one is afraid he is — that person whom he fears the world will not accept. Under the influence of this social mask an individual will behave publicly in a way which may be diametrically opposed to the way he acts in private. Moreover, the longer one identifies with this social veneer, the less conscious he will become of his own identity, until the mask finally supplants the man. Socially he may be a very well-adapted person, while he may be thoroughly unadapted to his own individuality. The persona is built on collective agreement, comprising those qualities which an individual feels he must necessarily project in order to be accepted in society. It is a false self — a concept of how one thinks society wishes him to be, rather than an expression of his true experience of Self. As a person acts and reacts within his environment, he builds this veneer layer-by-layer, modifying and perfecting it each time he encounters the outside world. This outer, social attitude will change like the skin of a chameleon to suit the particular situation, always with the purpose of gaining acceptance from and agreement with the external world. Its aim is always social, and therefore it seems logical to relate it to the Jupiter function.

Marc Edmund Jones has referred to Jupiter and Saturn as "soul" planets. Taken in the Jungian context, this would relate them to the functions of the "anima-animus", which reveals the inner, unconscious attitude which will *complement* the conscious attitude of the persona. It contains all those general human qualities which are lacking in the social mask. When the social mask is thwarted in some way, or fails to produce the desired results of recognition or social acceptance (the social function of Jupiter), then the Jupiter function will turn inward. This identification with the subjective world is felt as a compensation for what one has found unsatisfying in his social or professional life. An individual will turn his attention away from outer success, social expansion and personal aggrandizement, and will seek instead — often in an over-emotional, compulsive and irrational manner — so-called "spiritual" values and activities. He will place the greatest emphasis of his life on delving into his own unconscious mind and seek to develop that rather than developing his contacts with the world.

When a person turns from the outer to the inner side of his nature, a certain introversion will result. A man will tend to project feminine characteristics, and a woman, masculine characteristics. This has nothing whatever to do with their sexual identity but rather deals with the unconscious side of their natures. Such an introversion of the Jupiter function can often be related to the retrograde movement of the planet. The relationship of Jupiter to the persona and the anima-animus is a relationship in terms of the negative use of the Jupiter function in humanistic terms. For Jupiter to work in a positive manner, there must first be a vital sense of purpose in life. From this sense of purpose an individual will wish to participate with others in some greater whole of which he feels himself to be a conscious part. Ultimately, the Jupiterian urge toward growth and expansion should lead one to a full manifestation of his solar potential. Deviations from this ideal Jupiter development are generally caused by Saturn's role in the individual life. Saturn sets the pre-conditions to which Jupiter reacts — Saturn describes the society within which Jupiter participates.

JUPITER AND THE PERMISSIVE SOCIETY. A great deal has been written and said about the generation born after the last world war, especially in regard to its exaggerated use of the Jupiter function. The old, established restrictions and controls of Saturn seem to have broken down — most notably in the area of sexual taboos, and this generation is often credited with having gone to the dogs. The problems facing contemporary society are clearly those of Jupiter run awry. Over-population, over-production, waste, pollution, inflation, traffic congestion and even military arms stockpiling are all facets of Jupiterian expansion. It seems that we have all been on a Jupiter binge for the past thirty years, and are now experiencing a Saturnian morning-after.

However, just as a Saturn-recession naturally follows a Jupiter-inflation, the converse is also true. The affluent society was born out of the privation of the depression years. Parents who had grown up with very little in the way of material possessions determined to give their children *everything* they had missed. It was in reaction to the strong Saturnian emphasis in their lives that they created, through their children, the "permissive society". It is interesting to note that these children are now reaching young adulthood and are totally rejecting the materialism of their parents for a non-materialistic, spiritual life of contemplation. There is a general trend among young people to return to the soil and to rediscover the simpler joys of life. Young people today are rejecting the persona orientation of their parents' generation, with its emphasis on driving large cars, wearing expensive clothes and generally breaking their necks and hearts in an attempt to "keep up with the Joneses". Instead, they have swung the pendulum 180 degrees to an animus-anima orientation. Their lives, like their clothes, have become uni-sexual. They are more interested in developing their spirit than their back-hand. They scorn the fruits of technology, even to the extent of wanting their babies to be born at home. The term "permissive" applies not to them, but rather to their parents.

THE SEVEN CYCLES OF JUPITER. The cycles of Jupiter correspond to the numbers 12 and 7, principally because it takes approximately twelve years (actually 11 years, 10½ months) for Jupiter to make a complete transit of the zodiac, and because in an archetypal life-span of 84 years (one complete Uranus cycle) there will be seven complete Jupiter cycles. The general significance of the number twelve is self-evident, (Signs & Houses), but it also identifies the number of moons which orbit the planet Jupiter. This 12-year beat which describes the Jupiter pulse is a generic cycle which describes a condition of age common to all mankind. Everyone, simply by virtue of the fact that he has lived that long, will experience a Jupiter "return" at the approximate ages of 12, 24, 36, 48, 60, 72, and 84. The rhythm of these cycles will describe, in a potentially ascending spiral, an individual's attempt to grow toward being "more than an individual". They express the urge to expand not merely outward, but upward as well. Each new Jupiter cycle is potentially more than a simple repetition of the last. Each of these seven cycles, having its own significant meaning and purpose, will mark an important turning-point in the life of an individual. This does not mean, however, that they will necessarily correspond to significant *events,* for the turning-point may take place subjectively and may not even occur on a conscious level. What becomes possible at these times is the use of the Jupiter energy in a new and different way. As this new tide begins to unfold, it will affect one's relationship to society and one's participation in it.

The division of any cycle into seven periods is of universal significance and application. Blavatsky's *Secret Doctrine* gives numerous instances of such a seven-fold analysis and relates it particularly to what she calls the "Seven Principles in Man". These principles are 1) The physical; 2) The etheric or vital principle; 3) The astral, feeling and desire nature; 4) The inferior mental or intellectual; 5) The superior mental or true mind; 6) Buddhi — the spiritual soul; and 7) The Atma or pure spirit. These seven principles have their counterparts in all religions, in the ancient Egyptian and Persian doctrines, in the Kabalah, in Taoism and in the I-Ching. Plato speaks of them, and they are part of the Hermetic doctrine and of Buddhism. The accomplishment of the alchemists' Great Work also had seven phases. The seventh is the highest stage of illumination. Thus, the seven conjunctions of Jupiter with its natal position in an 84-year lifetime suggest that the complete fulfillment of the Jupiter function within the personality proceeds by seven stages and necessitates 84 years for completion.

THE TWELVE-YEAR JUPITER CYCLE. Because the Jupiter cycle has been linked to the number 12, each year of this cycle is associated with a Sign of the zodiac. The first year of this cycle is an "Aries" year, the second a "Taurus" year, and so forth. It must be remembered, however, that this zodiacal correspondence is related to the placement of Jupiter in an individual birth-chart and *is not to be confused with the Sign through which Jupiter is transiting.* If the natal position of Jupiter is 18 Capricorn, then the "Aries" year will begin when Jupiter reaches 18 Capricorn by transit and will last until transiting Jupiter reaches 18 Aquarius. In this way, and in relation to Jupiterian matters, the familiar meaning of each Sign can give its coloration to the Jupiter year in question. Also, the astrologer must always consider each year of the Jupiter cycle in terms of the Age Factor. This is especially true of the "Aries" year.*

The "Aries" Year — The Jupiter Return. This year begins with the Jupiter return and signals a re-birth of the Jupiter principle in the life. If a person wishes to earn more money, gain more prestige or social recognition, or assume a role of responsibility within the community, this is the time to begin working consciously toward those goals. People

---

*Editor's Note: The following sections not only outline the *general* meaning of the twelve phases in a complete Jupiter cycle, as correlated to the zodiacal signs, but also include interpretive guidelines for applying these general principles by using two specific examples — natal Jupiter located in the 1st and 10th houses. When natal Jupiter is found in one of the other ten houses, the reader should attempt to integrate the quality of the specific year (or phase of the Jupiter cycle) with the meaning of transiting Jupiter's particular house position.

should use their power of initiative and leadership in Jupiter matters if they want this new cycle to bear fruit. *They* must take the initiative, make the effort, and try out their possibilities on social, financial, religious and political levels for success to come to them. The "Aries" year is not a culmination, but a beginning. It is not, as many traditional texts hold, a time when honors and rewards come rolling in, but rather a seed-planting time. Each person will begin his Jupiter cycle in the House in which natal Jupiter is found. This natal House position determines the type of initiative required and will indicate the area of life in which the Jupiter urge will manifest. For example, if the Jupiter return occurs in the 1st House, the new initiative will be less outward, as in business, and more inwards, as regards perhaps some new social or religious ideal. Inward preparation for some future *new* social function may necessitate retirement from *habitual* social or "religious" activities. The new social function of Jupiter must be related ever more effectively, cycle after cycle, to one's basic life-purpose as it is revealed by the whole birth-chart.

The Aries period is especially useful for becoming more aware of the way in which the Jupiter function of assimilation works within one's biological and psychological organism. The problems one meets in the social, religious and professional life of his community will also be brought into focus at this time. If an individual is *conscious* that a new cycle is beginning and that he has a new opportunity to make more significant *use* of the Jupiter energies in his life, *then*, and only then, can something change in his habitual manner of growth and expansion. As another example, Jupiter in the 10th House indicates that a person is able to wield social power. The tests of his life, therefore, will be of the *use* he makes of his social position, prestige, wealth, or of his religious and psychological insights. Each new Jupiter cycle will present a new test in this area, based on the fruits of the previous cycle. Thus, the Aries year falling in the 10th House will not signal a time of inward retirement, but rather a challenge to grow *beyond* what one has been in the outside world. What will matter will be the end toward which one uses his influence in his social or professional field. To sum up, the Aries quality of initiative and leadership will be necessary at the beginning of each Jupiter Cycle, but always in terms of the natal House position and aspects.

The "Taurus" Year. During the second year of the cycle, one should see the new Jupiter impulse become more concrete. The new initiative should now bear some fruit and so the person may get some idea of what will realistically be possible or impossible — necessary and unnecessary. He should therefore renounce any line of endeavor that seems unfruit-ful. Using the example of natal Jupiter in the 1st House, the "Taurus" phase would coincide with the transit of the 2nd House. The new Jupiter impulse might demand an outlay of personal resources — financially, psychologically and physically. A new appreciation of one's innate possibilities and powers, or better management and organization of one's resources may be required at this time. The 2nd House accent will reveal whether or not the Jupiter opportunity, as it was understood in the Aries phase, has practical possibilities. It will also reveal whether the inertia of one's habit patterns and prejudices is stronger than the new impulse, and whether the individual can break out of his self-constructed mold. If he is able to do this and tap deeper layers of his being, then unsuspected powers within his nature will be revealed.

In the case of the 10th House natal Jupiter, the Taurus phase of the cycle can coincide with the 11th House transit. This suggests that any Jupiter impulse initiated during the Aries phase must be related to the *social means* at hand capable of making the person's vision a reality to others. One may have to tone down his enthusiasm, and he must not cut himself off too brutally from the people who have made possible his social success in the last Jupiter cycle. His ideals must be realistic, acceptable to his associates or community, or he might find himself alone and friendless, powerless to act constructively in terms of what his society *really* needs. The new Jupiter impulse should consider true social needs, not personal aggrandizement at the expense of others. If it does represent a possible answer to a social need, then the power of the community will certainly try to act *through* the individual, who will become a representative man in the social sphere related to his competence.

The "Gemini" Year. This phase will stress the power of communication with the environment. One may find himself reading and writing a great deal in the attempt to expand his mind and better organize his ideas. One may be tempted to live only in the mind and thus must make the effort to utilize his new Jupiter impulse in a significant and practical way. New relationships should be established within the social sphere as one begins to externalize his Jupiter energy. As this is a time for experimentation however, those relationships should not be forced into set patterns, but allowed to flow freely. They are the first objective test of the new impulse. If the Gemini phase coincides with the transit of the 3rd House, new contacts with and concepts of one's environment can help the Jupiter impulse to function better within everyday reality. A person should seek demonstrations and concrete proof of the value — or lack of value — of his new use of Jupiter. During this phase of the cycle an individual should see his new social or psychological outlook in its relationship to society.

If the Gemini phase corresponds to a transit of the 12th House, the person's capacity to be a true and efficient manager of some group aspiration will be put to the test. In this phase, an individual will either succeed in finding an answer to the subconscious needs of his group, or else he will tend to be overcome by ghosts of the past cycle. One's memories of past failures and one's "unfinished business" clutter a person's life and provide barriers to any forward movement. In this phase it will be decided whether the Jupiter cycle will really introduce new elements into the manner of one's social adaptation, or whether, through a lack of courage and will-power, the "new" will be a repetition of the old pattern in boredom or resignation.

The "Cancer" Year. The Cancer phase of this cycle corresponds to the first quarter or waxing square of Jupiter to its natal position, and describes a "crisis in action". This time should be used to consolidate the new trend. The "Aries" through "Gemini" years are a time of experimentation — no firm decision had to be made, and no definite direction had to be chosen. At the Cancer phase, however, a choice is imperative. One must decide both the form and the direction which the new Jupiter trend will take, and then allow himself to be limited by it. This does not mean that a person should give up certain goals or ambitions because of fear, or that he should limit himself too much by trying to adapt his new Jupiterian urge to fit some already established form or doctrine. Limitation in this sense means *concentration* — aiming in a specific direction like the Sagittarian archer, rather than scattering oneself all over the universe. The Cancer phase is a turning-point in the Jupiter cycle. Whereas in the Gemini phase the urge was to communicate the new Jupiter trend, to talk about it, the waxing square is a call for action. At this time one must choose the Jupiter social activity which best corresponds to what one truly seeks and desires to achieve. This period will set the direction for the remainder of the cycle, so the choice must be a personal one.

If this Cancer phase corresponds to the 4th House transit of Jupiter, then the attempt to consolidate one's position and to lay concrete foundations will be doubly emphasized. It is important not to feel that one has reached rock bottom and can progress no further; rather, the new impulse should be sufficiently well-formed and realistic to be developed further. In other words, during this phase an individual must find some stable base from which he may begin to act socially in a more dynamic and creative manner. Only an opportunity which offers a chance to lay the groundwork for *later* progress — especially during and after the "Libra" phase — should be considered seriously at this time. If the Cancer phase corresponds to the 1st House transit of Jupiter, then "consolidation" will mean that the individual must now decide to put his personality at the service of the collective or group enterprise which corresponds to the vision of the Aries phase. An individual should be prepared at this time to devote himself utterly and completely to that personage or collective work which best seems to represent his social ideals.

The "Leo" Year. As the Cancer phase is an important turning-point in an individual's effort to expand both socially and personally in some new way, the following Leo phase can only carry forward what has already been established. A person must go forward with faith and imagination, giving free play to his creative ability and his social talents. The dreams of the first quarter are now becoming a reality, and one should be prepared to take certain risks to see them realized. This is a time when one should not be afraid to show in some concrete way the values for which he personally stands.

If the "Leo" phase corresponds to a Jupiter transit of the fifth House, one's social expansion will depend more than ever on personal initiative. There may be problems due to over-optimism, especially in speculative ventures. An individual will act as if he has a real mission to accomplish, and he will be able to assume responsibility freely. At this time it is possible for a person to become the mouth-piece of some group which expresses those Jupiter values which he holds most dear. In any case, this is the time to gain social recognition for one's Jupiterian aims, and to increase one's self-assurance when acting socially. To be avoided are tendencies toward pride, arrogance and the type of mindless passion which blocks both the reason and the will. If Jupiter transits the 2nd House during the Leo phase, there will be a test of one's ability to manage and expand the scope of those things which he values, be they material or spiritual. This test may involve a choice between the desire to possess the social power with which a person has been theoretically entrusted, and the proper management of that power — holding it in trust for the good of all. If an individual uses the social power at his disposal simply to feed his ego or to gain social or religious privileges, then the entire Jupiter cycle will turn spiritually negative.

The "Virgo" Year. During the Virgo phase one reaps the results of his manner of social expression, which often requires changes in one's social behavior. A lack of success during the Leo phase should lead now to attempts at self-improvement. Here an individual will reveal his true spiritual stature by the quality of his response to this lack or defeat. It may simply entail the development of some new social technique, or more comprehensively, it may signify a complete self-consecration to the social ideal envisioned at the beginning of the Jupiter cycle. The crises which arise at this time will have to be met, especially in all those cases where the problems are due to one's egocentricity or selfishness. During this phase, an individual must be ready to grow, to serve, and to obey. Greater efficiency will be demanded in terms of what a person tries to contribute to the productivity and growth of his community. One must not be afraid of increased work and the need to develop his capacity to serve.

If this Virgo phase coincides with the transit of the 6th House, the person should work to relate himself ever more effectively to some larger social pattern, and to develop his sense of participation in society. This is the last step on the way either to some form of new social accomplishment (if the Jupiter cycle has developed in a positive manner up to this time) or to the realization that one has not been sufficiently realistic and therefore has not been able to mobilize his energies adequately in order to arrive at a positive result in his social life. If one's social behavior does not come up to the ideal he held at the beginning of the Jupiter cycle, then this 6th House Virgo phase will provide an opportunity to clearly realize the reasons for this failure. It is not too late to change. When the Virgo phase corresponds to the Jupiter transit of the 3rd House, there may be a need for discrimination in the manner in which one uses his new social or spiritual ideas. Here the response of one's neighbors or relatives to his ideas may force him to realize that, as he expresses them or tries to put them into practice, there is something which is not as worthwhile or practical as he originally thought. This can produce a crisis — the necessity to change something, either in one's way of thinking or in his behavior; therefore it may become necessary to acquire a new technique to remedy one's social and/or personal failings.

The "Libra" Year. The Libra phase marks the mid-point of the Jupiter cycle, the culmination of an individual's external efforts to establish new Jupiter values in his life. As one tries to change the character of his inter-personal relationships, to perfect them and make them more fulfilling, the new tide of Jupiter energies related to one's social and religious life reaches its high point. Whatever has been initiated during the Aries year and sufficiently consolidated during the Cancer year should reach a definite consummation of some sort in the Libra year. At this time a person may have to consciously adapt himself in some new way to everything Jupiter means in his life. If since the Aries year he has been purposefully preparing himself for the development of a new social or spiritual consciousness, then this Libra year can bring this trend to a culmination through some definite "initiation" into that greater social or spiritual whole of which the individual now *knows* he is a significant part. The desire to run away from oneself, to lose one's sense of identity in social activities or in a relationship, may be especially strong at this time. Additionally, the Jupiter urge may tempt an individual to lose his sense of Self by entering into projects or assuming tasks which are too ambitious. At the same time, however, there is the possibility for acquiring greater social prestige during this phase — forming important business liaisons, marrying, or at last finding one's true social or professional work.

If the Jupiter transit occurs in the 7th House during this phase, partnership propositions will offer opportunities for growth and expansion. This will be particularly true if such partnerships develop out of work already underway, or along a line which has been pursued since the Aries phase. Marriage is a possibility, as is some sort of promotion. In all cases, however, the sphere of one's personal contacts should widen. Future opportunities for progress will come from the new social and inter-personal relationships established during this Libra year. When the Libra phase corresponds to a Jupiter transit of the 4th House, the culmination of the social or spiritual efforts begun in the Aries phase will now lead to a strong sense of personal power. This will enable a person to establish his life on more secure foundations. One can now become a true representative man, fully aware of the new social role which his personality can play. The inner life should be richer, the feelings more expansive, and there should be an enhanced sense of self-confidence. On this one can build a broader and firmer foundation for his personal life.

The "Scorpio" Year. Whatever has been accomplished during the "full-moon" Libra phase should now be consolidated in the Scorpio year. Those realizations should now be substantiated socially, and this usually leads to the necessity for some kind of reorientation or revision of the Jupiter trend which has been seeking social recognition since the beginning of the cycle. One must consider closely the expectations one has from the new relationship of self to society initiated theoretically during the Libra phase. Problems in the practical working out of one's life-purpose through his new inter-personal relationships can crop up at this time. Unrealistic dreams must now be forgotten or set aside. In spite of the possibly idealistic nature of a person's love and his desire to share, any new relationship established on this basis must still take place within the framework of the existing social, cultural and religious order. Thus, in this Scorpio phase, there may be problems due either to the need to conform to this socio-cultural framework, or due to one's defiance of traditional values. This phase of the Jupiter cycle is the most important in terms of one's actual success. If a person is not realistic and conscious enough in his present social efforts, he is likely at this time to witness the failure of his efforts to relate his individual purpose to the social means at hand. Whatever happens, this 8th phase will reveal the concrete reality — success or failure — of the effort to become a socially harmonious and significant person.

If Jupiter transits the 8th House during this Scorpio phase, the need for some form of personal regeneration will be evident. If an individual wishes to be reborn as a person able to participate productively and effectively within the framework of his group, community, nation or culture, this is the most likely time. What must be avoided is the tendency to lose oneself in other people's wants or values, or in the established pattern of social activities of the "greater whole". It may be necessary to conform to certain social procedures in order to be socially accepted; however, one should never lose sight of his individual purpose. Thus, even after conforming, one may work to direct the social energies at his disposal toward his own ends. When the "Scorpio" phase coincides with Jupiter's transit of the 5th House, this period can be a test of one's personal behavior developed in the preceding Libra phase. The real worth of one's theoretically new social personality must be proved. In this an individual will have to be true to his own purpose, acting in a way which convinces others without hurting them. In this transit is the danger of expressing oneself through the persona-mask, especially if one is feeling inferior. Pride, anger, and lust must be avoided. They simply reveal that the person is not master in his own house, and that the energies of human nature are acting in place of the individual Self.

The "Sagittarius" Year. If the cycle has been positive up to this point, then the Sagittarian phase can be one of real social expansion. During this time one will see the new social activities or meanings introduced during the Libra phase begin to permeate society. The accent here should be on social management or organization, and on the extension of one's social power. One should make an effort to transform those elements in his social or religious life which relate to his own current Jupiter cycle. Social and ethical principles become important. An individual's assurance and expansiveness will come from the security he has gained by merging his energies with some group. If Jupiter transits the 9th House during this phase, the time is ripe for making long-range plans. Such plans should aim at the reorganization of one's social relationships in terms of the new social vision which that individual has succeeded in developing. One must be careful here not to over-do things, not to become carried away by a fanatical desire for personal aggrandizement. It will be possible to accomplish concrete objectives in the religious or occult sphere, and there can be an ecstatic loss of Self in mystical experiences. On more mundane levels, personal, professional and social opportunities may lead to contacts with foreign countries or a move to a new territory. One might also invest in new or distant projects at this time. Educational work, publishing, promotion, shipping, law, mail-order, or any work which requires traveling are among the possibilities of this 9th House transit.

When Jupiter transits the 6th House during the Sagittarian phase, there is the possibility of making good progress in one's work and, if necessary, it should not be difficult to find a new job. The person's best chances will generally come through his ability to apply efficient methods to his daily routine, whether at home or in the business world. In some cases, this period can bring a crisis of response to some new social or national need. Some things may have to be changed either in the body's responses or in the expression of instinctual urges and desires.

One must be prepared to learn a new approach to the skills he possesses, especially if the Scorpio phase has revealed weaknesses. A person must realize, however, that technique is not everything. His personal, emotional or psychological approach to the possibility of crisis can defeat his ability to use that technique. On mundane levels, government appointments, the civil service, production or personnel positions, public utilities, nursing and dietetics can offer professional possibilities at this time.

The "Capricorn" Year. The Capricorn phase corresponds to the waning square of transiting Jupiter to its natal position, and therefore presents another period of readjustment. What one has been working for since the beginning of the cycle should now be firmly established in a concrete way in one's social or professional context. One cannot expect further expansion along established lines, and it becomes necessary from this time forward to look objectively at the results achieved in terms of their value to the community and the growth of one's true Self. One should now ask oneself certain questions: What does my present job or career mean to me personally? What do I expect from it? Has it given me what I expected from it? Have I given all I could to my job or career? How much have I conformed to collective ideals and collective behavior up to now? How much can I afford to be more myself in the future within the limits of what society expects from me? If the answers to such questions show that the social or professional activities which a person has chosen have not enabled him to prove his true worth or to demonstrate effectively in public who and what he is as an individual, then the time has come for him to revise the situation thoroughly. Ideally, each individual should contribute to society what he essentially is. One's work in the world should serve to solve his personal problems and, at the same time, meet the needs of society in some way. It will not necessarily be the easiest type of work; however, it should be an occupation which will provide those experiences capable of stimulating one to be truly himself and to give truly of himself. Neither the job nor the place matter, spiritually speaking, but rather the opportunity to contribute something of value to others in terms of his own personality and uniqueness.

If the Capricorn phase coincides with the transit of the 10th House, there will be a particular need for readjustments in terms of one's career or public image. These will reveal publicly what one has managed to exteriorize of the Jupiter ideal established at the Ascendant. As this exteriorization is never complete and perfect, whenever the 10th House is emphasized, that is the time to admit to oneself that something is lacking and to accept the necessity of bettering one's performance. During this transit a person will have the prestige he merits, and he will be asked to prove his social, personal and professional capacities and skills publicly. This is the time to present one's creative work to the public and to rise to the social or professional occasion. If the Capricorn phase corresponds to Jupiter's transit of the 7th House, then the readjustments demanded by the Jupiter cycle will affect an individual's inter-personal relationships as well as his general attitude toward the world. One must prove the worth of his social ideals by the way he *acts* both in relation to other individuals and also to his community. In other words, one must readjust his social relationships so that they really do serve a purpose in some larger process.

The "Aquarian" Year. This phase of the Jupiter cycle is the time for a reconsideration of *all* one's social ideas and ideals — for realizing the need to give a new value to one's social activities. One will need common sense as he tries to evaluate, as calmly and objectively as possible, what he considers to be the *actual* needs of society, his friends and himself. This is a period during which one tends to build dreamcastles in the effort to compensate for what was found lacking in the Capricorn phase. It is also the time when an individual is inclined to be deeply affected equally by public approval of his efforts as by public condemnation. Although one can now enjoy the fruits of his public success and can even succeed in increasing the value and prestige of all that comes to him as a result of his Jupiterian expansion, this period should also awaken in him the yearning for new horizons.

If the Aquarian phase coincides with the transit of Jupiter through the 11th House, one can now enjoy the fruits of his efforts (providing that the 10th House phase has been positive). More importantly, however, this phase should see a clear understanding of what has been achieved in the complete Jupiter cycle. One must see the gap between the ideal and reality, and make preparations for a new cycle of Jupiterian accomplishment. Having decided what the new step into the future ought to be, one should concentrate his attention on the social means at hand, the friends and associates who have made his past ascension possible and who should be taken along in the new ascension. The principal danger of this phase is the tendency to be too utopian, or to cut oneself off completely from the past. In order to succeed, one must do his utmost to formulate his new ideals in a socially effective manner, in a manner acceptable to those who have followed in his footsteps up to this 11th House phase. Social assets are the key to one's future success. The people one knows professionally and the clubs and organizations to which one belongs will be his means to progress. The entertainment of important people, friends and family prestige can help in the realization of one's plans.

If Jupiter transits the 8th House during the Aquarian phase, one must now substantiate in a practical way the relationships entered into during the Capricorn phase. Here a person must put his managerial abilities to the test in order to increase the fruits of his common work with other members of the group. One may be called upon to correct and adjust many different problems arising from his inter-personal relationships, and to develop a real sense of deep human sympathy. Success will still come through partnerships, provided that one is prepared to pool his resources for mutual benefit. A co-operative attitude and personal charm can smooth the way. It is essential to be forward-looking at this time, and not allow oneself to be hampered by precedents. One must try to transform the ways of custom by demonstrating a new principle of conduct. Here it is important not to lose sight of the life-purpose which is described by a 10th House natal Jupiter. What one does during this 8th House transit will either help or hinder, on very practical levels, what one hopes to achieve as a public image of his individual reality.

The "Pisces" Year. This final phase of the Jupiter cycle is a period of transformation. The actions or decisions taken at this time can retard one's capacity to meet the new conditions and the new environment looming on the horizon. As one tries to go beyond the social, religious and political consciousness and activities which have until now commanded his allegiance, one may have to renounce much. The new Jupiter impulse will not be truly new unless, during the Pisces phase, one manages to discard those beliefs and attitudes which bind him to the past. During this phase one must assimilate as many unfamiliar and distant values as possible. The Jupiterian expansion should now include even more, especially that which challenges one by its striking difference or even antagonism. Only in this way can one prepare himself for a *new* Jupiter cycle; for greater understanding and greater love depend on an individual's capacity to include the alien and the unknown.

If Jupiter transits the 12th House during the Pisces phase, the trend of dissolution of attachments and of binding limitations takes on a very strong character. The natal Jupiter in the 1st House will never be a symbol of personal identification with some new social or religious ideal unless there has been some prior renunciation or relinquishment. Thus, the call to renunciation will come every twelve years when Jupiter transits the 12th natal House. It is only when the past no longer pulls and binds the soul and the mind that the spirit can act and lead one forward and beyond. During this final phase of the Jupiter cycle one must question his allegiance to society and social customs. If no change comes at this time, then one is not living as a free individual. The only true freedom resides in one's ability to change his allegiances according to his growth in spiritual, moral and social ideals. If a person resists change, then he also resists growth. However, when one becomes conscious for the first time that he is not growing because he has not wanted to change, then the opportunity arises to *use* that freedom. By renouncing one's petty values and narrow satisfactions, he may seek instead the attainment of greater and nobler goals. This is the pattern of opportunity presented every twelve years when Jupiter goes through its Pisces phase, and also when the planet transits one's natal 12th House.

If the Pisces phase corresponds to a Jupiter transit of the 9th House, then it will signify the opportunity to reassess and renounce those values and beliefs which form the basis of his 10th House natal placement. It will be specifically in terms of "9th House matters" that one will meet the conditions through which his old way of feeling, thinking and behaving should pass gradually into a new way. It may be through some religious experience, or through reading some philosophical work or listening to a teacher that one will transform his Jupiterian urge; or it may be through travel to a distant place or meeting a person from a foreign land that one will gain a new perspective and change his allegiances. In any case, this 9th House transit refers to an individual's effort to find out *why* certain things happen or have happened both in his inter-personal relationships and in his attempt to relate significantly to the outer world. The Pisces influence suggests the need to pass through crisis in order that he may approach the world in a new and freer way.

JUPITER'S TRANSIT THROUGH THE SOLAR HOUSES. When the birth time is unknown, the Solar House technique is often used. Because this technique is the one generally used when presenting astrology to the public through the mass media, it is often scorned by astrologers as too superficial to have any significance. In humanistic terms, however, Sun Sign astrology has a specific value beyond the scope of "popular" astrology. In terms of the Jupiter transit, this technique relates the general trend described by the Sign position of Jupiter to the Sun Sign of an individual. Thus, the passage of Jupiter through the Sign of Gemini in 1977 establishes first of all a collective mood and opportunity which will apply to *everyone*. The *mentality* of all human beings will be colored by Jupiterian characteristics, since Gemini rules the mind. People everywhere will tend to think more expansively, more optimistically; there will be much eager planning for more extensive relationships and a strong urge to grow through new contacts and new concepts. Each person will react to this *general trend* of thought in his or her own fashion, according to the individual natal chart. However, in a more general way, each person will also react according to his solar type. The general trend of thought related to Jupiter in Gemini will, of course, affect more particularly those people with the Sun in Gemini. Those having other natal planets in Gemini, or in the other Mutable Signs, will also feel the Jupiterian urge to expansion in a purely personal way; however, it is specifically each solar type (Sign) to which the "typical" interpretations are given. Thus, while Jupiter in Gemini will have a "1st House" meaning for those people born with the Sun in Gemini, it will have a "4th House" meaning for people born with the Sun in Pisces.

In other words, when Jupiter in Gemini transits over my Sun in Gemini, a general social trend is brought to a focus in my life through a transformation and stimulation of my vitality, my will and my sense of purpose or destiny which the natal Sun represents. This will be *particularly* evident through the experiences related to the *natal House* in which the Sun is found. But in solar astrology it may also be interpreted in terms of the *Solar House* through which Jupiter transits. In all cases, however, the Solar House will not show an individualized response, but rather *the area of the life in which the pressure of a collective trend will operate.* This trend is outside of the individual, and he reacts to it as a social being. Even if his life is changed by the pressure of such outside forces, the motivation is collective and not due to the *individual* development of the pattern of his own destiny.

While the transit of Jupiter through Gemini provides a general meaning which applies to everyone in the world, the fact that a particular person is born, for example, with the Sun in Virgo will give the astrologer a more specific framework within which to relate this transit. According to solar typology, Jupiter will be found in the 10th Solar House for the Virgo type. Thus, the astrologer may interpret this transit as indicating that the general expansive mental atmosphere — the trend to expand through the making of new contacts and new plans — will be particularly evident in the 10th House field of experience for the Virgo person. This could indicate the possibility of business opportunities or professional advancement, increase in social prestige or authority, a feeling of optimism and benevolent behavior when dealing with public issues, and even spiritual growth through the wise use of social power.

Although this technique is more general in its implications than the relation of transiting Jupiter to its natal position by Sign and House, it is still valid and should not be dismissed. Each solar type will respond to the general trend described by a transit in relation to the Solar House; and the more true one is to his solar type, the more true the Sun Sign interpretation will be. Since so many astrologers seem to rely more on transit indications than on progressions and directions, this Solar House interpretation of their meaning according to Rudhyar's humanistic approach will give them an added dimension.

THE INDIVIDUAL JUPITER CYCLE. In the humanistic approach, the individual cycle of Jupiter begins when that planet first reaches the Ascendant degree. Since the Jupiter cycle lasts about twelve years, and since the planet can be found in any of the twelve natal Houses at birth, the individual cycle will begin some time during the first twelve years of life. From that time forward, Jupiter can be used in an increasingly individualized manner in relation to one's basic life-purpose. According to the basic ideas on transit cycles put forward by Rudhyar, the first three Houses of the chart counting from the Ascendant (the first or Winter Quarter) refer to growth of the essential nature of the planetary function being studied. Therefore, as Jupiter moves from Ascendant to Nadir, the Jupiter function and everything related to it develop new facets in a subjective, interiorized manner. Nothing much may show in the outer life. This stage of the process is like the seed during the winter quarter of the year. The next three Houses, comprising the second or Spring Quarter, refer to growth in the individual's capacity to use the planetary function. Therefore, as Jupiter moves from the Nadir up to the Descendant, the quality of its function becomes clearer in the person's outer life. Something begins to happen, as if it were Springtime. The new Jupiter impulse begins to germinate and can be recognized for what it hopefully might become later on. New Jupiter faculties should be built as the individual tries to participate in a new way in the life of his community and to influence more creatively his society in the field of his competence.

The third or Summer Quarter refers to further growth in the use of the Jupiter factors in the life. Therefore, as the planet moves up from the Descendant to the Midheaven, the individual will show how well, or how badly, he can function within the social context. The way in which a person uses his newly developed capacities and means for social action, IF he has developed any at all (which is by no means certain), will now be clearly seen. Whether he is capable of becoming wealthier or gaining greater prestige, or whether he is growing spiritually through more effective participation and sharing in some form of organized religious or cultural experience will become apparent at this time. In any case, when Jupiter comes to the Descendant, the individual is supposed to have developed certain "tools", and, as the planet climbs to the Midheaven, he should try to use them with increasing skill and effectiveness. It will be during the Summer Quarter transit that the individual will be able to use the means of conveying his individual vision and the ideals which he has developed since Jupiter crossed the Ascendant in a truly conscious and responsible manner. From the moment Jupiter reaches the Descendant, he must reach beyond himself and meet people as equals. He must choose those people with whom he feels able to work out the new social vision he has tried to make practical. With them he will gain new experiences which he could not have reached alone. The aim must be to cooperate and to love — to assimilate into oneself what were previously alien or unknown values. One must also be prepared to accept many modifications in his attempts to blend his ideal vision with that of others.

Then, finally, comes the fourth or Autumn Quarter which refers to the growth of the person's influence on the basis of actual social achievement. The individual has had the opportunity to put his Jupiter function to the test in social or religious living and, if all has gone well, he should now become increasingly influential in the field of activity he has made his own. His social actions and example should now lead to concrete results. At this time, however, a greater question presents itself: What should he do with these results? A harvest will be made of the fruits of all his efforts since Jupiter crossed the Ascendant, and, especially during the 12th House phase of this cycle, the individual will be challenged to grow beyond what he has accomplished. His inner decisions as to how to do this will condition the new seed which can develop when Jupiter again comes to the Ascendant for a new twelve-year cycle. In those cases where the arrival of Jupiter at the Mid-heaven does not spell success because the person has not known how to share his Jupiter abilities with his social group in a positive way, this Autumn Quarter should be used to understand as fully as possible the reasons for this failure. By doing this, he will not build the essence of this failure into the seed of the new cycle which is forming at this time.

Uncreative, non-individualized people will naturally tend to experience each new cycle at the same level as the preceding one. Because they do not work *consciously* with the rhythm of the Jupiter cycle, neither their social nor their spiritual results can be clear-cut or individualized. They add nothing new to society or to their group and therefore cannot expect any particular reward or recognition. And yet it is just these unsuccessful people, often frustrated and fearful, who would benefit the most from the counsel of a humanistic astrologer. Through learning to work consciously with the tide of growth of their Jupiter function, they could certainly learn to live a more interesting and valuable life. When a person is living in a spiritually positive manner, he will not grow and expand through conforming to society's traditional ways, even though such ways could possibly bring him vast profits and social power. He will rather try to find how, while submitting to a necessary degree of social conformity, he can impress his own vision and sense of social purpose upon society. The creative individual will direct those means generated by human beings working and producing together in business, cultural, or religious realms and use them intelligently toward some future goal.

VI

The Saturn Cycle

Every individual has antecedents in the form of family, racial and, at the limit, human heredity. Thus, each new-born infant is a synthesis of collective elements, as well as — if one believes in reincarnation — the end product of an infinite series of manifestations as a divine soul. Astrologically, the symbol of this collective past is Saturn. The position of Saturn in a birth-chart thus indicates how history will condition the individual's future life development. Saturn defines the individual starting point — the universe has come this far before he arrived, and from this point he must move on in his own way. Saturn does not rule the future, but rather defines the past, the background and traditions, both racial and cultural, into which the native is born. The beginning of a cycle does not absolutely and unavoidably determine its end. There is in every cycle a middle point — the ceaseless Present — which symbolizes the creative power of the individual, the unpredictable factor in all life processes. The creative element is, however, only a *potential* and is not necessarily operant in a particular man or woman, since it can only operate when an individual becomes a relatively complete and integrated personality. When such an integration does not take place, the individual remains a passive specimen of his or her race, community and culture. For the creative individual, the present moment is always more than a mere result of the past. The Saturnian present moment takes on the visage of a taskmaster only to a person who is not individualized. In that case, he feels his originality bound by routine; his aspirations are leveled to the collective norm, and his actions are based on precedent and are therefore devoid of creative, and thus free, initiative.

In the natal chart Saturn brings energies to a focus; where Saturn is found by Sign and House there is some knot of destiny which is unavoidable. When Saturn forms conjunctions or oppositions to other planets in the birth-chart, some of the most basic secrets of that individual are revealed. Saturn conjunctions show the nature of a new situation confronting the incarnating Self, or a new relation to the family tradition, which will deeply occupy his consciousness. It will be a binding situation; and, because new and unfamiliar, it will require the person's entire attention during a great portion of his life. The basic experiences will stem from the planet conjoined to Saturn, and an understanding of these experiences may consume much time and energy, and may necessitate many repetitions. The person's task will be to detach from those experiences so that they will eventually lose their compulsive character. When transiting Saturn opposes the natal conjunction, the person will have his best opportunity to reach an objective understanding of the condition and thereby be free of it. Such freedom, however, can only come through fulfilling the task to which the conjunction points. Secondary moments of deeper awareness of the meaning of the conjunction can come when any other planet, or the Sun and Moon, opposes it. Again, however, it must be pointed out that awareness is only possible *PROVIDED* the native gives his conscious attention to the task.

Natal conjunctions with Saturn are often the symbol of psychological "complexes," especially if Saturn conjoins the Sun or Moon. A Saturn-Sun conjunction relates specifically to a father-complex. This may have come about either through some misunderstanding between father and child, or through the loss of the father at an early age. In any case, the native may feel the lack of a father's example and presence during the formative years when such an example is most important psychologically. The Sun-Saturn conjunction may also indicate *too close* a psychic link to the father. The first major opportunity the person will have to resolve this complex will come at the onset of puberty (at approximately the age of 15) when transiting Saturn makes its first opposition to this conjunction. At this time the problem may manifest as one of sex identification or rebellion against parental authority. The second major opportunity for resolution will come at the onset of middle-age (at approximately 45) with the second Saturn opposition. At this time the person may himself have a teen-age child going through the trauma of puberty, or he may be experiencing a second puberty, or he may experience an awareness of his father's mortality. If the person has not resolved his father-complex by the time of the final Saturn opposition around age 75, he will have another opportunity at that time.

There are, however, in the intervening years many secondary opportunities for such deeper awareness. The Sun, for example, will transit the opposition to the natal conjunction every year, giving the person a chance to re-evaluate the father/authority-figure in the light of his own solar purpose or "true nature." Monthly the Moon will transit that position, heightening one's instinctual awareness and the possibility of taking action to clarify the solar purpose. The annual transit of Mercury indicates a time when the person may use the principle of intellectual interchange to clarify his understanding. Intellectualizing the problem and giving it verbal expression can help the individual become more objective. With the transit of Venus very 12 months (approximately) the person may draw upon his basic values to find inner meaning in this life-conflict. The transit of Mars occurs every 2 years and will give the opportunity for outer expression of the father-complex. Directing the energy outward will further objectify it and free the individual from its compulsive nature. The transit of Jupiter to this opposition point every twelve years will provide a chance to place this problem in a larger frame of reference — to view it from a social standpoint rather than a purely personal one. Only once in a lifetime will Uranus transit this point. At this time a true integration may take place, provided Uranus is victorious over Saturn. How the individual will choose to use the Uranus energy will greatly depend on his age at the time of the transit.

A Moon-Saturn conjunction in the natal chart often indicates a mother-complex. The person may feel that he is an unwanted child, thereby building up a resentment toward the mother. This generally comes from the experience of a lack of maternal loving and can express itself in later life as either an insatiable need for mothering, or as an inability to express the mothering quality. This is often a difficult aspect, especially for women, since the Moon in a woman's chart also refers to her view of her own femininity. Thus, the resentment can be not only against her mother and women in general, but against herself as a woman. The natal configuration of Moon conjunct Saturn can manifest in a much more insidious manner than the Sun-Saturn conjunction because it often operates on an emotional or subconscious level in the form of depression. Like the Sun-Saturn conjunction, the opportunities for objective understanding will come when the opposition point is activated. In this instance, however, particular attention should be placed on the transiting Moon, especially in a woman's chart. The periodic discomfort often linked to the menstrual cycle (which is also a 28-day lunar cycle) may be closely linked to this configuration. If this is a problem, the individual may choose to use this lunar energy consciously to draw her attention to her own feminine nature, accepting rather than denying her biological function. It is interesting to note that the first opposition of transiting Saturn to its natal position in a woman's chart corresponds to the onset of menstruation, while the second opposition corresponds to the onset of menopause. Thus, a woman's child-bearing years are bordered by the first and second Saturn oppositions.

A natal opposition of Saturn to the Sun, Moon or a planet can be an easier aspect for the person to deal with, since the configuration itself inherently symbolizes the possibility for objective understanding. Moreover, transits will activate it by opposition twice as frequently — the Sun twice a year, the Moon twice a month, etc., allowing twice as many opportunities for objective awareness and understanding. In the case of Saturn opposing the Sun or Moon, the influences of the past, the family and especially the parents can be more easily synthesized. Rudhyar has observed that the natal conjunction of Saturn with the Part of Fortune is a strong indication of basic introversion and a tendency toward pessimism and self-pity. There is a curious sense of fatality, or of being compelled to act according to some dominant purpose imposed from without. This may isolate the person and make him feel heavy with the burden of the world. There are, of course, many possible modifications indicated by other astrological factors, so any natal Saturn conjunction must not be interpreted outside the context of the chart as a whole.

The Generic Cycle

Two distinct cycles of Saturn occur simultaneously in every life: the generic cycle and the individual cycle. The experience common to all human beings, the experience of age, is symbolized by the transit of Saturn to its natal position (the generic cycle). Allowing for variations because of retrograde motion, Saturn's sidereal period is approximately 29½ years. Thus, in a life spanning ninety years, Saturn will transit the entire birth-chart three times. Each of these transits is a complete Saturn cycle, beginning at its birth position and ending with its return. These three cycles indicate turning-points in the gradual unfolding of destiny and character and correspond respectively to the PAST, PRESENT and FUTURE.

THE FIRST CYCLE — SATURN THE PAST. This cycle begins at birth and concludes as the person approaches his 30th birthday. Here Saturn is expressed in terms of the collective past, that is, the heredity and environment into which the individual was born and out of which he must emerge in order to fulfill his birth potential. The bonds of Saturn, first experienced as the father-figure/authority-figure, then later as the strictures of family and social traditions, must eventually be broken. If they are not broken during this cycle, they will carry over into the next, manifesting in far more negative ways. Every child begins life as a totally dependent being, incapable of even the most elementary assertion of his own volition. As transiting Saturn moves away from its natal position, the child becomes progressively more independent and better able to divorce himself from his birth conditioning, thus gaining perspective on his parents, his dependency and all family patterns. Throughout the first cycle this separation frequently takes the form of rebellion; and, although much-bemoaned by parents, it is an important step in the growth process toward individuality.

The Waxing Square. The first "crisis" occurs near the age 7-8 as Saturn squares its natal position. Such squares, according to Rudhyar, often assume the character of a critical Mars aspect. At this waxing square there is the first attempt to emphasize the "I" against the pressures of the family and the environment. The child is said to have reached the "age of reason" and no longer responds to "because I said so..." For the first time he questions the God-like authority of parents and teachers. He will begin to express a desire to choose his own clothes and the foods he wishes to eat. If an established bedtime has previously been enforced, he will often make this an issue in which he attempts to assert his own volition. This can be a time of great conflict of wills as the child looks for more and more means of asserting himself. He wants to establish himself higher up on the pecking-order, to *be* an authority figure. Realizing that he has an advantage over someone smaller, he may become bossy toward class-mates or younger siblings, and if he has no younger brother or sister, he may ask for or even demand one.

As common brush with Saturn (the strictures of society) experienced at this age is being caught stealing. Before this age, when a child took something it was because he could not differentiate between other people's property and his own. By age seven, however, the concept of ownership is clearly defined, and the child knows that taking what belongs to someone else is wrong. What he is doing is testing the authority of society. Eventually the child will be caught, and he must be adequately reprimanded. The lessons of the first Saturn square, if not learned at that time, will carry over into anti-social adult behavior. A parent must realize, however, that in a seven-year-old these are merely lessons to be learned as part of the natural growth process.

The Opposition. The crisis at or immediately following puberty (approximately age 15) corresponds to the opposition of transiting Saturn to its natal placement. This entire period is characterized by drastic swings between childhood and adulthood. One minute he is too young and the next he is too old. As the emerging individual makes his first attempts to fly on his own, he finds that being grown-up isn't at all what he thought it would be. With freedom comes responsibility, and the greater the freedom the greater the responsibility. Although the problems of sexuality and pairing relationships seem paramount during this period, they are only a part of the crisis. The mind is also developing its objective faculties and is used as a means of critical evaluation. This is the real turning point of adolescence — not merely a biological awareness of sex and social relationships — but much more deeply a confrontation with and objective evaluation of the family, all authority figures and society itself. In our society, this also includes the media and government.

In his attempt to separate himself from the strictures of parents and family, the teen-ager frequently adopts an attitude of overt rebellion. The poor parents cannot do ANYTHING right. He objects to everything, from the food they eat to their basic moral values. The peer group replaces parents, teachers and sometimes the laws of society as the final authority. He adopts a "siege mentality" of us-against-them, and popularity among his peers is the ultimate goal at this time. The emerging individual will adhere to their codes of dress and behavior with an almost religious fervor. This is a natural step toward full independence, but until one can move beyond this dependence upon group approval, the ego will not continue to develop in a creative sense. Evasion of responsibility is another natural phenomenon of this age. Usually it appears as an avoidance of household chores, but sometimes it assumes a far more drastic and potentially damaging aspect — early marriage. Most marriages which take place early in this cycle are doomed to failure since their purpose is not to establish a relationship, but to run away from home and parental restriction. Prematurely detached from his peer group by selecting a single mate, the individual may feel as though the ground itself has been pulled out from under him. The reaction is often to run from the marriage, and once again he finds himself "running away from home."

If Saturn (the laws of society) did not come down hard on him when he stole that first piece of bubblegum at about age seven, then the teen-ager may again test the system with further theft. This time it may be with the co-operation of his peer group. Each time he gets away with it, the object becomes either larger or of greater monetary value. Just how far can he go? Sooner or later Saturn will catch up with him. Through this period it must be remembered that the teen-ager needs some established authority to rebel against. If no disciplines have been placed on him, then he will go as far afield as necessary to find an outlet. Parents who provide their children with total latitude are doing their offspring no favor, no matter what some books may say. This is the true meaning of "spoiling a child".

The Waning Square. Whereas the crisis at the waxing square (age 7-8) is primarily one of action, the crisis corresponding to the waning square at age 21-22 is essentially a cerebral one, a "crisis in consciousness". This is the time when the bonds of dependency on the parents can finally be broken. The individual is recognized by society as an adult with all the attendant privileges and responsibilities. He can drink, vote, marry and sign contracts without parental permission; if he breaks the law he will go to jail. By this time he has often completed his education or apprenticeship and is ready to embark on a career and be self-supporting. Now is the time that he can move out into the world without running away from home. The parent-family bond, which has been diminishing since the age of seven, should not be of major concern at this time. The problem now is that the individual must finally separate himself from the peer group and stand alone. There is a strong awareness that true "individuality" is mental rather than physical. The person may, at this time, become a loner, isolating himself from the group. This can be a highly analytical time, with much energy spent on philosophical questions.

The severance from the past should also include breaking the bonds of old attitudes. Once having freed himself from the dependency on parents and peers, the individual is ready to establish a one-to-one relationship and take his place in the social scheme. Breaking with the peer group does not necessitate becoming a hermit, for the only true freedom is in the mind. If the individual still carries a dependency need, he will marry a mother or a father no matter what age he is, and will never be able to establish a truly adult relationship. If he cannot break away from the peer group, he will never establish true friendships and will forever be "keeping up with the Joneses".

THE SECOND CYCLE — SATURN THE PRESENT. The new cycle begins just before the 30th birthday, as Saturn returns to its natal position. This is often a year of choice which determines the direction of the life, the type of associates one values, and the profession or business activity he adopts. The second cycle is an antithesis of the first — it is the cycle of potential productivity. Throughout this cycle, as one struggles to make a living and produce something of value within the community, Saturn manifests primarily as the taskmaster. The individual is obliged to act according to principle, fulfilling a definite function or role in society as significantly as possible. Here Saturn is the force which constrains and steadies the present through the compulsive routine of existence.

Personal development through the second cycle is, however, totally dependent on the growth and degree of maturation achieved during the first cycle. If, at the end of the first cycle, one has emerged as a creative individual ready and able to use his full potential, then the second cycle will be one of ever-increasing creativity and productivity. On the other hand, if one has not emerged from the first cycle as a complete and whole individual, if he remains bound by the strictures of society, the demands of his peer group or a dependency upon parents and family, then the second cycle is likely to be a warped or inverted repetition of the first. This is not to say that if the challenges of Saturn aren't fully met before the 30th birthday that a person is doomed to a meaningless existence, but only that he will still be resolving conflicts at the age of 45 which he should have resolved when he was fifteen. There is always another chance, but the second time around, the patterns are more deeply entrenched and their resolution more difficult.

As the new cycle of Saturn begins, the individual finds himself confronted with new situations and new limitations which condition and define his destiny (the pattern of his consciousness and character) for the coming thirty years. This is a psychologically critical time since people are acutely aware that something has ended yet barely aware of what lies ahead. There is a tendency to evaluate the past cycle, not in terms of its value as a learning experience, which is what it is meant to be, but in terms of productivity, which is what the following 30-year cycle is supposed to be. At the time of the waning square (age 21) many people set goals related to their 30th birthday. "If I haven't made it by thirty..." is an oft repeated phrase among people in their twenties. The unspoken implication is that one will give up if he has not achieved his life-goals by that time. What he will do with the rest of his life if he does "make it" is not considered. Fortunately, since most people do not "make it" by age thirty, they still have another full Saturn cycle ahead of them to achieve, to grow, to accomplish and to fulfill their creative potential. The return of transiting Saturn to its natal position affords an opportunity to reevaluate the dreams and goals of youth in the light of maturity. Many times the ambitions which seem meaningful at the age of twenty-five appear markedly shallow at thirty. This is a time to stop and take a careful look at one's life before plunging on.

The Waxing Square. The actional crisis in this second Saturn cycle, paralleling the childhood crisis at age 7-8, occurs near the 36th year. At this time the individual should be well along the road to maturity, and his basic reactions to life should be clearly evident. The primary question here is whether or not they become *self*-evident. Before being able to use his full power, the individual must finally separate Self from what society has told him he is or should be. This is a period of digging around for one's own roots, of finding one's own foundation. The sense of "I" is strong, but where do "I" belong? Through this period the individual may thus experience a strong feeling of isolation. In finally releasing the past he may feel that the pins have been kicked out from under him. In this he will experience true freedom only when he acknowledges that he *himself* pulled the plug, thus truly accepting total responsibility for his own life. There is an acute awareness at this time of empty spaces, and the individual may attempt to fill them either with people or with material goods. The understanding that *space* is a necessary precondition for growth may come hard, yet until it does, one will become a consumer stuffing the empty corners of his life with possessions. The urge to own property at this time is an expression of the desire to establish a permanent foundation. It is the outward manifestation of the foundation being established within. Both the waxing and waning squares of this cycle, according to Rudhyar, partake of Jupiter's characteristics.

Jupiter, being the polar opposite of Saturn, is capable of compensating for Saturn's restrictions with financial rewards and social success.

The awareness of age, which first appeared at the time of the conjunction, begins to be a definite issue. In a youth-oriented society the individual suddenly finds that he is being judged "too old". Many job opportunities are closed to applicants over thirty-five, and although one may be in prime physical condition, there is a growing awareness that the body will no longer take the punishment it once did and bounce back as readily. One's contemporaries always remain the same age, but the person watches his children and his parents growing older almost before his eyes. An awareness develops that if unresolved differences still exist between the person and his parents, they must soon be resolved. His parents are no longer immortal, as they seemed when he was seven; and, if he does not lose a parent at this time, he will experience the death of his parents' contemporaries. Time is growing short. He knows that he no longer has forever to make things right between himself and his parents.

This can be an especially critical time for a woman, since thirty-six marks the beginning of the final quarter of her fertile years. Even to a woman with several children there comes the knowledge that if she is going to have another child it had better be now. To a woman who is childless, this issue can be the source of great despondency. It may have once seemed that she had plenty of time to think about children later, but at age 36 time is running out. It will be interesting to observe the generation born after World War II, who are now approaching their Saturn return. A disproportionately large number of these people have opted, for one reason or another, not to have children. When these women reach their mid-thirties, will there be another baby boom not unlike the boom which produced them?

The Opposition. A crisis of reevaluation occurs at the time of the opposition (age 44-45). It is an assessment of all that one has built as an individual since the age of twenty-nine. The keynote here must be OBJECTIVITY. The evaluation must be made according to one's personal values, rather than the expectations of family, peer group or society in order for the individual to find true meaning in his existence. Although a period of crisis, with a clear objective understanding of his life-purpose the creative power of the individual can fully emerge. This can be an experience of real illumination — the gateway to an individual's most creative and productive period — age 44-59. If problems are encountered at this time, one may be certain that the root of the trouble lies in the fact that the person has remained immature, inwardly uncertain and frustrated in some important direction. An awareness of this may lead one to try and make a new start before it is too late, to experience at 45 what he has failed to experience at the right time in the past. If the gap between the ideal and reality is too great, then the sense of frustration, failure and impotence can force one to give up the struggle toward individualization, and he will eventually resign himself to a personally meaningless existence according to the collective norm.

The problems of the second opposition can closely parallel those experienced at age 15 during the first opposition. Once again problems occur in the area of sexuality and pairing relationships, and these are compounded by the hormonal changes which accompany menopause. A woman is near or at the end of her child-bearing years, while a man sees his sexual potency greatly diminished. Both feel their physical desirability ebbing away. The signs of aging are clearly visible; and, according to the collective values of a youth-oriented society, this is a tragedy which must be avoided at any cost. The dues for membership in the "Pepsi generation" run higher and higher — hundreds of millions of dollars for cosmetic surgery, hair dye, vitamins, hormone therapy, weight reduction, and a myriad of goods and services which promise eternal youth. The emotional cost cannot even be counted. For many it is a bottomless well of frustration and anger, and death becomes a fearsome reality as one chases his lost youth. For the first time the native experiences his comtemporaries dying of so-called "natural causes".

At this time one frequently experiences the death of a parent. He may, on the other hand, find the teen-age situation reversed as he assumes responsibility for a parent who can no longer care for himself or herself. If a parent-complex remains, it will generally transfer to the native's relationship with the boss, corporation or marriage partner. The avenues of rebellion are, however, limited. One is usually too old at forty-five to change jobs, so divorce becomes a viable alternative. In fact, divorce is seen as a solution to many problems at this time, if the marriage is now judged responsible for all the problems that one blamed on his parents when he was a teen-ager. A new mate will reaffirm one's sexual desirability, regenerate one's empty life-style, revitalize one's sagging career. Just as many teen-agers run away from home to get married, many so-called adults are doing the same thing. They are literally running away. Peter Pan-like disappearances at this time are not uncommon.

The Waning Square. The crisis in consciousness which comes at the age of fifty-two (with the waning square) parallels the crisis experienced at age 22-23. Once again the individual is faced with the need to sever himself from his established patterns of behavior, feeling and thinking. At this mid-point of one's most creative and productive years, one is challenged to take a chance and to try something new. When one accepts this challenge, the Jupiterian character of the square becomes most evident. Life expands in a social sense as one attempts to broaden his horizons. At this time many people return to school and find that new interests begin to open to them. Personal satisfaction can be found in creative expression — painting, music, photography and gardening to name but a few. There is also an urge to get out into the world and make a contribution to other people. Freed from financial responsibilities toward their children, many people use this as an opportunity to travel — to take the dream vacation they have always planned but never really thought possible.

These are the peak earning years. Unfortunately, one also realizes at this time that he has risen as high as he will go in the hierarchy, and for someone in a low-level position there may seem to be nothing left but to wait passively for retirement. In this case a sense of defeat can take over, and life itself becomes meaningless and futile. For others, however, this may be the time of a major job change. By taking a chance and trying something new, one can vastly expand his creative potential. However, in order to do this one must first free himself from the hindering memories of past failures, especially those linked to the experiences which occurred at the opposition (age 44-45). If one indulged oneself in juvenile behavior in the mid-forties, then this square signals the time when the piper demands to be paid. If the health has been abused, then problems may occur in that area. Such problems may be severe enough to demand a forced retirement, but generally they are merely a warning that one must change one's life-style. The body is no longer capable of absorbing punishment without showing ill effects.

By this time the "children" are adults in their own right and must be recognized as such. This necessitates a revaluation of the parent-child relationship. One must finally let go of his children and accept a position of zero influence. The reward for this can be grand-parenthood, a responsibility-free relationship in which one is able to lovingly indulge the grandchildren without the necessity to discipline. For many this is the greatest of all Jupiterian rewards. However, the parent who deserted his children at age 44-45 may now find that his children want nothing to do with him. Such revenge is often expressed by withholding the grandchildren. Just as the parent-dependency bond is often forcibly broken by death at the time of the opposition, the peer-group bond begins to be dissolved by death at this time. The realization that one is ultimately alone, that he cannot depend on parents, children, mate, friends or career to provide his life with meaning and creative satisfaction will drive some people to despair, while it brings others to the peak of their individual potential.

THE THIRD CYCLE — SATURN THE FUTURE. Just before the 60th birthday Saturn returns to its natal position for the second time, and the final cycle of life begins. Here Saturn tries to gather the essential meaning of the life into a form of consciousness or seed-symbol which can guarantee immortality. The psychological crisis which occurs at this time parallels the crisis at the first Saturn return. Once again the individual is acutely aware that something has ended; however, in this case the awareness is that his youth is gone, his vitality is diminishing and his productive years are nearing an end. There seems to be nothing left but to wait patiently for death. The real challenge at this time is to see that there is yet another cycle of life which is only beginning.

In ancient times, sixty was considered to be the age of philosophy, of wisdom, because only through wisdom is it possible to integrate significantly the individual contribution with the real needs of the race. Rudhyar has pointed out that a creative mind — artist, scientist, statesman, writer — usually does not leave his mark upon his time before reaching the age of sixty. The works he performed during his second Saturn cycle impress themselves upon the generation born at the time the works were produced. This impress is the foundation of the socio-cultural immortality possible to the creative mind. It is proof of the successful synthesis of individual purpose with the collective needs of the race. This is the goal toward which every creative person should work after the Saturn opposition of the forties. In such cases, Saturn symbolizes the seed, and its third cycle refers to the gathering in of the harvest of life. The seed, which will be bequeathed to future generations for them to plant and harvest, is an individual's immortality. The tragedy of contemporary society is that the end of life is not regarded as an age of wisdom. Elder citizens are not expected to play a creative role, and therefore it is most difficult to give a positive meaning to Saturn's third cycle. If there are so few spiritual leaders in the world today, it is because our society does not really call for spiritual leadership. People have placed their faith in production and technology, and so we have great producers and eminent technicians, products of Saturn's *second* cycle. The collective consciousness is stuck in the second cycle and will remain so as long as the cult of youth is glorified and only productivity is worshiped. In trying to prolong the period of productivity and avoid the reality of age, we are avoiding wisdom as well. Perhaps unconsciously we fear to seek the wisdom which age *can* bring, because if we were wise we might have to change some of our cherished ideas concerning productivity.

The fear of age cannot be blamed solely on society's lack of reverence for the wisdom and strength of its senior citizens. It is more profoundly a fear of death. As long as an individual feels that society expects him to keep on producing or to get out of the way and make room for the younger generations, this negative attitude toward aging will persist. If, through a knowledge of the meaning of Saturn's three cycles, more individuals will try to grow in wisdom and so become wiser in their human relationships and understanding of life's problems, then it is possible that their light will eventually be recognized. Society may then slowly learn how to entrust to its elder citizens some of the functions now inadequately performed by younger minds still filled with the fever of productivity and ruled by ambitious egos. In furthering humanity's spiritual future, one is also furthering his own future, and that future extends beyond the crisis of growth which we call death.

The Individual Cycle

In addition to the generic cycle of Saturn, which produces its critical turning points at approximately the same ages for everyone, there is an individual way of measuring Saturn's impact, relating the transit of Saturn to the Houses of the birth-chart. If the birth-time is unknown, significant data can also be found in noting Saturn's transit through the solar Houses. The starting point for the individual cycle is the conjunction of transiting Saturn with the natal Ascendant. This will occur at some time during the first twenty-nine years of life and signals a time when the native will be able to begin working with Saturnian energies in an individual manner. During the period between birth and the Saturn-Ascendant conjunction, one will feel the social dimension of Saturn imposing limitations from without, however much one tries to rebel against them. From this it would seem that the earlier the age when Saturn transits the Ascendant, the easier, relatively speaking, it would be for one to *use* Saturn in an individual manner. In such a case, the person is potentially able to mature earlier than the person whose Saturn-Ascendant conjunction occurs in his twenties. Here, however, it is important to note the age factor (see Chapter II). This information will give a deeper understanding of the basic Saturn problem in the life. The astrologer must consider the seven-year period in which the conjunction occurred, and also the specific year of that period during which it was exact.

In one example, transiting Saturn conjoined the native's Ascendant at the age of 4½ (in the fifth year of the first seven-year period). At that time she was diagnosed as having a heart murmur and was confined to bed for several months. During that period she had no one to play with, she had not yet learned to read, and, since it occurred before the advent of television, she was left with only her imagination to keep her company. The age factor in this instance corresponds to the Organic Level, in which both the physical body and the psychological faculties are being formed. In this case a life-pattern was established. Every major aspect of Saturn which followed was marked by illness. As it occurred in the fifth year of the seven-year period, creativity and self-expression were intimately bound up with the problems of health. It was not until she recognized this link and began to deal with her necessity for creative self-expression that the health problems could be resolved.

In another example, the Saturn-Ascendant conjunction occurred in the third seven-year period (age 14-21) and, because of retrogradation, in both the second and third years of that period. On the basis of the age factor an astrologer can conclude that the basic problem for this individual was in the area of psychological development. The second and third years suggest strong conflict (especially emotional conflict) followed by a decision which was then acted upon. Before this person could truly individualize, he had to become consciously aware of the dominant influence of the family tradition and especially his father.

When Saturn comes to the Ascendant, the seed of that planet's cycle is sown. At that time some decision is made, either consciously or unconsciously, in freedom or in bondage to fate, and the direction and significance of the new cycle is established. The subsequent transit through the first quadrant (Houses 1, 2 and 3) is a period of maximum subjectivity in terms of Saturnian activity. Outwardly the fruits of the old cycle dominate, while the person tries to develop inwardly a new type of ego-consciousness. The success of this process will depend largely upon the individual's capacity to *assimilate* the fruits of the old cycle without letting them dominate his consciousness. He must learn to *use* the results of outer social experiences (related to Saturn's transit of the upper hemisphere of his chart) as a foundation for some new trend. New responsibilities enter the life, and this will progressively modify the new pattern of his destiny. The task for him now is to grow in essential being and to reconsider many things which the conscious ego had taken for granted up to that time.

This period of Saturn's transit often coincides with what seems to be an eclipse of the individual's objective success. Because the accent here is on subjective development and the capacity to meet new responsibilities, the person's attention will not be drawn toward the outer life. This is as it should be, for if the person tries at this time to maintain his outer power, he will be doing so in terms of the old attitudes which it is now his task to modify and renew. If he acts in his habitual ways, the new opportunities offered by Saturn's new cycle will not be grasped, and instead of growing the individual will merely repeat what he has already learned.

One must consciously focus one's attention on the experiences of the House in which Saturn is transiting. If one is truly attentive to the type of experience symbolized by this House, then he will find the best opportunities to develop his sense of Self and his sense of responsibility. This does not mean that life will be easier, but that the experiences during the transit of that particular House will provide the person with what is *most necessary for* him, even if the experiences are difficult, in order to grow and mature. Of course Saturn's transit through a House, especially if it simultaneously conjuncts or opposes natal planets, will always compel the attention in some way. If one concentrates his attention elsewhere at that time, then what Saturn asks him to do will be an unwelcome intrusion into his plans and he will tend to meet the confrontations in a negative instead of positive manner. What must be learned is to give full attention willingly and readily to what Saturn asks and to accept the new responsibility it entails. After having evaluated clearly and correctly the implications of this new responsibility, one must assume it without reservations. The crux of the Saturn problem is always a matter of recognition, clear realization and adequate formulation — it is a test of courage. The challenge is to the individual's capacity to adjust his outer life and behavior to the new field of responsibility — to the new NEED of the conscious ego.

Saturn Transits the First House. The best opportunities for inner repolarization are possible during this transit, since nature, society or perhaps health problems will in some way challenge the individual to reconsider his attitude toward himself. During the first twenty-eight years of life, the Saturn transit of the First House specifically symbolizes the influence of the physical father, the development of a consciousness of one's place within the family structure, and incidents basic to the biological development. It will measure the type of security and awareness of one's place in the world which are normally provided by the father's influence (or lack of influence, for one reason or another). It relates to an individual's consciousness of his roots — racial, ancestral and personal. Saturnian action during this first 28-year period of life is usually based on family and cultural tradition. Even if one rebels against it, tradition still dominates the consciousness. The Saturnian experiences of these first twenty-eight years make the person acknowledge that he *must* fit himself into some specific group or community, thus enabling him to play a definite role in his particular society. Saturn forces one to realize that he was not born into a vacuum, that he can never fulfill his creative potential except in *relationship* to some greater whole (community, society or universe). This relationship will give coherence, direction and purpose to life.

The first time Saturn transits the First House, the ego is given its first chance to renew itself at a new level of individual selfhood. This will manifest through certain destiny-making experiences. Life will appear more serious, and events will test the moral strength of the character. A good deal of self-discipline may be demanded, and it will be much to the native's advantage even though he may not altogether like it. In order to gain a more concrete and precise understanding of oneself and of the purpose of one's life, it may be necessary to learn the lesson of conformity to certain social and traditional standards. On the negative side there may be a tendency toward gloom, depression and lack of self-confidence due to fear or feelings of inferiority. A reaction against such tendencies in the form of blustering and aggressiveness is merely the reverse side of that same coin. Either way it manifests, the purpose is the same — to learn greater stability in one's individual behavior and a deeper sense of personal responsibility and integrity.

This same transit occurring later in life accentuates the need to assert one's individuality, either through or against the social traditions into which one was born. The goal should be to gain stature and esteem in one's own eyes through self-discipline. Such discipline may be self-imposed, or achieved by accepting inwardly a discipline imposed from without. One must remember that much of what happens at this time will be the result of the way in which one has related to the world, professionally, socially and personally, during the past fourteen years (since the time Saturn transited the Descendant). If one's social ambitions have been realized, he will know that his work has been worthy of reward. This transit will prove the truth and the value of the principles by which one lives. If, on the other hand, the individual has failed to make any visible gain or if loss and trouble dog his footsteps, then one must conclude that there is something basically wrong in the way he has been living. It becomes imperative now to deepen one's sense of self and to undertake some fundamental change of attitude. Perhaps the individual has set himself impossible goals or has proceeded on false premises. During this First House transit one may analyze the path he has followed in the past and rectify what mistakes he can.

Above all, one should not have Saturn leave this House with the idea that the world is a cold and dreary place where no one appreciates him, for the attitude adopted here is likely to persist through the subsequent phases of Saturn's personal cycle. Even if individual success has been achieved, one should not expect an easy life. The tendency now will be toward added responsiblity — extra demands of all kinds will be made on one's energy, time, finances and patience. The most important thing will be one's attitude toward what is demanded of him. One must remain positive and centered even if things appear dark and foreboding — and even if life seems littered with the very obstacles one has been trying to escape. One is meeting his "dweller on the threshold", his shadow, and he must recognize it as such before he can face it and then overcome it. The Saturn transit of the First House therefore presents us with what

Rudhyar has called the "test of isolation". Here one must face every experience with the conviction that through it he will be able to realize more deeply who he is as an individual. In order to do this, one must not identify himself with the experience itself. What is needed is a conscious adjustment to it, but without any loss of one's personal integrity; not a constant and rigid way of responding to life, but the capacity to make ever more distinct the expression of one's true identity through the Saturnian structure of the conscious ego.

Saturn Transits the Second House. Here the challenge of Saturn along the road toward personal maturity will be how to use one's possessions to express that new facet of one's true identity, which one has theoretically come to know during Saturn's transit of the First House. The deeper understanding of the basic problem of destiny revealed in the First House demands now a review of the means available — both inner and outer — to solve this problem. Either these means are, in themselves, a limiting factor, or the individual is not sufficiently aware of the tools at his disposal, of the innate powers and faculties with which he was born. One must therefore become more objective toward his assets, both material and psychological, and realise that now he has the opportunity to use them in a more conscious and responsible manner. In order to so use his possessions, however, one must have become aware during the First House period of the need and purpose which demand such a responsible use. This need or purpose is different for each individual and can manifest on different levels of being and awareness. During youth this purpose may simply be the challenge to incarnate more fully into the physical body and psyche, and to assume responsibility for the correct and purposeful use of all one's faculties on all levels of consciousness. At this stage it becomes necessary to realise that the "I" is distinct from both the physical body and the feelings and thoughts through which this "I" expresses itself. It becomes necessary also to take responsibility for their misuse rather than to believe, as so many do today, that such misuse is due to factors outside oneself.

Assuming responsibility for one's own body and its instincts, and for one's feelings, emotional impulses and complexes means detaching the "I" consciousness and evaluating them objectively. The beginning of all true spiritual living is the detachment of the "I" from its vehicles of expression — the body and the psyche — and also from the collective social values which dominate one's particular life-situation. This means that in the first two phases of the Saturn cycle the "I" must realize as clearly as possible that it is *distinct from* the body and psyche as well as from the individual's heredity and environment; at the same time it must establish a responsible *relationship* with these elements. Without this distinctness and objectivity it will be impossible to meet purposefully and intelligently the needs of either body, psyche or society.

The Second House transit is the time to look at one's body, to go over the way in which one has been using it in the past, and to decide what changes in this use will be necessary if one wants it to be a fit vehicle for the particular task or lifework to be performed. Now is also the time to review all the facts and ideas one has accumulated, to review all the established values which make one see certain things as good and worthwhile and others as bad, worthless or dangerous. One must discover whether these values were established on a personal foundation, or merely because one's parents, family or society have impressed them on him.

If an individual finds that he has been using his assets in the traditional manner, spending or wasting what he owns according to the custom of his social class or the dictates of temporary "fashions", afraid to be different from what the average man or woman does or thinks, then now is the time to transform this inherited sense of values and establish his own values. Saturn transiting the Second House makes one realize that the purpose of possessions is *to provide the means by which he may give substance and weight to what he is.* The individual can only become aware of what he is by using what he owns. At this time a person must prove what he is, to himself and to the world, by his individual and responsible use of his ancestral inheritance and of whatever possessions he has acquired. This means that, if necessary, one must be prepared to transform his possessions to fit the new purpose of his true self. This also means orienting their use so as to be able to enter into fruitful relationships with others. Even more, this Saturn transit challenges the individual to come into full possession of his own unique powers and faculties. Such a mastery of one's means can only come through significant, purposeful and creative *use.* One will never be able to experience and then reveal his real self unless he *uses* his powers and faculties to that end.

Saturn Transits the Third House. This is the time to act in the environment according to the new purpose revealed in the First House transit and with the means developed during the Second House transit. As the individual tries to act in a new way in reference to his everyday relationships, he will meet varying reactions, some favorable, others limiting or even hostile. Whatever happens exists to demonstrate the quality of one's purpose and the degree of mastery over one's powers and faculties. Through these Third House experiences, the individual is meant to find out how much is an illusion or ideal and how much is real in his estimation of Self and his powers. Experience during this transit will show one the best way to *relate* one's new sense of Self to people and things. One must dare to experiment with ideas, feelings and various ways of doing things, for in this way he will discover his limitations and what actions will be necessary to overcome them. The challenge here is to develop the capacity of *conscious* and purposeful adaptation to the requirements of the environment. This is another way of saying that one must now *deepen* his intelligence in relation to the very practical, concrete and immediate problems which are met in the Third House. One must search for the deeper meanings of such problems and test the efficacy of his faculties. Saturn will set limits which will oblige one to focus his energies in well-defined areas; therefore it will be important to recognize just what these limits are and accept them, before one can work to transform his potential into effective power.

On more mundane levels, this transit will force one to deal constantly with the petty problems of daily routine. Discord may arise with the people one meets every day — family, neighbors, tradespeople and fellow commuters. All of these people may become boring or irritating by upsetting one's routine, or by making greater demands on one's time and perhaps also on one's purse. Inanimate objects may also seem to take an almost fiendish delight in wrecking one's plans — the tire goes flat just as you're pulling out of the driveway late for an important engagement; household gadgets refuse to function or develop a habit of disappearing just when needed; letters get mislaid. As the mountain of petty annoyances grows, one is apt to wonder if the world is taking its spite out on him personally. And yet Saturn has a method in this seeming madness. If the daily routine has been disrupted, one must be at fault somewhere. Perhaps good use has not been made of one's time, or it may be that one runs his life on a helter-skelter basis with no order whatever. So along comes Saturn and binds one to a routine, like it or not, until the value of time and the desirability of order has been learned. One may have liked the people in his neighborhood well enough as long as they made no demands, but now is the time to learn the mutual nature of such obligations.

Such things will happen, especially if one has made no *conscious* effort to deepen his sense of self and the value of what is his, both materially and psychologically. If an individual has made positive efforts to contact the self in depth in a new way since Saturn crossed the Ascendant, then the problem of the Third House transit is that of objectively recognizing the limitations which life imposes on his efforts to prove his personal worth in everyday relationships. These limitations need not be understood as being inimical, but should be seen rather as necessary to growth. Limitations will enable one to define more clearly his real character and the resources at his disposal. Outer defeat may be just what is needed in order to discover oneself in an inner way, to learn a necessary lesson, or to clear up some karma. The experiences of this transit should be used to test, one by one, all those powers and faculties which one has decided to use during the Second House transit. The person may even choose the environmental situations which will enable him objectively to test his strength, endurance and his capacity to respond or adapt to change. Voluntarily he can test the quality of his sympathy, helpfulness, love and co-operation. Such deliberate training of self and its power would be the most positive way to use Saturn's transit of the Third House.

The negative implications of this transit will occur only when the individual has no such positive attitude, and, rather than consciously choosing to act, he waits for things to happen to him. However, a negatively oriented person can be helped most at this time by an astrologer who explains that the purpose of present difficulties is to enable him to discover his limitations and to force him to find new ways of being himself and using his resources. He must use thought and develop intelligence by trying to *relate* to all the facts of his daily experience. An integrated personality is the result of a healthy and significant relationship between all the parts of one's nature — physical and mental, internal and external. Where integration is lacking, Third House experiences teach us our lack. Balance is reattained by *acting out* what one thinks is right. Actual experience is the teacher at this time.

Saturn Crosses the Nadir and Transits the Fourth House. This starts a new lap of the path toward personal maturity. The new trend begun when Saturn crossed the Ascendant should now show concrete results. One has, theoretically, established a new attitude toward his destiny, and has worked on both his material and psychological resources in such a way as to be able to fulfill this destiny in a more conscious and purposeful manner. Finally, in the Third House, he has tested in actual daily living the efficacy of this new use of his resources and knows what he *really* has at his disposal and in what direction he must go. Now comes the time when one must establish a new base of operations, the new foundation from which he will go forth to challenge the world in order to realize his new objective. Whatever changes may come when Saturn later crosses the Descendant and then the Midheaven will be but extensions or expansions of the projects begun as Saturn enters the Fourth House. Therefore, here one should concentrate on the strength and stability of one's foundations, as his future success — particularly for the coming fourteen years — will depend on them.

In any decision made at this time, this long-range perspective must be taken into account. There may be a change of residence, the establishment of a new home, business, marriage, professional position, or even a new outlook on life. Whatever it is — and usually with this transit there are many opportunities to step out of the usual pattern of one's life — one must bear in mind that what is started now will have to be worked at in a personal way until Saturn reaches the Descendant, and then in a social way until Saturn comes to the Midheaven. One should therefore choose something related fundamentally to the deeper needs of his true self and destiny. One may choose to break away or cut himself free from old ties, old habits, old localities or positions. Young people may want to leave their parental home, while older people may decide to go into retirement. In other cases, the decision may not rest in the individual's own hands — life may force him out on his own in spite of a desire to cling to his old ways. The changes characteristic of this transit are seldom comfortable at the time. In order to use this transit positively, one must establish first of all the long-range objective in terms of Saturn's transit of the first three Houses. He must then be willing to sacrifice those aspects of his old life-style which the achievement of his objective makes necessary. He must stand on his own feet, secure in his own truth and ready to accept new obligations. At the same time, however, one will have to distinguish between those obligations which are rightfully his responsibility and those which could be more correctly termed impositions. Finally, plans must be adopted for a slow start. In spite of the chaotic quality which may often create a false sense of the need for speedy action, the rate of progress is not likely to be rapid.

This transit also raises the question: On what basis shall I make my decision, and to what purpose must I use the knowledge acquired in the Third House concerning myself and my abilities? All depends on whether what has been learned and experienced since Saturn crossed the Ascendant now enables one to establish a new sense of power and security, or whether the efforts at incorporating this new destiny have brought only hurt and defeat. In either case, the individual must now relate what he has discovered to that in his own life which he considers to be absolutely basic, sound, solid and stable. For the immature individual, this Fourth House transit is not easy, particularly for young people living in the cities. The frame of reference constituted by the family, religion and social traditions is no longer stable. Youth is subjected now to so many conflicting points of view and values, both within the home and without, that it is practically impossible for them to feel that they have a solid and trustworthy foundation and a valid frame of reference from which to evaluate and understand their experience. Not being able to find stability outside themselves, they are obliged to find it within. This is a new trend in evolution. Instead of seeking outer stability — a permanent home, a permanent job — a person today is constrained more and more to seek stability within himself. He is urged to reach toward his own center, which is, at the same time, the earth center. He is asked to build a "global personality". He must work, especially during these Fourth House periods, steadily toward inner harmony and integration, toward becoming master of his own house, capable of acting from his own center.

Saturn Transits the Fifth House. Here the feeling of *what* you are and *who* you are has to be acted out for the world to see. What matters now is how the individual releases the power of his personality. The capacity to act out what he truly is as an individual (Fourth House experience) and to fulfill the purpose of his life without doing harm to anyone is now tested. One must be prepared to allow others to experience him as he is through his actions and creations. The *quality* of one's self-expression is here the important factor. If the feelings expressed now as emotion are purely egocentric, based on possessiveness or fear, then the *individual* is not acting, but rather is being used by the negative energies of human nature — pride, anger and lust. Whenever the Fifth House is accentuated, one must question whether his expression aims at an expansion *of* self, as a conscious ego, or at an expansion *through* self of a purpose to which he has dedicated his personality. Through bitter experience one learns here that the urge to personal expression in terms of purely personal desires and needs — the desire for progeny, the yearning for fame, the projection of self into the being of the beloved — never produces the desired results. The individual must adopt here what Rudhyar calls the "transpersonal way", the effort to build the personality as an engine so that *through* the individual something greater than the personal self may manifest. He will be no less an individual, but because he will have understood that he partakes of a greater Life in company with other individuals, the power of the universal whole will be able to create through him. The resulting creative accomplishment will then have meaning and value for that part of the world which he is able to contact. Any form of self-expression which does not take into account the needs of others or of society is doomed to failure.

Fifth House problems derive from an exaggerated self-consciousness. As one is continually preoccupied with the impression he feels he is making when he acts or creates, he becomes over-independent, wanting to force his way of doing and feeling on others. On the other hand, through a lack of Fourth House equilibrium, he may become more and more suspicious of other people's motives. Acting in a hesitant manner, unsure of himself, he can become prey to feelings of inferiority and rejection. Instead of taking offense at the slightest provocation or insisting on what he considers his due, the individual should try to give of himself without counting the cost. Therefore, when Saturn comes to the Fifth House, there are basic choices to be made in relation to how one would release the powers of his personality. Will he act now simply to make his mark upon others or upon society, to have his own way in everything, and to prove the strength of his ego in a battle of wills; or will he become a pure channel for more-than-personal powers according to the part he should play, together with other individuals, in the greater whole?

Truth, spiritual identity, dharma: are various words to define moral selfhood in effective and adequate act. The truth of an individual consists in all the activities necessary for the complete and correct performance of his life-purpose as an incarnate self. All that is necessary; nothing that is not necessary. In purity and in truth, freedom and necessity become identical. The individual is spiritually free as he fulfills his essential purpose, and in no other way...For an individual to be free to do anything he might wish or conceive has no meaning in itself. The only freedom is that of performing all the acts that are necessary for one's inherent spiritual purpose. (Rudhyar, *Triptych-The Way Through*)

On a more mundane level, the test of the Fifth House is the degree of mastery of the energies of human nature. This mastery will enable one to act in terms of his true individual purpose. As long as the ego identifies itself with the energies of human nature, the latter will tend to use him. When the ego gives way to anger or lust, the true individual identity has abdicated before the power of an emotional impulse which makes the ego act in a compulsive manner. The instincts of human nature are only concerned with organic satisfaction, self-defense and self-aggrandisement. If they dominate one's actions in the Fifth House period, it will be because one's true identity was not established within an integrated personality in the Fourth House period. What is expressed in the Fifth House will then be the manifestation of one's weakness and frustration, his lack of roots and stability; in short, his feelings of inadequacy. If *conscious attention* is paid to the manner of personal expression as well as to the quality of what is being expressed, a great lesson can be learned from Saturn's transit of the Fifth House. In trying to become an ever-purer channel, the meaning inherent in one's true individual identity will emerge.

Saturn Transits the Sixth House. Here we come to the final phase in the effort to improve the technique of expression of one's true individual identity. Having released the powers of the personality on the basis of one's personal feelings and will to self-expansion during the Fifth House transit, one will find that the results of this self-expression usually lead to a crisis. The more ego-centered one has been, the more likely he is to realize that now something must be changed in his attitude. The ego must become consciously aware of its limitations and its mistakes. It must now decide that its way of expressing emotion is wrong if it brings pain or suffering, that the feeling must be subjected to some form of discipline and must be directed to new values which are less ego-centered and more universal.

As Saturn transits the Sixth House, one is forced to realize that what he does, feels or thinks has not come up to the First House ideal of behavior, achievement and success. The individual becomes acutely conscious of a lack, of a need for improvement either in being or doing.

Perhaps egocentricity and selfishness have led to defeat in one's attempts to prove oneself through relationships both with individuals and with society in general, in spite of one's talents and mastery of objective techniques. This precipitates a crisis, because suddenly one realizes that he must somehow transform his personal attitude toward life, himself and perhaps even toward God. This crisis may take the form of a need to serve and obey, to adapt one's efforts to the needs of some revered person or cause which seems to embody those qualities to which the true self aspires. One may be placed in some subordinate position, such as the armed forces, or perhaps be loaded with thankless, petty jobs which give one no chance to shine. Circumstances can pile a mass of detail work before him to impress on him the need for organization and adequate preparation. There may be a growing dissension around him which forces him to make adjustments in his everyday relationships. In short, life will call for a maximum of adaptability, patience, and a willingness to assume one's own share of the weight.

Service has been described as the willingness to recognize that the individual is but one cog in the machinery of life. It is a first lesson in learning that the whole is greater than any of the parts. All of one's relations with other people will run smoothly only if each helps the others and all work toward the common good. With this Sixth House transit, the individual becomes a member of the group, with the special task of helping the others. He must subdue his personal desires rather than make the futile attempt to force life to meet his private demands. Circumstances now can place a heavy load upon him — more work, especially insignificant routine tasks which repay in small coin compared to the time and labor involved. Illness in others may require that he shoulder *their* tasks as well as his own, or even take on the actual job of nursing. Personal relations will demand the utmost tolerance. There may even be personal illness through which the soul may try to impress upon the body the need for a revision in attitude. Illness may, on the other hand, simply be the result of the defeat of one's vital energies which are unable to cope with the challenge to grow stronger or to transform one's way of life.

The deepest aspect of this transit is what Rudhyar calls the "test of suffering".

> ...suffering is a sign of human greatness not yet fully realized, or wantonly wasted....Suffering can never be a goal or have a value in itself. It is a training in objective understanding and emotional severance; a test in endurance of our will and our faith....Suffering is the condition for breaking man's identification with the "less" as he climbs on his way to the "more". It is the pressure of his greater destiny upon his attachment to his lesser goals....Here, the great and subtle lure which distracts many a soul is: self pity. "Why has this happend to me?"

To this, there are varied metaphysical answers. The one practical reply, however, is "Because you do not know yet what your full power and your essential goal are." Not yet. Not yet. (Rudhyar, *Triptych-The Way Through)*

If one finds himself confronted by some crisis of transformation, one must discover to what extent his natural abilities have been twisted by the pressures of family, religion or the moral attitudes of his society. He must be very sure that he is not facing his present crisis simply as a member of a group, allowing other people's ideas to condition his present response.

Saturn Crosses the Descendant and Transits the Seventh House. Here begins a new social emphasis in life. During the past fourteen years, the individual has been challenged to reconsider his attitude toward self, to deepen his contract with his true identity and to improve or renew his technique of expression. Now, and for the fourteen years to come, one must broaden his base of operation with the aim of stamping his image and purpose upon society and assuming greater public responsibility. As transiting Saturn has moved from the natal Ascendant, through the six Houses below the Horizon to the natal Descendant, everything that one has done has proceeded from the self. The individual has been trying to learn more about himself and how best to express himself significantly and harmoniously. At the Descendant there is a basic change of emphasis. Here one leaves the sphere of personal being to meet the test of human *relationship.* One's inherent purpose and destiny, as well as what or who one feels he essentially is as a person, can only be revealed or demonstrated as he *acts them out* in relation to others within a greater sphere of activity.

The transit of Saturn through the Seventh House will force one to realize that he must change his self-image as he moves into the objective world of things and entities outside his personal control, but with which he must establish a relationship. The question each individual must answer for himself is "How must I act in relation to other individuals and to the larger whole of human activity in order to reveal and demonstrate, to myself as well as to others, the essential purpose of my existence such as I am able to understand it at the present moment?" Most people are conditioned by their personal point-of-view or biases, not seeing things and people as they really *are,* but as they appear through the glasses of revered traditions, education, personal desire or precious memories. Saturn will now reveal the degree of one's conditioning, one's fear of change or of experiencing the dynamic transformations continually necessary in a life of human relationships. If one refuses to change, then he also refuses the possibility of significant participation with others in the life of society. Individual selfhood and purpose of destiny need not change, but one's *relationship* with the world must change continually.

One's own needs and those of his partners must fit harmoniously together so that these mutual relationships may be constantly adjusted to the requirements of the group, business or society within whose framework these relationships have their meaning. What must now dominate the consciousness is the effort to establish a significant participation in the life of society, not only as an individual self, but also as a creative partner of others. This participation will become concrete, if all goes well, when Saturn reaches the Midheaven.

In terms of the more intimate relationships to which the Seventh House refers, Saturn's transit here emphasizes the need to assume such relationships on a basis of equality, objectively and with open eyes. Any association which is based on the psychological projection of an Image onto the other person is actually based on self-love, and will reveal either its inadequacy or the need for personal transformation if it is to endure. A Seventh House relationship must serve some purpose *as a relationship*. It must exist within some larger framework, be that racial, social, cultural or spiritual. As Saturn transits the Seventh House the individual may discover that the function, life-purpose or group with which he has previously identified himself is now alien to his deeper nature or to the new facet of his destiny revealed since Saturn crossed the Ascendant. If this is the case, then the transit will help one find his true function in society. Experiences of frustration or hostility, or even a crisis of separation such as divorce, may be necessary to lead one to this discovery of self. It may seem a rocky path through a landscape of emptiness and isolation, but such experiences must be accepted objectively as necessary to the end-goal of self-knowledge. It is through the results of his relationships that one must prove, both to himself and to the world, the validity of the function he has chosen to perform.

Cooperation must be the keynote of this Seventh House transit. Having emerged from a fourteen-year period during which personal problems were related to one's individual development, one will attempt to control the world around him as he has during the last fourteen years. This attitude will not work now. If, however, one has mastered the harder requirements of work and service during the Sixth House transit, then the lesson of cooperation should be simpler. In any case, an individual can control circumstances now only by cooperating with them — it will be of no use trying to pit one's strength and ego against the world. Often the transit of Saturn through the Seventh House elicits a view of the world as a gloomy, cold and hostile place, bristling with enmity on all sides. This immediately places one on the defensive, encouraging one to strike first for self-protection, or to attack life with a battering ram because he is sure that success must be wrested from the world by force. Life, however, is the stronger, so the individual will find himself slapped down time after time. This can happen when an individual has not realized that he must fit his selfhood into the structure of society and cooperate with others for mutual progress and protection. The anxiety and resentment come from a fear that one's individuality will be submerged, that relationship will negate self.

In the Seventh House one should decide to meet life half way, to recognize the rights of others if he wishes to maintain his own rights. One must come out of himself and become more objective toward others in his environment. Marriage problems can arise because one has never seen the partner as he or she *really is*, having been too preoccupied with himself. Business problems can arise simply because one has never really tried to understand other people's needs or to adapt what he has to offer to the common good. The lesson to be learned is that nothing in the world of relationship can remain static. Most problems in this sphere arise from a tendency to crystallize one's attitude toward others or the world at large in terms of accepted standards of behavior, official titles and traditional contracts. One must now learn to meet others with an inner freedom which permits creative transformation.

Saturn Transits the Eighth House. One must now focus his attention on the fruits of all his relationships, both with other individuals and with the outside world. The quality of these fruits will depend on one's capacity to relate significantly and as an individual to intimates, business partners, social groups and to the work of the world. It will depend also on the degree of one's conformity to established patterns in social attitudes and activities. Having related according to a presumably new understanding of one's life-purpose and individual identity (since Saturn crossed the Ascendant), what is now being tested is the concrete way in which one will act to realize this purpose through his relationships. The individual must concentrate his attention on the practical working out of his ideals of relationship, love, and conjugal happiness, as well as on his plans for business profits. Plans and ideals must now become social realities through constant effort and perhaps prolonged or repeated activity. The socio-cultural order, with its particular rules and customs, will inevitably impose modifications on one's ideals and plans. The problem is how one will react to this outside framework. Will he conform utterly to its dictates, or will he strive to defy convention for its own sake? Between these alternatives is a path of compromise. Whatever one experiences now as he tries to remain true to himself, while at the same time relating in a creative and free manner with others, will reveal the degree of personal maturity he has achieved, as well as the quality of his sense of relationship.

At issue here is the *use* to which the native will put his sense of individual identity, so that his relationships may produce both value and "wealth". It is no longer a question of using his physical, material and psychological assets to make his individuality a concrete reality, but rather of orienting what he himself has established (in the Fourth House) toward the most complete and harmonious participation in some activity of the greater whole. What matters now is the quality of those shared experiences, as it is the sharing itself which creates social consciousness. Although one may have a steady purpose behind his relationships with reference to the social whole, he must keep them dynamic and creative, adjusting them constantly to the needs of the moment. A dynamic relationship must continuously meet the ever-changing requirements of each participating individual's growth, as well as the demands of society. In the Eighth House such a relationship is now challenging the separative tendencies of the ego. The process of shared participation in a social organism demands that much which belongs to the personal life must now "die". Much must be given up, often including the outer means upon which one has relied to insure personal security. "Shared participation" will now demand a deep modification of one's long-cherished individual "sovereignty". The native may have to transform the "master" concept, change his notion of ownership into managerial ability, and realize that he has developed his individuality in order to participate in some vaster organism of being. One can now *create* through his relationships.

Problems related to material security in partnership, finances and business may occur during this Eighth House transit. The person may have to face much necessary reorganization in these spheres and, in fact, in everything where intimate relations are concerned—marital or business partners, parents or other relatives who may be contributing to a common domestic fund, clients whose money he handles, or the public (in case the native is an accountant, cashier or auditor who handles public funds). Problems may also arise in relation to money or objects which have come to the native unearned. These include legacies, dividends, payment of debts, prizes and gifts. Problems of security may also arise at this time for people who have retired, especially if they are dependent on a pension or income from investment. At this time, the first step toward freedom from financial worries is to establish a stable economic base. This may entail refinancing and starting anew if debts have piled up, or simply reorganizing one's business or domestic budget along more conservative lines if accounts are running above income or if one needs to live off capital. One should not be afraid to accept partnership or cooperative offers, and to make use in every way of the partnership experiences and opportunities opened during Saturn's transit of the Seventh House. If one has learned to see the world and his relation to it in proper cooperative perspective, he should not experience severe problems now. To be on the safe side, however, one should make precautions against future need a part of his present program. Moving along well-tried, familiar lines, one should become more conservative in his business propositions. Saturn conserves as well as constricts.

Saturn Transits the Ninth House. Here understanding must be born. Whatever results have come from one's efforts to meet the implications, the new vistas and the challenges of the life of relationship must now be understood. During the Eighth House transit, what seemed important was the amount of benefit or loss, pleasure or pain, experienced in relationships. In the Ninth House period, the question arises HOW and WHY these relationships have led to the kind of results one has experienced. One must also try to understand the purpose and the value of these results, both in terms of his overall destiny and also in relation to his society. The Ninth House deals with those facts and lessons of experience which derive from the effort to understand and come to terms with the ceaselessly expanding vistas of human association and human commerce. It refers to philosophy, to the abstract mind, and to the law, and is also related to long journeys, foreign affairs and contracts, diplomacy and higher education. Additionally, it is the field of religion and mystical or prophetic experiences and dreams.

According to the nature of the Eighth House fruits of one's relationships and participation in society, one will now be involved in one or more of the activities symbolized by the Ninth House. If one has had problems with relationships or contracts, he may now be involved in lawsuits. If he has been repeatedly frustrated through conjugal, family or social pressures, he may try to compensate for this through religious or philosophical study. Psychology, philosophy, religion, and the study of law and custom are means to attain knowledge and understanding when facing problems in cooperation or love. They also enable one to understand the place he can occupy in the world and how he may orient himself more consciously toward activity in society. They help one to know how and where his various relationships fit into the larger pattern of the present-day world, and how, with his associates, one can benefit from current social trends. In any case, this is the time to learn how to use intelligently the tremendous energies generated by human cooperation and production, whether in business or the realm of culture. The individual will grow in maturity to the extent he is willing to assimilate what is unfamiliar or distant, to include what at first seems alien, disturbing or seemingly unusable. This can lead to greater understanding, greater love, and eventually enable the person to fulfill the greater destiny which awaits him at the coming Midheaven transit.

The task as Saturn transits the Ninth House should be to *enlarge one's vision and understanding* of the place he wishes to occupy in the world, and so to fix his attention on a firm purpose and the means necessary to attain it. One must remember that one can only attain that place and that success which one can clearly visualize. This may necessitate gaining a new perspective on the world at large and on one's possible place in it. The aims, however, must be clarified, made practical and sound, and must be based on one's actual qualifications rather than on an ideal, dream or vision of impossible things. Such a vision of one's potential and his place in the world may develop through traveling or working in a foreign country. The person should do all he can to increase his contacts, study worthwhile subjects and learn languages as a means to expand his participation in the world. He should study metaphysics, religion, philosophy, so that his understanding of relationships may also expand on a mental plane. One must be prepared to exert oneself in these directions, for understanding does not come without effort and without the sacrifice of many previously held conceptions, limitations and habits. For those who did not cooperate with the trend of regeneration begun in the Eighth House, this Ninth House transit may have to teach its lesson through suffering and deprivation.

In the deepest sense, Saturn's transit of the Ninth House presents a test of the *significance* of one's relationships, both with others and the world at large. He must ask himself if what he is doing and producing is really filling the needs of his true self and society. He must make an effort to understand the *real meaning* of what has been happening in his life, especially since Saturn crossed the Descendant. He must try to understand *why* his intimate relationships have led to his present situation and be ready to renounce the unnecessary and the unattainable.

> The test of significance is the challenge to any man and any association —whether in marriage or in business, in politics or in cultural fields—to accept no participation that cannot be significantly defined as to its character, procedure and purposes. To be significant is the requirement of any relationship, and significance is the crowning and soul of mutuality; creative harmony, the formulation of effective and productive love. (Rudhyar, *Triptych-The Way Through*)

Saturn Reaches the Midheaven and Transits the Tenth House. Here the person comes to the crowning moment in the Saturn cycle, when all he has strived for since Saturn crossed his Ascendant (and especially, since the transit of the Descendant) will be judged in terms of its social value. The person will now learn what the world thinks of him and the values he presents. The individual begins to prove his worth when Saturn crosses the Descendant. He learns to adjust his activity in accordance with the activities of others, adding something of his own to the effort, and in return, receiving something new from them. During the Eighth and Ninth House transits, one becomes more deeply concerned with common forms of shared participation. He learns from precedents or he rejects them, studies laws and customs regulating social intercourse, and perhaps expands his understanding of people, cultures and religion through study or travel. Now the person must prove himself and the value of his actions by taking a public or professional stand.

Confronted by this "test of position," one must demonstrate his capacity to assume the responsibilities of his personal or professional influence and authority. Under the best circumstances, the position in society achieved at the time of this transit should be the proof and consecration of what one has achieved as an individual. The *manner* of fulfilling one's tasks, rather than the nature of the tasks themselves, is what is important. The attitude toward one's work and the way it is performed will determine one's true individual status, both social and spiritual. It should not be forgotten that the manner in which one participates in the work of the world is first conditioned by his early home life, by whatever complexes or fears he may have developed then, and most importantly by his revealed capacity to reach personal maturity. Because of this, one's present success or failure in reaching a position of relative social power and prestige is deeply related to the character of his relationship with the parents. The individual now gives to society whatever he has succeeded in building into himself from those ancestral and racial gifts which his parents bequeathed to him.

This transit will mark a test of the strength of one's public standing. In matters of prestige, authority and profession, one will see his greatest triumphs or defeats during this time. No matter where one stands on the social scale, his standing in the professional sphere, in matters dealing with superiors or the public, or in the realm of culture will now be in the limelight. Saturn in the Tenth House is a time of harvest. One collects the fruits of his labors at the jobs, projects or relationships begun when Saturn was transiting the Seventh House. The nature of this harvest will depend on how much has been extracted from one's opportunities and on the amount of honest effort the person has put forth to attain his ambitions. This Tenth House transit is, however, also likely to be accompanied by some form of restriction, either on one's time (due to added responsibilities) or on one's professional scope, authority or income, if the trend has been negative. Whatever happens, the important thing now will be the individual's attitude toward events and his willingness to adjust to circumstances. At this time, it would be wise to strive for security and to consolidate one's position, rather than to seek further expansion along established lines.

Saturn Transits the Eleventh House. The results of the public influence achieved since Saturn crossed the Midheaven will confront the individual during the Eleventh House period. Having struggled eagerly and perhaps persistently for many years to achieve something in the world, one should now have what he thought he wanted. The problem of the Eleventh House transit is what to do with the success or with the concrete outer situation in which the individual now finds himself. Whether the goals have been trivial or of true social significance, one has had to participate in the activities of society. He is now confronted with either positive or negative results. All that matters now is the *use* one will make of his success or failure. Success must be *used* wisely, imaginatively, consciously and purposefully. Failure must be met with courage and its causes sought so that the lessons learned from it will become a springboard to new achievement in the future. This is the only way to avoid falling passively into some form of social servitude.

Whatever the results now, their cause will be found in the way in which one sought success, in the methods used and in the spirit behind them. The search for success is not only an outward-directed effort; it is also the attempt to give meaning and value to one's ego. The sense of who or what one is obviously is linked to the awareness of the place one holds in his society. The way an individual meets the test of the Eleventh House will depend on whether his ego has experienced success or defeat in the Tenth House. If he has experienced success, then he will naturally want to enjoy the fruits of this success, to show his friends and the people with whom he is professionally related what a fine fellow he is. He may want to enjoy with them the profits of his business and the wealth which came through the partnerships established during the Eighth House transit.

If on the other hand one has experienced failure, then the tendency will be to protest, to show resentment and to try to revenge oneself on those whom he considers responsible for his failure. There may now be an effort to transform the conditions which brought about this failure or loss of ego prestige; however, if the ego is not strong enough to react positively toward its failure, then there may be negative or even violent manifestations during this Eleventh House transit. When one meets the outer world in too egocentric a manner or with fanatical discontent, then the Saturn transit can bring feelings of social isolation and friendlessness. One becomes bitter, despondent and filled with feelings of "what's the use". There is a price to be paid for overly-reckless gestures against society. Man's greatest tests are met in the succeedent Houses. In the angular Houses the individual comes to experience himself, his private and public status, and other individuals; however, in the succeedent Houses the individual must decide how to *use* these experiences and energies made available to him. The way in which he carries out these decisions is what tests and proves his true individual worth. The Eleventh House is the last of the succeedent House tests; the strong individual *must* dare to challenge the past, the status quo in himself and in society. Refusing to conform to decadent patterns of social behavior and with the faith and wisdom necessary to stand alone, one can become a channel for *creative* "divine discontent".

To the average person, attaining high social position, fulfilling the responsibilities of that position as best he can and enjoying the fruits thereof, is seen as highly desirable. Saturn introduces into this vision a feeling of emptiness and discontent by making one realize that the cycle is not yet finished and that many things he wanted to do at the beginning of the cycle (Saturn in the First House) have not been realized. The Eleventh House transit should make one aware of all that is missing from the Tenth House accomplishment so that one may orient his attention to some new adventure of the spirit. The individual is asked to develop a new vision, new ideals and concrete plans for social or professional improvement, and to work towards them. Quick recognition of these efforts should not be expected, since one is in the final phases of the Saturn cycle and all that has gone before weighs heavily upon him. What is necessary, above all, is the attempt to extricate oneself from the social pattern to which one has for so long conformed. Then, when Saturn returns to the Ascendant in a few years time, the individual will be ready to break free and set out in a new direction.

Saturn Transits the Twelfth House. In this last stage of the cycle one may either consolidate his past successes into a seed which will lead to a new cycle of growth in maturity, or meet the accumulated results of his failure to reach the maturity possible during the closing cycle. Actually, both success and failure become unavoidable confrontations at this time, since no life is all success or all defeat. However, these confrontations are usually on a psychological level in the form of conscious or unconscious memories, some giving hope for the future, while others take the form of frustrations, fears, or the denial of life itself. All those wrong things one did in the past and the right things one did not do return to haunt him. What is important now is the courage to face this compound entity made up of one's past, to *understand* it, and to emerge free from its oppressing influence by the time Saturn reaches the Ascendant. Much depends on the Eleventh House experiences which the individual has just lived through, for now he meets the results of either his passive conformity to the social pattern or his rebellion against it. Either the social trends which he has blindly followed will influence him—whether he likes it or not — or society will try to punish him for his "anti-social" behavior. If society refuses his efforts to bring about some new vision, he may decide to bear it courageously.

This is the time to try to give some new and individual direction to past conditioning, environmental and hereditary. One must use the past and synthesize it into some revealing message which will give a creative meaning to the closing cycle of activity. This is the time to question the *value* of one's life, and of all one has done, felt and thought. Once this is clear, the person may then decide what *new* value he will be able to offer the world in the coming Saturn cycle. On a more mundane level, one now meets the results of his social and professional failures or frustrations, as well as of his successes and wealth. Social rewards for past services or work—academic degrees, prizes, political "plums", and social honors—can all come as Saturn transits the Twelfth House. More importantly, however, one meets here the less obvious results of the methods he has used to gain his Tenth House accomplishment. The individual will now be reminded that certain kinds of success give rise to enmity and resentment or may have caused suffering to others. Here he will become aware of the negative as well as the positive results of his successes.

The confrontation with obstacles born of one's past deeds is always strongest when one tries to make a new start. All sorts of ghosts and fears appear and inhibit the individual from taking the new step ahead. This is the Twelfth House crisis. The real battles of one's life are fought and decided *within* oneself. In this the individual is completely alone—with no one to hinder him or judge him; he must answer only to himself. Everything that has gone into making the character what it is can be found in the Twelfth House—courage and fear, faith and suspicion, self-knowledge and self-deception, self-help and self-destruction, self-interest and self-deprecation, creative abilities and phobias—all these are stored in this House waiting to be called into use in time of need. At this time, one's responsibilities and problems are of a most personal nature, perhaps almost invisible to others. Little or no help comes to him from outside sources, and he can make little progress toward worldly goals. If one confines his aims to things which are measured by the personal satisfaction they can give, then he can accomplish miracles in the way of becoming a bigger and more able person. If, however, he persists in fighting against the current, striving still for public recognition and making efforts only where he thinks they will bring material rewards, he is moving towards trouble in the form of frustration, ill-health and loss of self-esteem.

The first line of defense should be honest self-analysis. One must look at himself critically and then decide where and how he can improve what he sees. Study of any kind will help, and what is studied does not matter much. It may be study to improve oneself professionally, artistically or spiritually, to develop a latent talent if only for diversion. The real benefit comes from proving to oneself that the thing can be done. The tendency to defend oneself *against* oneself must be avoided. If there is fear and suspicion, they will be products of the individual's own lack of self-assuredness, and no alibis will change the fact. Distrust of others can lead to loss of friends, business losses, or actual thefts. Imaginary wrongs and fear of deception may bring these very things into being; self-pity can cause more responsibility and work to be piled at one's door; and last but not least, all the unhealthy thoughts and feelings can bring on real ill-health. Therefore this House has been called the dumping ground of experience. The function of this phase of Saturn's cycle is to weed out the wrong ideas of Self and to strengthen the right ones before the new cycle begins.

TRANSITING SATURN AND THE PROGRESSED MOON. Although this book is devoted to a study of transits, Saturn and the Progressed Moon both refer to the urge to be a particular being different from all others; therefore, they must be considered together. An astrologer must, in some way, take the Progressed Moon's cycle into account when attempting to find out what, at any moment, is the basic challenge on the path to personal fulfillment and maturity. Saturn and the Moon together establish the structure and the quality of the conscious ego. Saturn gives to the ego both its form and its distinctive qualities. It therefore refers to the manner in which each person tries to be different from all other people. The Moon refers to the quality of the ego's adjustments to other people and to the environment. Harmonious and mature living depends on an individual's capacity to maintain a flexible equilibrium between his effort to be a distinct individual and his need to adjust himself harmoniously to changing outer circumstances and the crises of inner development—that is to say, to maintain a balance between Saturn and the Moon.

While the Saturn transit cycle lasts 29½ years, the progressed Moon cycle lasts 27-1/3 years. Thus, ages 27-30 and 56-59 are especially significant for—as discussed in Chapter II—these age periods potentially refer to the most important readjustments in the lives of each individual. It is because the motions of transiting Saturn and the progressed Moon describe cycles of approximately the same duration that Rudhyar has suggested that the astrologer should study these two cycles together. However, while it is logical to emphasize the movement of Saturn through the Houses, since both Saturn and the Houses are "structural" factors, Rudhyar has shown that the *Sign position* of the progressed Moon is of greatest importance. The position of transiting Saturn by House and Sign enables the astrologer to know *where* and *how* to act at any given time. The Sign and degree (especially the symbol for that degree) of the progressed Moon indicate those faculties, qualities of character and kinds of energies which *should* be used in order to meet the challenges of life successfully.

As an example, let us examine the case of Jimmy Carter, 38th President of the United States. He was born on October 1, 1924 in Plains,

Georgia at 7:00 AM CST according to his birth certificate. This puts 29 Cancer on the Midheaven and gives an Ascendant of 26.06 Libra. The last time Saturn came to the Midheaven by transit was in May 1976, and at the time of his election it was intercepted in Leo in the 10th House. The progressed Moon entered Libra and the natal 12th House in July 1976 and was at the 5th degree of Libra at the time of the election. According to the humanistic approach, the Midheaven begins the quarter of the birth-chart which refers to "growth in influence". Since we are dealing with Saturn, and especially because Saturn is the rising planet in his birth-chart, close to the natal Ascendant, it can be said that Carter identifies himself personally with the Saturn trend toward personal maturity and responsibility. A new cycle of responsibility began for him in 1953 when Saturn crossed the Ascendant. At that time he was a naval officer serving aboard a submarine. He might have continued as a career officer in the Navy; however, in 1953 his father died and he left the service to return to Plains and look after the family's farming interests. Thus, during the autumn of that year his life set into a new pattern—the seed of a new destiny was planted.

In 1961, at the time transiting Saturn crossed the IC, he was elected to the Georgia State Senate, where he served from 1962 to 1966. Then, as Saturn transited his 5th House in 1966, he made an unsuccessful and perhaps premature bid for the Democratic nomination for Governor of Georgia. Almost immediately after the primaries he began quietly to build a political base on which to run again in 1970; and in 1969 he announced his candidacy. At that time transiting Saturn was crossing his Descendant. Saturn's transit of the Midheaven, which signals a possible time for public recognition, was in Carter's case the high-point in his effort to attain personal maturity and to assume social responsibilities. The fact that he was elected President of the United States shows that his growth as an ever more mature personality since 1953, and particularly since 1969 when Saturn reached the Descendant and the opposition to its natal place, has made it possible for him to become an instrument of national destiny. A new period of world responsibility now opens for him. Between 1976 and the end of 1982 (which will be the middle of his second term, should he be re-elected) when Saturn crosses the Ascendant and returns to its natal place, his influence on a national and global level can grow and be consolidated.

Now what does the progressed Moon add to the meaning of the Saturn transit? The progressed Moon entered the Sign Libra in June-July 1976 at the time of his nomination (which has also been called a "coronation") by the Democratic party. It also entered the 12th House according to the Placidean House system. Carter's natal Sun is also in Libra and in the 12th House, a position that Gandhi also had. During the

Libra phase of the progressed Moon cycle, the personal self is asked to adjust more completely to the life of some greater social or spiritual whole. The goal is to free oneself to be an integral and significant part of that whole, and thereby to be able to participate fully and consciously in its activities. This Libra phase often coincides with an individual's finding the real work which he was destined to do. There is also a danger of losing oneself in things too vast for one's personal capacities. In any case, since the Summer of 1976, life has demanded of Carter that he fully display his natal Libran qualities, especially since both his natal Sun and Ascendant are in that Sign. He has had to represent a greater social and spiritual reality in his person; he has had to show publicly that he was dedicated to human society, ready to defend human qualities and values and to fulfill human needs.

In the Sagittarius rising chart for the United States on which Dane Rudhyar has written extensively, the Sign Libra is on the Midheaven. The accent on this Sign in Carter's natal chart, and the fact that his progressed Moon was in Libra at the time of the election, links Carter strongly to the U.S. chart. This may be interpreted as a national feeling that Carter was a representative man for the nation's ideal effort to establish a new society. The fact that the progressed Moon (with the natal Sun) was in the 12th House at that time is also significant. The 12th House is the final phase of the House cycle of experience, but it is also the gestation phase of some new venture. It would seem that Carter's administration will focus its attention upon the development of some future new condition. The new administration inherits a heavy burden from the past, and only time will show whether Carter is able, through a personal victory over the pull of the past, to shape the national conditions which his administration has inherited toward new and more harmonious ends.

The student will find it worthwhile to study the symbols for the first five degrees of Libra which were emphasized from June to November 1976. The symbol for the 5th degree of Libra (the degree of the progressed Moon at the time of the election) is especially significant. The symbol reads: "A man revealing to his students the foundation of an inner knowledge upon which a 'new world' can be built".* Rudhyar interprets the keynote for this symbol as follows: "The necessity for the youthful spirits to learn from a Teacher who through his long experience has been able to reach solid and illuminating truths, i.e. 'seed ideas'." In earlier commentaries, this symbol suggested: knowledge and experience being put to the test; proof of works; greatness calling its own to itself; and positive transfiguration of the consciousness of personality by the new Eon (Age).

---

*See *An Astrological Mandala* (Random House), pp. 170-175.

In the week following his election, Carter's progressed Moon entered 6 Libra. The symbol for this degree reads, "A man watches his ideals taking a concrete form before his inner vision". The keynote is "The need to visualize clearly one's dreams or ideals in order to make them truly effectual". Other commentaries include confrontation with one's goals, inevitable confrontation with the results of one's ideals, lessons to be learnt from these, and willingness of heart. When Carter began his administration at the end of January 1977, the progressed Moon was in the 8th degree of Libra. The symbol for this degree is "A blazing fireplace in a deserted home." The keynote is "The need to realize that even through the most empty hours a spiritual power is ever ready to welcome and warm up the wayward consciousness returning to center." Other commentaries include: constant presence of unseen, sustaining agencies in every worthwhile activity, great depth of initial effort, social sustainment, and the ever-renascent HOPE for a re-beginning. This example is meant to show how revealing it is to take transiting Saturn together with the progressed Moon in order to understand the deeper implications of "events" in the life.

VII

The Jupiter-Saturn Cycle
The Development of a Social Destiny

When approaching a birth-chart, an astrologer must seek to understand not only the unique destiny of the person, but also how that destiny will fit into the social context existing at that person's birth and during his formative years. No one is born into a vacuum. At birth an individual enters a complete social environment; he becomes not only a member of a family, but also a participant in a community and society. His identity, and also his social destiny, will be shaped by the cultural, economic, political and religious values of that environment. These influences, either subtle or pronounced, communicate to the emerging individual the *kind* of social participation expected of him. To understand how an individual will react to these influences, an astrologer must look first to the planets Jupiter and Saturn. Saturn indicates how that person should envision his *place* within the family, community and country, while Jupiter shows how he will *participate* in that family, community or country. Saturn describes *where* the person belongs, the kind of environment and activity which correspond to his individual limitations and gifts. Jupiter shows the feelings of social participation or devotional aspiration which the person has toward the people with whom he must live. Together these two planets indicate the individual's most natural way of adjusting himself to the activities of his family, social or professional group, and society. At every moment Saturn consolidates and makes concrete the type and quality of social participation envisioned by Jupiter.

It follows therefore that the phase of the Jupiter-Saturn cycle at which an individual is born will show basic attitudes toward his place and participation in society. It also indicates the possibilities for change in one's social position, professionally, politically or religiously. Therefore, the astrologer must study the transit cycles established by the successive conjunctions of these two planets every twenty years. The natal Jupiter-Saturn phase determines the ages at which a person will experience the transiting Jupiter-Saturn conjunctions during his life-time. These must always be considered in terms of the Age Factor (see Chapter II), since the impact of these conjunctions is totally different at different times in the life. For example, if a person is born during the waning phase of this cycle, he will experience his first conjunction when still a child. The transiting conjunctions offer basic opportunities to develop a more constructive and fruitful social sense, and to participate with any person or group in a mutually beneficial way. Such changes in one's social sense are psychologically necessary in every life, and the transiting conjunctions to the natal chart also show the extent to which a person has *made use of the opportunities* life has presented him. If one is living purposefully, then each conjunction should reveal the beginning of a change in his social sense, in the way he relates to other people in a social context. In those cases where an individual has failed to make use of the opportunities of the last Jupiter-Saturn cycle, the conjunction's position in relation to the natal chart can show the astrologer the causes of the resulting frustration, feelings of guilt or social defeat. When an individual is thus able to see the root-cause of his failure and take responsibility for it, rather than blaming it on chance, he will be able to take his destiny in his own hands and make his own luck.

A word of warning must be interjected here. According to the humanistic point of view, astrological symbols point to *potential* opportunities and not to outer facts. Nothing extraordinary need happen at the time of a critical phase in any planetary cycle. These cycles refer to processes of psychological growth, rather than changes in one's material fortunes. The conjunctions, squares and oppositions of transiting Jupiter to transiting Saturn, as they relate to the natal chart, bring to a focus a definite phase in a process of transition, development and fulfillment (or of disintegration) of the individual's manner of relating to his community. The astrologer cannot know in advance whether a specific person will respond to this negatively or positively. A negative response to the challenge of the conjunction can lead to a second crisis at the time of the opposition, making it necessary to change in some objective way and in clear consciousness what was done or not done earlier. The opposition will then show that the crisis is in reality a challenge to bring about the changes in one's social behavior which the individual refused to do at the time of the conjunction. The natal position of Jupiter and Saturn show the particular phase relationship between these two planets, whose cycle began with the conjunction which occurred before birth. Since the conjunctions of Jupiter and Saturn correspond to new social trends and family patterns, they will inevitably affect persons born *later in the cycle* when those trends have taken on a more concrete form. For this reason it often happens, especially when birth occurs during "critical phases" in the Jupiter-Saturn cycle, that one's social adjustments are deviated and frustrated by external events or trends which began some time prior to birth.

People do not become neurotic or maladjusted all by themselves. The relations which they seek to establish, and especially those which they fail to establish both with other people and with the activities of their community, are equally responsible. Finally the state of society and the prevailing social norms which must be adjusted to are important factors. The humanistic astrologer must take these facts into account when trying to understand the Jupiter-Saturn transits. The complexity and rate of change of today's societies make it impossible to give a set astrological formula and an invariable technique for the interpretation of the Jupiter-Saturn cycle. However, a study of the conjunctions, squares and oppositions during this cycle in their relation to the natal chart, especially during the part of the life already lived, will give to the psychologically oriented astrologer extremely revealing data.

Although twenty years elapse between one conjunction and the next, the basic rhythm of the Jupiter-Saturn relationship is, according to Rudhyar, a 60-year rhythm, since every third conjunction usually takes place in the same zodiacal Sign. For example, in 1842 the conjunction was at 9 Capricorn, the 1901 conjunction was at 14 Capricorn and the 1961 conjunction at 25 Capricorn. During an average life-span Jupiter and Saturn can be said to "return" three times to the same aspect or phase relationship they had at birth. Of these three "returns", the third repetition is the most important because, when it occurs at age 59, each planet also returns to the zodiacal position it occupied at birth. At this time, therefore, a person's entire social sense can be completely renewed or more strongly reaffirmed, and he has the opportunity to relate in a new and more significant manner to the social activities of his community.

Although the cycles established by the successive conjunctions of Jupiter and Saturn are particularly significant for people who have a public destiny or who assume important social responsibilities, they can also be significant for others; for any person is capable of realizing suddenly that he or she *could* live a socially more significant life. The time when an individual first becomes aware of the role he *could* potentially play in society generally coincides with a major phase of the transiting Jupiter-Saturn cycle *provided that* this phase contacts the natal chart in a significant manner. Although people who have already assumed some important social or political function are more acutely tuned in to changes in the Jupiter-Saturn transit cycle, mainly because their natal charts reveal strong Jupiter-Saturn activity, the ordinary person can make simpler and more personal changes at the time of the major phases of the cycle. Everyone will find it necessary at some time in his life to adjust in a new way to his social environment, to make important changes of attitude or profession, or to make a new start at the close of an old cycle of activity. At such times the astrologer must look to the Jupiter-Saturn cycle in order to understand better what is involved in such changes.

THE JUPITER-SATURN CONJUNCTION. These conjunctions begin new cycles of development in an individual's approach to the life-long problem of effectively relating his conscious ego (Saturn) to the social activities of his community. When the birth hour is known a personalized meaning can be given to these conjunctions according to the natal House in which the conjunction falls. In cases of an unknown birthtime, the solar House can also give valid, although less individualized indications; it will be of a more external nature and must be referred to what the natal Sun represents, the vitality and basic soul-purpose of the individual. If understood in this way, the solar House position of *any* transiting planet can give pertinent information which will complement the indications furnished by the natal House position.

The transiting Jupiter-Saturn conjunctions occurring during the 20th Century are:

1901	Capricorn 14
1921	Virgo 27
1940-1	Taurus 14, 12, 9
1961	Capricorn 25
1981	Libra 9
2000	Taurus 23

The 1940-1 CONJUNCTIONS reached their opposition phase in April, 1951 in Pisces-Virgo 28; in October 1951 in Aries-Libra 8; and for a third time in February 1952 in Aries-Libra 15. The following waning square phase was exact in August 1955 in Leo-Scorpio 16, and again in June 1956 in Leo-Scorpio 28. The 1961 CONJUNCTION reached the waxing square in July 1965 in Gemini-Pisces 18. The opposition occurred on December 31, 1969 in Scorpio-Taurus 3; again in March 1970 in Scorpio-Taurus 6; and for a third and final time in November 1970 in Scorpio-Taurus 19. The waning square was exact on June 4, 1975 in Aries-Cancer 18; July 29, 1975 in Aries-Cancer 25; and for the third time on March 10, 1976 in Aries-Cancer 27. The 1981 CONJUNCTION will reach its waxing square in Pisces-Sagittarius 9 in April 1986, and the opposition in 1989-90 in Cancer-Capricorn 10 and 22. The waning square will occur in 1995 in February-March in Sagittarius-Pisces 14, and in November in Sagittarius-Pisces 18. In order to give these phases a more concrete meaning, they should be applied to one's own natal chart.

In the 1st House the individual may react in a very personal way to whatever challenges come at the beginning of the new social-political-economic cycle. He has to discover and bring to a clearer focus of consciousness what he potentially is as an individual ego. The best way to accomplish this will be through *utilizing* the very pressure that social conditions of the moment exert on him. **In the 2nd House** this conjunction challenges one to gain a new perspective on the *use* he makes of his inherited or acquired social and cultural gifts. It will become increasingly more important, as the Jupiter-Saturn cycle evolves, to make concrete and workable what one has to give to society as an individual. One must use his inborn muscular strength, his mental abilities and intuitions, and also his social position, to enter into *more fruitful* relationships with other people. **In the 3rd House** the Jupiter-Saturn conjunction challenges one to use whatever social sense he has in a new and better way in his daily contacts with his environment. This means that one should now try to live according to some well-defined social or cultural purpose through which he can demonstrate concretely what he is. He must also be as practical as possible at this time.

In the 4th House the challenge of the new Jupiter-Saturn cycle is focused upon one's home life and one's ability to make concrete in his everyday personality whatever vision and understanding he may have of the larger, social realities of life. It may be necessary in the coming years to put down new roots and to find a greater stability in one's social or professional life. **In the 5th House** this conjunction will find the individual asked by society, and by his own inner destiny, to creatively contribute something new to his community. Having been born in his particular circumstances has a purpose which the social pressures or challenges of the present time may reveal more clearly, specifically in terms of the faculties or powers necessary to the outer realization of this purpose. One should give freely of himself as an inspirer and educator. **In the 6th House** the challenge of the new social, cultural and religious cycle is directed toward a person's capacity for service, endurance and self-discipline. He may have to learn new techniques in order to meet the needs of the times. This House shows one's basic response to the social situations in which he finds himself. Some facets of this response may have to be transformed so that the contribution he makes to the productivity and the growth of his community may have positive results.

In the 7th House one begins a period in which the challenge is to gain a new sense of human relationship and of the value of one's community participation. The 7th House is the foundation and testing-ground for all future public, professional, and socio-cultural achievement. Therefore, one should try now to orient his interpersonal relationships so that there may be an effective, significant and creative participation between partners in the work of the world. One should make certain that his relationships are not selfish and isolationistic. **In the 8th House** the social challenge to an individual is self-regeneration. This may affect the awaited results of one's established partnerships, whether it be in marriage, business relationships or group contacts. One has the chance now to review his habitual instinctual-emotional and social-cultural patterns of activity, feeling and thought in his relationships, and to change the purpose of such relationships. **In the 9th House** the new Jupiter-Saturn conjunction can bring problems of social adjustment and also lead to greater awareness in the field of abstract thinking, philosophy and religion. One is now asked by life to make a determined effort to grow spiritually beyond his existing limitations. To do this a person must be ready to assimilate many things which are unfamiliar to him. He must also be willing to include in his world outlook ideas which up to now have seemed alien, disturbing and perhaps unusable.

In the 10th House the challenge of the new cycle can bring opportunities affecting one's professional life and social status. These may involve changes in the way one assumes and discharges responsibilities in his community. Decisions now can make or mar one's power as a social or professional leader — "by your fruits you shall be judged." Since this is the time to ask oneself how he would like to be judged by society and posterity, he should determine exactly what he is ready and emotionally free to do with his professional, social, cultural or religious abilities. **In the 11th House** the new Jupiter-Saturn cycle can provide one with the opportunity to change his ideals and to gain perspective on social processes or functions which interest him. The individual must be ready to associate spontaneously with others who could help him to realize such changes. One's recent social success or failure can lead to a new creative departure, provided he has not identified himself too closely with his struggle for achievement. In any case, the way in which one now *uses* the experiences and the energies born of his professional or public activity will prove his true worth as an individual. **In the 12th House** the new adjustment to social realities has to be made as a "last look" at an ending phase of personal experience. Something has come to seed from one's ancestral, social, cultural or religious past (one's individual karma). The challenge now is for a person to extract from this seed the foundation for *a new life*, for the new cycle that confronts him. It also means having the courage to repudiate the ghosts of the past cycle. A social crisis now is the outcome of the way in which he has worked out his relationship to his family and community. It is a transition between what one must face up to, out of his past, and the call of a new beginning.

THE OPPOSITION PHASE in the Jupiter-Saturn cycle will bring to some climax, fulfillment or critical confrontation whatever was started at the time of the conjunction. This will be followed by a slow disintegration and will relate specifically to the natal House in which the conjunction fell. In regard to one's attitude toward social, cultural and religious matters, anything begun at the conjunction which was a constructive departure from one's old pattern will bear fruit at the opposition. The type of fulfillment will be suggested by the Houses of the birth-chart in which the opposition of Jupiter to Saturn falls.

THE JUPITER-SATURN SQUARE. Since this book is being written during the waning square of the Jupiter-Saturn cycle, it seems appropriate to discuss this phase of the cycle in detail, especially as it relates to the individual birth-chart. This waning square brings to the fore the necessity for self-criticism, as well as a general tendency to criticize society, the government, national institutions, economic trends and all authority figures. This comes as a result of experiences occurring after the opposition of these two planets, the most recent being between December 1969 and June 1971. Since the *present* Jupiter-Saturn cycle has been rather negative because of a wide-spread tendency toward over-production, the social awareness on which our current social behavior is based is at a critical phase. Many wasteful habits are now being questioned as the cost becomes increasingly difficult for the average person to bear. At the same time there is an inner challenge to understand the social implication of this glut of over-production, over-expansion and over-indulgence. It has become a time to assess the true value of technology, the golden calf of the 20th Century. Out of this self-criticism should come a reorientation of the relationship of the individual (individual comforts) to society (the needs of the greater community) which can potentially lead to a new beginning in 1981.

Of the two planets, Jupiter is the faster moving, more positive, activity-initiating planet. It is therefore the challenger in this cycle. The natal (or solar) House containing transiting Jupiter and the natal planets which Jupiter activates constitute the dynamic focus of the challenge to one's personal growth. Jupiter describes the basic social problems facing the individual at the time of the square (waning or waxing) in this cyclic relationship.

Jupiter in the 1st House — Saturn in the 4th House. This is a period of spiritual testing, a crisis of growth which strains one's relation to his society. One will have to determine where he stands socially and individually as well. There will be a need to balance individualism and conservatism, to expand within and to solidify the position without. This can be a period of great self-realization, especially in the development of one's self-reliance. There should be a practical inspiration challenging one to build his personality anew on the foundation of one's personal beliefs. At home one should assert himself, yet with gentleness, not allowing the conservative side of one's nature or parental influence to dominate his life and hold him back. It is not that a person will lack individual power at this time--if anything, the individual approach to life will be too dominant. However, it is not free, conditioned as it may be by a sense of fatality or by moral precepts.

Jupiter in the 2nd House — Saturn in the 5th House. Here one is tested by life at perhaps his weakest point, his sense of possessions.

Financial problems may arise and force one to be practical and to use common sense in all matters. It may also be that a person has spent too much in order to please a loved one, or becomes emotionally indignant at the treatment he fancies himself receiving. Financial worries should not be allowed to get one down. This is the time to develop one's latent powers, to make the most of hereditary or accumulated possessions. Care should be taken, however, not to squander one's assets, even though one may have to use much of his capital to meet speculation losses. Whatever happens in a material sense, it may be difficult to bear the emotional stress and strain of a sharp readjustment of financial or ancestral values.

Jupiter in the 3rd House — Saturn in the 6th House. A sharp examination of one's intellectual values is indicated at this time. This may involve strenuous work, the demands of which may lead to a complete immolation of Self in service. This is a great test, and some sort of conversion may be indicated. The challenge is to face the new unswervingly. Health may be a consideration and should be watched, especially one's psychological health. Difficulties with one's relatives or within one's immediate environment may arise, and meeting them will test one's strength and patience. One should be extremely careful of the letters he writes at this time. If it is necessary to write, one should be aware of a tendency to over-commit oneself or to make overly optimistic promises. These could possibly endanger one's job or position. This, above all, is not the time to allow one's judgement to be swayed by subjective considerations.

Jupiter in the 4th House — Saturn in the 7th House. The difficulties and tests in evidence here may result from a strong arousal of one's personal feelings, primarily in relation to one's life-partner. Additionally, there is the more general difficulty of meeting the outside world and its standards of behavior. One should try to remain as emotionally poised as possible for outbursts, or effusiveness may be met with coldness or unresponsiveness from those he loves. This situation requires strength of character, the capacity to stand firm. Some will achieve a relative mastery of their fate while others may fall apart. Cheer up and take things easy is the best advice.

Jupiter in the 5th House — Saturn in the 8th House. At this time a person may be extremely agitated and emotionally upset. One should be cautious of lawsuits, contests of wills, inheritances, and all business deals in general, and not take for granted any rights he feels he has. He would be well advised NOT to speculate, as pride may lead one to fly off on inflated ventures. If one has speculated and did not let go in time, there may be difficulties during this transit. Business partners can be a bit sour and may tend to curb, rather nastily, one's further efforts at investing or expanding through forceful action. They may not be right in their attitude, but that will not deter the strength of their antagonism. However, giving free rein to self-righteous indignation can be dangerous. This transit is a time to learn about one's own emotions, about what is and what is not spiritual, and to relax one's own shows of self-assurance.

Jupiter in the 6th House — Saturn in the 9th House. All attempts at personal expansion are to be discouraged at this time. The sobering discipline of service is now the order of the day, and any flight from the mundane realities of day-by-day living will bring trials and sorrow. One must be practical both in his flights of imagination and in his estimation of just how much work he is capable of performing. Some people may experience either an intensification of their devotional nature or be severely tested in their loyalties to a cause or a personality whom they had taken for an ideal. It may be that through pride one feels ready to throw overboard all sense of devotion or subservience to others, and to assert himself as a leader. This may be good, but only if done rationally and within the boundaries of common sense. Emotional stress may tell upon one's physical health, and some people may indulge in self-displays which could, in extreme cases, verge on paranoia. During this transit one should keep faith and cheerfulness and know that self-abnegation is the key to success.

Jupiter in the 7th House — Saturn in the 10th House. An emotional storm may erupt at this time affecting one's marriage or close relationships. One's public or professional life may also be shaken. Care should be taken in all partnerships, and especially in one's contacts with people in authority. Whatever happens must be seen as a psychological test. It may be that one's professional, spiritual or social ambition is tearing him away from loved ones and is causing trials in one's interpersonal relationships. At this time care must be taken not to sacrifice too much to one's ambition. On the other hand professional difficulties may be due to one's having lost himself in his own conjugal bliss. A recent intimate relationship may have led one to a reconsideration of his professional activities and as a result, one is now faced with difficult problems.

Jupiter in the 8th House — Saturn in the 11th House. One must watch his business associates every moment during this transit and not trust anyone too much. Conservative advisers or friends may be against one's expansive business moves. It is important not to let outworn, traditional ideals or prejudices hamper one's social opportunities, yet one must be cautious since contracts and agreements can be unsound. Subtle tests occur in one's business life, and one should rely primarily on one's own judgement. Here the worth of one's ideals is challenged through the need for making them concrete realities, and one must now incorporate them as practical ideals of living. This situation may make a person restless, and he will have to consciously relax to remain emotionally steady in his relationships with friends, advisers or business partners. This is no time to become involved with occult groups or spiritualistic seances.

Jupiter in the 9th House — Saturn in the 12th House. This may be a period of ruthless reformation, a "holy war" within one's inner nature. In such a crisis one must become a focal point for the power and the ideals of his social group or nation. The karma of the group or nation may be upon one's own shoulders; therefore, living up to what is demanded of one will be a great test. An individual must mobilize all his inner resources and use his understanding of life to the utmost. In some cases a trend toward long journeys develops which may be essentially fortunate; however, much can happen during such a trip and one must be careful not to land in dangerous places which could lead to confinement. Psychological difficulties can become prominent because of a wrong understanding of religious matters. At this time, one should not lay too much store in dreams and omens, or in so-called messages from the "masters". This is a time to conquer spiritual pride. It would be well to examine immediate situations carefully, and not jump into anything which might destroy the spiritual or social gains possible.

Jupiter in the 10th House — Saturn in the 1st House. This situation often revolves around an ever increasing demand made upon the individual by his profession or by society in general. It is a test of power and responsibility. Can a person, by rallying to the task, meet the demands of the group? One may be ready to try, even though he may feel weighed down by the task. This confrontation will require having to watch one's public standing carefully. Either one's sense of professional responsibility is already great, or he will realize that public matters need more of his attention. One must be careful at this time not to let mental strain get the better of one's health. In other cases, the great task now seems to be that of active participation in social or religious movements, or in some cause wherein the individual has authority. One's physical and psychological past has led him to his decision of self-renunciation and utter consecration to that which is supra-personal. If one refuses now, and if he clings to the narrow limits of his conscious egoism, he will be shattered. Safety is to be found in losing oneself so that he might find a greater SELF in which alone he will discover security and inner peace. One must not be afraid. He should mobilize all his energies for extreme social exertion, shatter his own self-centeredness, and put all his powers at the service of a cause.

Jupiter in the 11th House — Saturn in the 2nd House. This transit indicates a spiritual test in which one's ideals will confront one's inherited nature. An individual will have to make a difficult decision which may be a turning-point in one's life. One must face the issue, alone if need be, for friends and advisers are not likely to help. It is important to hold oneself steady and not to force any social issues at this time, as one can lose financially and morally by doing so. In some cases, financial difficulties involving friends or social organizations may come to a climax. One may have to spend money to save, or to please, friends and maintain one's social position. This can be especially true if one is involved in responsibilities relating to clubs, fraternal or humanitarian organizations and the like. One may have to choose between wealth and ideals, although the latter will seem more valuable just now. Those who were enthusiastic about backing one may not be able to live up to their promises, or it may be that one is not financially able to assume his own share of the obligations. Controversies and tests of patience or endurance are therefore likely in these areas.

Jupiter in the 12th House — Saturn in the 3rd House. This may not be an easy time. For example, one may meet trials through relatives and neighbors. It will be necessary to remain serene and to use common sense to solve one's immediate problems. Neighbors or relatives are not necessarily negative factors in the situation. If in trouble, one may be able to fall back on them, or at least to receive their sound advice and perhaps an equally valuable dressing down for one's past behavior. The intensity of living may cause mental fatigue at this time, and one must therefore learn to relax. Mental instability can also cause severe tests of strength. On psychological levels, there may be an inner test of one's capacity to meet some binding condition in the environment. If a person has thought and acted wisely in the past, he may be able to realize previously unconscious ideas or hopes. One should therefore concentrate on form, and try to see the pattern behind all changing appearances.

VIII

The Uranus Cycle

In the humanistic approach, the three planets beyond the orbit of Saturn symbolize stages in human development which are "transcendent". These planets represent new factors affecting human activity on both social and individual levels, factors which continually upset the status quo, both in thought and action on all levels of society. Since their discovery, Western civilization finds itself in a state of crisis, due in part to the fundamental social and economic changes introduced by modern science and technology. Additionally, repercussions are felt on the personal level as individuals find themselves in a perpetual state of upset. In an attempt to meet this constant state of crisis, different schools of psychology have appeared, each emphasizing its own approach to the problems of modern life. As Rudhyar has pointed out, the present widespread emphasis on the use of psychological techniques, including astrology, is the direct result of the need to meet this universal state of crisis.

There is a general tendency to over-react, especially on an emotional level, to the word "crisis," to view it as something dire and dreadful which must be avoided at all costs. The more recent schools of psychology define "crisis" as a *phase of growth*, either of the individual or society. It has purpose and meaning in relation to the overall development of the human personality or the collectivity passing through such a phase. Crisis is necessary to this development, although the *form* it takes is not inevitable. Change, transition and transformation are necessary ingredients of human experience, but this does not mean that violent revolution or war are the only means of bringing them about socially. In the same way, a personal crisis of growth does not *necessarily* produce illness, neurosis, insanity or tragic loss. There seem to be two distinctly different fundamental aims to the psychological treatment of crises. The first, and unfortunately the most common, is to try to re-establish the state of so-called normalcy which the crisis upset. This is the aim of both the social psychologists and the Freudians and can be linked astrologically to the Jupiter-Saturn level of functioning. The alternative aim, first put forward by Carl Jung, is to *use* crises as challenges to greater growth, as means to induce an inner metamorphosis of the personality. This attitude can be linked astrologically to Uranus and Neptune. The humanistic astrologer knows that such crises are often stressful and disturbing. It is the point of change/no-change at which the person must either make a conscious decision or become the victim of fate. He must either act or be acted upon. The point of change is never comfortable or comforting; however, in order to attain personal maturity, crises must be met, understood and assimilated.

This approach takes the person well beyond the level of "self". Whereas on the Jupiter-Saturn level one is challenged to become *a greater and better individual* rather than merely to accept the status quo, on the level of Uranus-Neptune he is challenged to become *greater than an individual*. As one changes his frame of reference, his life assumes a meaning on the collective or even universal level, rather than the purely personal one. Ego desires become secondary, and one finds significance in values which have meaning whether he, as an individual, exists or not. Instead of meeting people in terms of his own desires, one seeks a greater reality toward which he can work with others. A person then is able to express the universal significance of Uranus and Neptune. If one simply wants to be "normal," like everyone else, then the crisis of Uranus and Neptune will seem destructive, something to be fought against until things return to the familiar, comfortable old-shoe existence he had before. The problem here is that the "normal" routine will never again be as comfortable as it once was, leading to an end result of fear, frustration and having suffered for naught. Such a result spells spiritual defeat. The humanistic astrologer can assist his client to find positive meaning in Uranus and Neptune crises and to assume a positive attitude toward them by first of all, advising the client of their expected duration. Secondly, the astrologer can point out the apparent purpose of the crisis and its transformational impetus in the life and character of that individual. Here the astrologer must consider not only the entire birth-chart, including life-time progressions, but also the age factor. With this information a person can work consciously with the changes which the crisis is challenging him to make, instead of fighting them.

From the humanistic viewpoint, Uranus acts positively as the revealer of greater worlds and more inclusive truths. Uranus is the inspirer, that force which forever tries to transform the autocratic and set ways of Saturn. The universal values of which Uranus is the symbol cannot be reached today except through some kind of revolt against the privileges and the domination of crystallized Saturnian behavior patterns. This revolt, however, need not be based on hatred or feelings of revenge which would lead to negative expressions, such as anarchy and revolution on the social level, and bizarre behavior and eccentricity for its own sake on the personal level. These are manifestations traditionally attributed to Uranus. When Uranus challenges, one must seek the means to give a new purpose, direction and meaning to life from a frame of reference larger than the personal ego. Passive subservience to the dictates of an unquestioned tradition and way of life must be changed into a dynamic, positive and creative search for new and more encompassing values and goals. In doing this, the individual must not destroy the Saturnian boundaries of the self, but try to make them more adaptable and less limiting. He must be willing to allow what seem alien elements to enter. One must question the belief that one's personal set of traditions, both racial and cultural, are inherently and spiritually superior to all others. He must be open to the possibility of acting in unprecedented ways and of undergoing a basic change of attitude in order to relate to others according to more-than-personal values. The natal House position of Uranus will indicate the field of experience in which one will most likely have to undergo a deep personal change, where in fact he will often have to deal with upheaval. One's individual purpose will be to work consciously with Uranus, to learn to understand and welcome the purpose of this metamorphosis. Without this conscious effort to *use* Uranus in the matters of the natal House, no transformation will be possible, and Uranus will work through social circumstances to bring upheavals that will seem meaningless and have a disintegrative effect.

Because an increasing number of people experience a complete Uranus cycle of 84 years in the course of their lifetime, individual characteristics can be given to Uranus, which is not possible with Neptune or Pluto. "Individual", however, does not mean "personal." Positive Uranian action presupposes individualization as its foundation, a consciousness open to what is new and *more-than-personal* in its implications. Unlike Jupiter and Saturn, which refer to a person's progress within the limitations of the values established by his birth — his racial, national, cultural and religious framework — Uranus opens the door to the collective unconscious. It is the path to what Jung called "individuation," to that metamorphosis which enables one to realize that his ego is not the central ruler of his personality.

Uranus provides a clue to the type of genius an individual may have; on more ordinary levels, it points to an adventurous spirit or a strong restlessness. This may mean an inner urge to break away from the life conditions which have brought dissatisfaction or failure. It is the power to start anew. As long as a person seeks happiness or success along established, socially acceptable lines and limits himself to the Jupiter-Saturn level of consciousness which leaves no place for spiritual or social metamorphosis, the Uranian energy within him will make him experience such dissatisfaction or failure. Only when a person becomes dissatisfied with the status quo and begins to search for different values does Uranus becomes active within him, shaking him out of his life-rut and urging him to initiate the changes which some new vision or goal presents. When Uranus begins to function, the conscious ego, conditioned as it is by Jupiter-Saturn heredity and environment, is filled with "divine discontent". One realizes that the values of his conscious ego are too limiting and limited, and that he must seek the means to free himself from the life-pattern established by his family and social milieu. The vision of more universal values enters one's life, a vision which will enable him to understand himself in a new light.

When significant transits of Uranus to the natal Sun, Moon, Saturn or "ruling planet" occur, the astrologer must interpret the social or familial disturbances in terms of a personal metamorphosis which will be the purpose behind those outward events, keeping in mind any natal aspects between Uranus and the Sun, Moon, Saturn or ruling planet. If there are no significant contacts at birth, then the transit of Uranus over those natal placements will not necessarily have a deep, personal significance. However, whatever Uranus touches in the birth-chart by transit will tend to be highly stimulated or upset. The potential challenge will always be presented for a person to *use* the planetary function thus stimulated at a more universal, less personal level. If one does not succeed in giving this transcendent goal to the transit, then it will simply coincide with some insignificant external change or meaningless upset. The transiting aspects of Uranus to other planets provide individual opportunities for growth, or can lead to the partial loss of one's personal integrity if the challenge of Uranus is not constructively met. This mysterious power within the psyche seeks to *transform* the essential character of the personality, to make one a fundamentally different person from what he was before the Uranus challenge. This difference will oblige one to test the validity of his earlier state of affairs, both within and without. Social ideals and values will be seen in a new light, and probably as limiting factors in terms of the new vision. One will therefore take steps to *radically alter* his relationship to them.

THE GENERIC CYCLE OF URANUS. The 84-year transit cycle of Uranus symbolizes a progressive effort toward radical transformations, both social and personal. The cycle can be divided in several different ways into sub-cycles: seven 12-year cycles, twelve 7-year cycles, and three 28-year cycles. Implicitly or explicitly in each of these sub-cycles, the number seven recurs, a number significant not only because Uranus transits each Sign of the zodiac in approximately seven years, but also because of its numerological import, as will be discussed below. Jung tells us that numbers have an archetypal foundation, and he defines number psychologically as *an archetype of order* which has become conscious. Numbers, in other words, are *not* inventions of the conscious intelligence, but spontaneous products of the unconscious — the unconscious uses number as an ordering factor.*

---

*See page 456-458, Vol. 8, Collected Works, 1972.

The 28-year Cycles of Uranus. In dividing the Uranus cycle into three 28-year sub-cycles, Rudhyar has likened them to the three "births" in a human life. The first is the physical birth, while the second and third occur as transiting Uranus forms waxing and waning trines to its natal position. The trine aspects offer two moments particularly propitious to a spiritual metamorphosis of the personality. Those who have read Rudhyar's *Astrology of Personality** will remember his cabalistic analysis of numbers. As he explained, by the operation known as "cabalistic addition" the number 7 produces or implies the number 28: 1+2+3+4+5+6+7=28. This means that the number 7 *potentially* contains the number 28. To put this another way, the characteristic nature of 7 is worked out in 28 phases (27 phases plus a 28th phase which will be the fulfillment of the cycle as well as the seed of the new cycle to follow). The number 27 is the third power, or cube, of the number 3: 3x3x3=27. The third power of 3 represents 3 operating on *three levels of being.* The number 3, linked to the trine aspect, is the number which refers to the plane of Ideas *before* they become concrete or embodied through the operation of the number 4 (the square aspect). Thus, the number 27, as the third power of 3, refers to the operation of Ideas on all three levels of being. A new Idea must pass through 27 phases of operation before it can be said to pervade the complete human being. Then, during the 28th phase, the Idea can be expressed through some creative act. This is why Rudhyar says that the 28-year cycle pertains to man as a *creative individual.*

In relation to the Uranus cycle, the word "Idea" is not merely a thought held by the brain, but is what Jungian psychology calls an *archetype.* It is an emanation of the universal Mind which has both form and energy, and which is capable of *impregnating* the whole person on all three levels of his being. An archetype is synonymous with a primordial image. The idea of God, an all-powerful divine Being, is an archetype, a primordial image within humanity's collective psyche. So is the prophet and the disciple of the prophet through the myth of the sun hero. Jung has shown how the most powerful ideas in history go back to archetypes. This is as true of the central concepts of science, philosophy and ethics as of religious ideas. In their present form they are variants of archetypal ideas created by consciously applying and adapting these ideas to reality.

A further reason for dividing the Uranus cycle into three periods is the dialectic process thus activated. The same process is used to analyze the three Houses in each quadrant of the birth-chart: first action, then reaction, and finally the integration of the latter with the former — thesis, antithesis, synthesis. Rudhyar has explained this as follows:

---

*Pages 230-231 in 1st Edition, 1936.

When a Life-Impulse or Idea (an archetype or primordial image) strikes an already formed organism — a man, a nation or the human race as a whole — *it takes time* for it to impress itself upon this organism. The Idea is perceived, then formulated. It upsets the "old order". It produces a revolution, sudden or gradual, indeed it is always a gradual process with one or more flare-ups. That process of impregnation takes 28 phases.

Then reaction sets in. After the thesis we have now the antithesis; the "old order" of consciousness fights for its life, while the very substance of the organism slowly adjusts itself to the new Idea-Impulse. The "masses" change while the "leaders" make desperate efforts to stem the tide. Finally the third 28-year cycle begins, which brings about the synthesis of what was valuable in the old with what was really permanent in the new — or rather what the organism as a whole *has proven ready to incorporate.**

This threefold Uranian process is the life-foundation of a person who is able to become more than a simple expression of his race and traditional culture, one who achieves the status of a creative and integrated personality. During the first 28 years of life, the Uranian Idea-Impulse which corresponds to one's true individual identity slowly descends. This first cycle is involutionary. If all goes well, there will be 28 phases of progressive incorporation of the Ideal into the concrete reality of a living person, which is the reason for birth. As this progressive incorporation takes place, a person will gradually emerge out of the psychic womb of his family, nation, culture and religion, establishing his individual character and destiny.

At what Rudhyar has called the *"second birth"*, the true identity of an individual is fully incorporated and can begin to manifest creatively. The effort to express this true identity in a creative manner will usually bring about deep conflicts between one's identity — the Ideal — and all that has been inherited from both his personal and social past. Many people find it difficult to realize how little their ideals are *really* embodied in their behavior. One *thinks* he is living true to his ideals, while most often he merely tries to ignore everything he does not like in his personal and social inheritance, thus living an illusion of his true nature. *If* one succeeds in remaining true to his vision and essential identity during the second cycle of 28 years, then at the age of 58 the potential of a *"third birth"* will arrive. For this to be possible — and it is, unfortunately, a very rare possibility, even for those who have tried very hard to be real "individuals" — one must first have come to terms with his past. He must have succeeded, in Jungian terms, in assimilating into his conscious ego some of the contents of the collective unconscious. This means becoming a true man of wisdom, radiating through his personality that spiritual essence which it was his destiny to manifest. Such a condition of individ-

*From an article in *American Astrology* magazine

uation is a balanced synthesis of all the collective elements which, together with the Idea-Impulse of his spiritual identity, form the conscious being. The fruits of this synthesis should then manifest in one's life from age 56 onwards. This analysis of the Uranus cycle has been incorporated in the interpretation of the 7-year periods in Chapter II, "The Age Factor".

Multiples of Seven. The number 7 is a basic measure in occult philosophy, and the division of any cycle into seven periods seems to be of universal application and significance. Dividing the Uranus cycle into seven 12-year periods links it to the Jupiter cycle, which lasts 11.8 years. This means that Uranus upsets and transforms the Jupiterian religious, psychic and cultural forms according to a rhythm of 7x12. The division into twelve 7-year periods, which includes the three 28-year periods already discussed, links the Uranus cycle to the cycles of Saturn and the progressed Moon. This is especially significant around the critical years 27-30 and 56-60. The progressed Moon cycle, the lunation cycle and the Saturn cycle all approximate the 28-year Uranus cycle. Because the Moon and Saturn refer to the development of the conscious ego and the Uranus function is to transform that conscious ego and its contents, this link exists between their cycles.

Rudhyar has established in general terms* the meaning which can be given to the seven periods of twelve years each, and this interpretation applies equally to each year of the 7-year cycles. The meaning is directly related to the manifestation of the Uranian transforming type of forces: In the **first year or cycle** the new Impulse is felt, usually in a very confused manner. This entire period can be described as a groping toward a new condition of being. In the **second year or cycle** the new Impulse gains substance, arousing the depths of one's nature. There will be a resistance from one's past; memories, complexes, social inertia and fears oppose the new trend. In the **third year or cycle** the first stage of exteriorization of the Impulse occurs. This can be likened to a "vision". As the archetypal form is more or less clearly revealed, one may experience loneliness and perhaps despondency, for the vision may seem unattainable and the means for realizing it most inadequate. In the **fourth year or cycle** the embodiment of that Impulse-Idea can occur through a period of conflict and struggle. Power may be released through the organism, or there will be a fruitless return to the past. The mid-point of this period (3 1/2 years or age 42) will mark its most important turning-point. *This is the Plant stage.*

In the **fifth year or cycle** consciousness, beauty and creative activity can occur in direct proportion to the progress which has been made. This will bring the Impulse-Idea to its finest and most vigorous period. *This is*

---

*In various articles in *American Astrology* magazine.

the Flower stage. In the **sixth year or cycle** one should gather in the harvest of the Impulse-Idea and evaluate its success or failure. This should be a time of dedication to the future and self-sacrifice. *It is the Fruit stage.* In the **seventh year or cycle** the seed of the future cycle is being formed. What was developed through six preceding years, or 72 years of the larger cycle, will come fatefully to a culmination. To the degree that there has been fulfillment and clarity of consciousness, there will also be freedom. This is the *Seed stage.* All of this is an abstract formula which can only be meaningful when applied to a specific case and in regard to a particular period.

The Twelve 7-year Cycles. In this division of life into twelve 7-year periods, Rudhyar related each period to a Sign of the zodiac.* This means that, *from the point of view of the transforming Uranus function,* the first seven years of life will constitute the Aries period, the next seven years, a Taurus period, and so on. In thus relating the twelve periods to the Signs, we may notice that the three "births" mentioned above correspond to the three Fire Signs. In Aries there is a birth of the physical body as an independent entity at the level of generic and instinctual human nature. In Leo, there is the *potential* birth of the individual Soul, permitting the assertive independence of the conscious ego or mind to make some form of original contribution to society. In Sagittarius, there is the *potential* third birth into the light. This action of the spirit normally comes to a climax every seventh year. Thus it occurs according to the Sign related to the period, and at the level of operation indicated by the particular seven-year period. This means that the characteristics of the Sign will help an astrologer to understand the nature of, and above all, the level at which possible Uranian transformations may take place.

The Aries period — **birth to age 7.** Uranian crises during these years will predominantly affect the basic instinctual reactions one has to life.

The Taurus period — **Age 7 to 14.** Uranian crises during this period particularly affect the sexual and emotional nature.

The Gemini period — **Age 14 to 21.** Here the effect of Uranian crises is principally mental and can modify one's social sense and adaptation to parents, family and friends.

The Cancer period — **Age 21 to 28.** During this period Uranus works mainly on the intuitive faculties and on all that affects the establishment of one's conscious ego in society.

The Leo period — **Age 28 to 35.** This is a most important time for Uranian crises, as they can indicate the possibility of freedom from parental influences and a birth into a truly adult way of life.

---

*Horoscope magazine, January 1950.

The Virgo period — Age 35 to 42. This can be the time to take a fresh look at one's way of life, deciding on changes in one's personal attitude or work. This will be especially true if one's efforts to establish an individual and responsible approach have not been successful in the past. Much will depend on the experiences of the preceding 7-year period.

The Libra period — Age 42 to 49. This is the turning-point of the Uranus cycle — the opposition to its natal place. It can be a period of deep psychological reorientation, or there may be spectacular social success if the previous Uranus crises have been met in a positive manner. Otherwise, there is the possibility of some form of psychological upheaval relating to one's intimate, social or professional associations.

The Scorpio period — Age 49 to 56. Uranian crises at this age can lead to deep occult experiences if the development of the planet's cycle has been positive up to this time. Otherwise, there may be sexual upheavals, emotional conflicts and attempts to regain one's lost youth.

The Sagittarius period — Age 56 to 63. This is the time of a theoretical "third birth". As this experience is rare, however, the astrologer must interpret what happens after the age of 56 as an outgrowth of an individual's attempts to lead an independent life since the age of 28. If all has gone well, this should be a period of harvesting the fruits of past efforts. There could be a birth into wisdom and the capacity to communicate the fruits of one's work to others.

The last three periods of the 84-year cycle of Uranus theoretically continue what the Sagittarius period began. The end of life, from the Uranian point of view, can be a period of abstract thought and social fulfillment, making a person ever wiser and more understanding, a "power behind the throne," or a teacher of this greater understanding.

Having established this level of Uranian activity according to the age of the client, one must then look at the transits which Uranus is making to the natal planets, and at any particularly strong aspects from the progressed planets (especially the Sun and Moon) to natal Uranus occurring at the same time. The year of the 7-year period during which the transits or progressions are exact will then add more detailed information. It must be repeated that *nothing necessarily need happen* on an external level at the time of such Uranian aspects, and *nothing* entitles the astrologer to predict the outcome of such confrontations. He should emphasize to his client that these aspects will call into operation the innate freedom of the individual as a spiritual entity, and he should never suggest anything to his client which could produce fear or uncalled-for expectations. The only positive preparation for Uranian crises is the complete willingness to face *whatever* may happen, with complete faith in the spirit within who is the real initiator of the transformation process.

This analysis of the Uranus cycle, although on a generic, universal level, is surprisingly significant in most cases and well worth taking into account. One should write down what one considers the main events in his life within the framework of these 7-year periods to see how their meaning can be illumined. As most people usually have little idea of what events are really significant in their lives (for most people notice effects rather than causes), it will be enlightening to see the changes in consciousness according to the Uranian periods and aspects. In this way one will learn to look behind the superficialities of life and become more conscious of essential values. Let us take the example of marriage, or any other strong pair-bonded relationship. If a person marries during his 23rd year (the 2nd year of the Cancer period, which is the normal period for establishing a home), the deeper reason for the union *may* be a psychological complex or need for breaking away from the influence of his family. If, on the other hand, that marriage or union occurs during the 28th year, it may have a connection to the potential of the "second birth" and therefore have a deep spiritual significance. In cases of marriage or psychologically close relationships, however, unless the partners are of the same age the meaning of the union will be different for each of them.

As an example of how to employ this technique, we may examine the chart of President Jimmy Carter at the time of his election in November, 1976. At birth Saturn was in 1.55 Scorpio and the Moon in 13.47 Scorpio. At the time of his election, transiting Uranus was exactly on the midpoint of this wide conjunction. Carter was 52 years old in October, 1976 and was therefore living through the 4th year of the 8th (Scorpio) 7-year period of his life. The events at this time therefore bear a strong relation to his use of this Scorpio power, the power born of identification (in this case with the American people). Carter's natal Moon and Saturn in the Sign Scorpio indicates his yearning to be identified with vast groups and with the deep currents molding human destiny. He wants to feel power, to be a channel through which the power generated by collective movements can be used for what he considers to be a creative and positive purpose. His success as President will depend on the quality of the purpose which he personally serves. Uranus transiting this Moon-Saturn pair provided a very real challenge to his personality, especially as transiting Neptune was approaching the conjunction to his natal Jupiter (exact between December 1976 and November 1977) at the same time. In other words, Uranus and Neptune were asking him to grow *beyond* success and satisfaction on "normal" levels of experience, and to give a new meaning, purpose and direction to his life. As President, he will hopefully direct this new purpose toward the life of the American people and nation in terms of some larger, more universal frame of reference than his personal (or the national) ego.

His presidency is meant to introduce a dynamic, positive, creative search for new, more encompassing values and goals. The personal and national ego must become more adaptable, less limited, and more willing to allow what appear alien elements to enter in. Through Carter, America could begin to question its belief that its own set of traditions and culture are inherently and spiritually superior to all others. He could open the country to the possibility of acting in unprecedented ways and of relating to other nations in terms of international, global values. The Scorpio period in the Uranus cycle is a "regenerative" phase which is meant to substantiate and strengthen whatever has reached fulfillment in the life during the preceding "Libra" period. October 1976-1977 being the 4th year of the 7-year period, the Scorpio trend touched bottom, so to speak. In the formula just presented, this is a period of conflict and struggle on Scorpio levels, a period of release of power and, because of his election to the Presidency, a consecration of efforts.

THE INDIVIDUAL URANUS CYCLE. Although transiting aspects from Uranus to one's natal planets refer to individual opportunities for growth, the more strictly individual meaning of the Uranus cycle is revealed by the planet's movement through the quadrants and Houses of a person's birth-chart. The House framework in humanistic astrology refers to individual factors because it is an expression of the axial rotation of the Earth — a movement peculiar to the planet Earth and therefore individual. The orbital revolution of the Earth around the Sun, on the other hand, has a collective significance, since it is a movement common to all the planets in our solar system. The Signs of the zodiac are an expression of this collective movement, referring to collective elements in human nature, elements common to all human beings. For this reason, humanistic astrology, which is a person-centered astrology, gives more importance to the Houses than to the Signs.

Analysis by quadrant is a basic technique in Rudhyar's humanistic approach to transits. It establishes a four-fold rhythm of spiritual unfoldment in terms of Uranus' natal House position. In this technique, the *individual* Uranus cycle begins at the time when it reaches the nearest Angle by transit. For example, if Uranus is posited in the natal 2nd House, the individual cycle will not begin until it reaches the Nadir.*

When Uranus Crosses the Ascendant and Transits the 1st House it creates a challenge to growth in essential being, in the quality and scope of one's life-purpose, and it demands an active change in one's personal outlook. This can be an inspired change based on a deeper perception of spiritual realities, or it may be a peculiar restlessness which makes one generally dissatisfied with the conditions of his life. At this time, an individual should develop intuition and be open to new ideas and new ventures. He should be ready to take the necessary steps to transform the present implications of his life and his relationship to society. In some cases, people tend to become fanatical, eccentric, anarchistic breakers of idols. They can radiate inspirational and exalting or disturbing and unsettling influences. Psychologically, a person should try to open him-

---

*See Chapter I, "The Humanistic Approach," for more on this topic.

self to the collective unconscious through dreams, meditation or other subjective means, to go beyond the conventional and traditional and to tap deeper resources within himself. Life now demands that one be himself with full independence. In that way one may give a new slant to accepted values and have the courage to break with the limiting factors in his present situation.

When Uranus Transits the 2nd House, a transforming energy begins to operate within a person's background through strange upsets or spectacular revelations, causing him to doubt the value of the existing order of things. All one has inherited is activated, and new powers may be revealed or new faculties manifest themselves. The challenge will be to *use* them fully and for a more significant purpose than before. A person at this time must find concrete means to substantiate the new vision shown by Uranus in the 1st House. He must concentrate his attention in those spheres where there seems to be a social demand for his physical, psychological or mental abilities; otherwise his desire to be "different" or "original" during the First House transit will never become socially effective. But he must be careful not to betray his new ideal just because the inertia of habits and social conventions creates obstacles. The strong personality *uses* these habits to demonstrate his vision — and thereby repolarizes them. The weak personality lets the collective habits use his vision, which thereby is distorted and materialized.

When Uranus Transits the 3rd House, the call to a new order affects one's everyday life and his mundane contacts with the environment. As one becomes aware that the trend begun by Uranus' transit of the 1st House is not automatically adapted to the conditions of his daily existence, one may develop nervous tension and restlessness of mind as he tries to adapt the new to the old. This transit is a decisive phase in a person's effort to incorporate new or deeper values. Either one proves himself capable of living a transformed life, or else he realizes that external circumstances are too strong for him to change. One must be prepared to change one's environment if necessary, or at least to change one's mental concepts. At this time one must discover new ways of being oneself, and one can see how the different parts of his personality are related to each other. One should not be afraid to provoke crises as he tries to demonstrate the new way of perceiving things and ideas which his Uranian vision requires. Such crises are necessary in order to make one aware of the practicality or impracticality of the way he has chosen to express his new truth. Thus he will learn to differentiate the utopian and ideal from the truly possible.

When Uranus Crosses the Nadir and Transits the 4th House, the time has arrived for one to express that part of his essential nature of which he has become conscious since Uranus crossed the Ascendant.

Habitual foundations and feelings can become quite unsettled as a result of the new impulse seeking expression within the personality. It may no longer be possible for one to hold on to his established home-life, for something appears to undermine the fundamental way in which he was taught to face society. Uranus in the 4th House can shake the ground from under one's feet. A person may be uprooted by war, revolution or social pressures, or by necessary changes of occupation, sudden losses, or conflicts with neighbors and family members. The important question now is how one will react. Perhaps the most important decision an individual can make under this transit is to change his desire for outer security into a desire for inner stability. To achieve this stability, the center of gravity of one's whole being must be shifted from the conscious ego to the Self. When one reaches the Self, he also reaches the common global center, the source of all truly dynamic and creative spiritual activity. If he manages to experience the center of his own personality as being one with the center of Humanity (which is one of the deepest messages of the 4th House), then his subjective awareness will take on a totally new quality. Instead of a non-adaptive and introverted being whose life is based on a passive participation in society, one will become a productive energy source, inspired by the center of all energy. One will constantly attempt to express through conscious living and creative activity what remains for most people a subjective and unconscious part of their total being. Uranus in the 4th House can be a taproot linking the conscious ego to the riches of the collective unconscious.

When Uranus Transits the 5th House, the possibilities will depend on the type of inner and outer stability gained during the 4th House transit. If a person has not yet found his individual center and is still ego-controlled in his expression, then this 5th House transit can be an upsetting factor leading to a loss of Self in illusory, utopian ideals or unsound speculations. If, during the earlier phases of this cycle, one has succeeded in transforming his personality sufficiently to give expression to more universally valid goals, then the 5th House transit will signal a time of creative action on a level which transcends tradition. It will then be possible to manifest one's true inner genius, inventiveness and originality. A person will act and create with the aim of *relating* himself to others in a significant manner, rather than simply *expressing* himself by projecting an image onto materials or other people. He will act purposefully and significantly in terms of the real needs of society, because his center is one with the center of all.

When Uranus Transits the 6th House, a person is apt to go through a personal crisis, either willingly or unwillingly. Because the way one relates or expresses himself in the 5th House is never perfect or final, in the 6th House he will likely feel a need to transform his manner of expression, to experiment with life, seek out new techniques and reorient himself toward the future. Continual readjustments to present social needs may become necessary, and this may involve sudden changes connected, for better or worse, with one's work. During this transit one must neutralize the causes of his past failures and inefficiencies in expression; he must overcome the final resistances so he may become a clear lens through which a higher state of being may be focused as Uranus crosses the Descendant. Whenever Uranus succeeds in its mission, the whole being and the whole life are utterly transformed. One is a different person after a Uranian visitation, and the future must be worked out in terms of this difference. This is the work of the 6th House transit.

When Uranus Crosses the Descendant and Transits the 7th House, a growth in one's power and sphere of influence should be evident. If a person has had a positive reaction to the Uranian energy, he will have the power to reform and regenerate society. He will meet the tests of objective life freely and courageously. One will make his relationships more spiritually significant by this ability to transform them. During this transit, many unexpected or inspiring experiences (love or hate, association or conflict) may completely upset a person's conception of what his established life-pattern should be like. Many readjustments will be necessary in order to meet the needs of the social whole. Nothing can remain crystallized; all past attitudes, contracts and patterns of interpersonal relationships are questioned. Uranus asks that one become inwardly free of set standards, of what seem to be clear-cut and obvious assumptions. For this reason, a person can become a disturbing influence in his relationships during this transit. He may, on the other hand, find that his relationships are upset by the independent or eccentric behavior of his partners.

When Uranus Transits the 8th House, one's capacity for self-renewal will be put to the test on very concrete levels. The world will now see the concrete results of the transformation process which began when Uranus crossed the Ascendant. These results can be either positive or negative; either the social and material effects of the process will be *strengthened,* or the effort to transform oneself will peter out through a lack of willpower, courage or faith. Ideally, this is the time to open new paths for the activities one engages in with associates and a time to transform habitual or customary procedures in business or group activities, to introduce new principles of conduct which will be less selfish and traditional, or to form associations for the sake of new and unusual purposes. This transit is not a time for utopian idealism, but for the *practical* working out of one's new vision of Self, relationship or business. The time for dreams and theories is over. A person must now *BE* what he has envisioned. One must *act* as a reformer and a creative pioneer, a founder of new precedents. Action in one's chosen spiritual or social field will be the only way to know the value of the vision he is trying to serve and to prove it to others. Even if a person should now experience the shattering of his ideals or suffer from adverse criticism, ostracism or social isolation, such experiences will teach him that he has not adapted to the reality of his times or taken the *real needs* of others into consideration in his actions. This can be a most useful acknowledgement for one's future development. Self and others, Self and society are in constant interaction. One will fail in his relationships if he puts too much emphasis on one pole of the relationship and disregards the other. He must learn, when Uranus transits the third quadrant, that it is the *relationship between* Self and others, between Self and society, which must be transformed, rather than either of the poles.

When Uranus Transits the 9th House, one has the opportunity to give a new and more creative *meaning* to his relationships through an attempt to discover the reason for his 8th House success or failure in social participation. One can discover new truths, new laws and new lands while trying to understand how and why he arrived at his present life condition. Under the stimulation of unfamiliar and even alien and disturbing ideas, this is the time for a change of mind and heart. It is a time of doubting the significance of one's relationships and the value of all that those relationships have produced. According to what criteria is one judging the value and significance of his love relationships or business partnerships and what they produced? What value do others place on one's personality since he plunged into the world of relationship as a transforming force when Uranus entered his 7th House? Such questions are important during the 9th House phase of the Uranus cycle, for one must find out for himself whether his relationships are meaningful to his destiny and whether his social or business activities are worthwhile to the community. Has one been behaving in a responsible manner in his relationships, or has he simply been drifting along in an unconscious manner? One's experiences during this 9th House transit can provide an answer to some of these questions, and the answer may not always be to one's liking. Nevertheless, if a person wants to expand constructively — spiritually, psychologically or socially — he must know where he stands as an individual, and personal goals must be grounded in reality.

When Uranus Crosses the Midheaven and Transits the 10th House, the scope of one's social and professional influence should grow. It is time to initiate progressive changes in his social or professional environment, and to inspire new trends. A person may be pushed to assume a role in some social, professional or national situation which puts him in the limelight, for better or worse. Since Uranus entered the 7th House, the efforts to share one's particular genius and vision with the world have had concrete results. In spite of social lies and personal fallacies confusing one's sense of Self and his spiritual goals in life, a person will be able to realize now how much of his true, individual nature he has been able to express through his social activities. Success, in terms of Uranus' transit of the 10th House, is not necessarily success in the eyes of the world. What matters most is one's ability to contribute his own personal truth to society as a result of personal fulfillment. In spite of outward success, if one feels personally empty, he can then be sure that he has not constructively followed the path of Uranus. Essentially, what matters is not a person's profession or the exact type of work he is engaged in, but rather what he can contribute to others and to his profession out of his own personality. If one has been working in the conscious, humanistic way with the Uranus cycle, then he has been trying to build a real place and function for himself in society ever since Uranus entered the 7th House. The test is one of creative participation — trying to become personally and socially more efficient in the use of one's creative power. When Uranus reaches the Midheaven, something may happen to make one grow beyond his *apparent* Saturnian limits. Society may then recognize one's individual capacity to assume collective power, and one may even experience a consecration of all his efforts towards this end.

When Uranus Transits the 11th House, there is a call to take the lead in cultural or social reform, to be the guide towards new collective goals. A person should dare to look for vaster horizons and give his attention to what may seem unusual or mysterious to most people. Building up one's faith in man's capacity to create a better future, he should interest himself in forward-looking groups or movements. If the 10th House transit led to a real achievement or mastery, then the 11th House transit will point to creative activity for some future-oriented, more-than-personal goal. A person must now prove his worth through the use he makes of the power, energy and experience acquired through his social or professional achievement in the 10th House. If the 10th House transit has had negative results, a person is likely to mobilize his rebellious energies *against* society and against the conditions and people he thinks are responsible for his failure. There is danger of destructive experiences and various forms of insanity or escape into an artificial paradise through drugs or alcohol. One may link his destiny to people or groups who desire to express their resentment or hostility. Foolhardy, violent acts and words at this time can lead to negative 12th House experiences.

When Uranus Transits the 12th House, the impatient search for new social values which began in the 11th House will continue. One must try to identify himself personally with collective attempts at social reorganization. He can be vested with dramatic responsibilities toward society, and can receive unexpected recompenses for his past achievements. Psychologically, this is the final phase in the cycle of Uranian transformation. Those forces of transformation have been working out what a person is capable of realizing ever since the 1st House beginning of the cycle. They have led to concrete results, both personal and social, during the 10th House transit. Then, in the 11th House, Uranian "action" became most evident. Through the 12th House transit, the impulse to transformation begins to die out. By accepting the failures, as well as the successes, of one's rebellion in the 11th House, the cycle must be brought to a significant conclusion.

As Uranus ends its cycle, the need for personal and social transformation is no longer so important. A *new need* for transformation is looming on the horizon, and it becomes increasingly necessary to change one's orientation. Attention must not be hypnotically focused on one's past success or failure to work with Uranus' transforming energy. He must instead prepare for some new revelation. Like John the Baptist, one must will himself to be reborn, in spite of the knowledge of his shortcomings and also in spite of his success in some particular set of circumstances established by the cycle now ending. Uranus is the planet of "divine discontent". It makes a person dissatisfied with his achievements and helps him to realize the inadequacy of the methods he has used to arrive at his present condition. In the 12th House, then, Uranus will expand the value of what one has realized by showing that this accomplishment is not an end in itself, but only a first step, a turn of the spiral, leading to ever-greater accomplishments and realizations. One must now gear his consciousness to the means at his disposal to transform and renew his habitual life-pattern. The spiritual essence which has animated the closing cycle is now seeking to be reborn in another form. One will have another chance to express it in a new way, provided the weight of unfulfilled expectations does not obscure his vision.

THE IMPORTANCE OF NATAL SATURN IN AN EVALUATION OF URANUS AND NEPTUNE TRANSITS. In different ways, both Uranus and Neptune challenge everything that Saturn stands for. If an astrologer does not know the level on which the Saturnian ego of an individual is operating, he cannot constructively interpret the progressive challenges of Uranus and Neptune transits throughout the life. The first thing to know about an individual's Saturn is whether it is functioning through an established tradition, culture, or religion of which the individual is only a passive part or whether it operates as an individualizing power. In the first case, the two universal planets can hardly be said to work on an individual basis, for the person is not yet individualized. Their transits will therefore measure *external* events aiming at the destruction of a limiting Saturnian order. Through some form of upheaval the person may be shocked into an effort toward individualization. In the second case, when Saturn represents a strong conscious ego, these outer planets can measure his attempts at individual metamorphosis happening *within* his personality. In this second case, however, the astrologer must also distinguish between the rigid ego which is still closed to all new things or to whatever does not seem logical and right (while at the same time being proud of that rigidity) and the type of ego consciousness which is firmly structured, but which is also an open window to the world within and without.

The complexity of the situation would render it foolish to attempt to outline fixed meanings for the transit cycles of these two outer planets which would be true for everyone. Additionally, when dealing with progressions and transits, the natal chart must be maintained as the most important basis of the astrologer's deductions. *Nothing* can come from the progressions or transits which is not already present, in seed form, in the birth-chart. It is very difficult, moreover, to decide whether a person's Saturn, Uranus and Neptune are likely to manifest in a positive or negative manner in his life. If that person and his or her birth-chart are well-known, certain tendencies and potentials can be surmised; however, even then the results of their action are always uncertain. One must first study the natal situation, paying particular attention to the Saturn-Uranus and Sun-Uranus aspects. Even if no aspects are found, the astrologer should note the *phase* of their relationship on the basis established by Rudhyar in *The Lunation Cycle*. However, this must be done in a very particular way. The usual manner of analysing a phase is to take the aspect made by the faster moving of the two planets to the slower moving planet, as one takes the aspects of the Moon to the Sun in the lunation cycle. This is the valid procedure in both progressions and transits where one is dealing with moving objects. The birth-chart, however, is a structure in space. It represents the archetypal form of an individual for a given life-time, and thus Rudhyar speaks of it as a mandala. Because of this, aspects can be taken in *both* directions, and it is no longer a question of which planet is the faster. In other words, if there is a natal square between Sun in Cancer and Uranus in Libra, this square can be analysed as a "first quarter phase" square of Uranus to Sun, or a "last quarter phase" square of Sun to Uranus.

In the first case, the person would be trying to find out how Uranus *releases* solar power on a universal level, and how a freedom from environmental influences and a crystallized ego-attitude can best be obtained. As it is a first quarter square, it can be concluded that actional crises which occur as one attempts to establish himself in the community will be the means to bring about a confrontation between universal goals and the status quo. In the second case, the astrologer would be studying the mechanisms through which Uranus functions. The waning aspect indicates how the Sun specifically contributes to Uranus' operation within the personality, and the effect of the Sun on all Uranian activity. As this relationship is shown to be a last quarter square, the transforming Uranian action would be conditioned by the capacity of the solar purpose. This would then precipitate a crisis in consciousness leading to a revision of values and a reconsideration of conscious motives. In terms of our present aim, which is to discover how Uranus might operate in a given life, the Sun should be considered as the "positive" factor and Uranus the "lunar" factor. Thus, its phase relationship to the Sun is that of a first quarter or waxing square.

In considering the Saturn-Uranus relationship, Saturn must be taken as the "positive" or solar factor, and Uranus as the "lunar" factor, because we want to discover how Uranus challenges what Saturn stands for. Therefore, if Saturn is found in Cancer squaring Uranus in Libra, the Uranus challenge would produce crises in action. Such crises test the validity and the strength of a person's Saturnian structural integrity at some level. Circumstances can upset his sense of security or his place in life accorded him by the social standing of his family. Psychologically, things can happen which would shatter his ego-pride and his intellectual concepts, forcing him through experiences which might be painful, to restructure his consciousness according to new and less limiting values. Such an analysis is, of course, very schematic. It is impossible to give standardized cookbook meanings to planets and aspects which would be true for any and every real-life situation. Furthermore, an astrologer must not limit himself to only the study of Uranus-Sun and Uranus-Saturn aspects. He must make a complete study of the birth-chart, noticing all the other aspects to Saturn as well. The purpose of mentioning these examples has been to make it quite clear that the interpretation of the transit cycles of Uranus and Neptune are dependent on the level at which Saturn functions in a given case. Going further into detail is not within the scope of this book and would lead too far afield from the subject of transit cycles.

This much can be added, however: the present crisis between generations is a direct result of the current trend to extol the individual. As each young person tries to "do his thing", everything which Saturn establishes on social levels, and which is necessary to an orderly, organized social and cultural life, is no longer seen as a positive mold within which to establish one's activities. Saturn can take on the oppressive role of taskmaster or judge, symbolizing all those *external* forces which limit one's freedom of action. Of course, if the young person is not at all interested in "doing his thing" and adapts himself harmoniously to the established life-patterns of society, then although Saturn may be "harmonious", it will not be working in an individualized manner. On the other hand, when a person rebels against the collective aspect of Saturn, then Saturn can potentially become an individualized energy force, a symbol of his personal ego-structure. In that case, the Saturn problem in one's life will change. The quality of his ego-structure will be totally different after he has freed himself from Saturn's external social rule. He may become a proud individualist, forcing himself onto the world through Mars. He may, on the other hand, manage to remain open to the world and use his Saturn energy as a focusing lens for Uranian inspirations. Unless this second alternative exists, Uranian and Neptunian crises will strike from without through collective events aimed at changing the Saturnian social order. There will be nothing he can do about it, unless such collective events, revolutions, wars or economic crises awaken his latent will-power and force him to take a clear individual stand. One cannot determine which of these two alternatives will apply merely by looking at an individual's natal chart.

The Saturn-Uranus Cycle

Uranus is the symbol of everything that disrupts the normal patterns of action and reaction, feeling and thought. It is that force in life which obliges a person to realize that world conditions change, and that human needs also become different as a result. Psychological growth necessarily requires a ceaseless process of self-transformation and self-questioning, upsetting one's static ego security. Uranus is a constant reminder that spiritual living is not essentially a lovely, devotional attitude toward lofty ideals and transcendent experiences, but rather the *incorporation* of a new life-attitude, a new way of meeting the challenges presented in both the outer and inner environment.

The contacts between Saturn and Uranus reveal the constructive value of inconsistency. Both social and personal needs change, and an individual who is open to the creative forces of his inner being will, through Uranus, answer these needs with a new attitude or a new kind of behavior. The challenge to become a greater and more inclusive individual is usually felt at the crucial turning-points in this cycle. At such times, the "greater" initially tends to appear as the enemy of the status-quo. Therefore, if the challenge is accepted, one must inevitably break with his traditions on some level of existence. He must become strong enough emotionally to follow a line of thought or action which may not fit into his habitual life-pattern. He must be strong in the faith that the present inconsistency is the threshold of some new order of consistency for the future. Symbolically, then, he must pit Uranus against Saturn. Habit patterns will always resist change; and when the pressure of some creative challenge is felt, the ego will experience a sense of impending doom, generating fear and resisting change. The ego is the Saturnian structure of man's consciousness. It is the expression of one's capacity for consistency in behavior, and it is the foundation of one's conscious sense of "I". Although a consistent ego-structure is obviously necessary, the tendency will be to crystallize such a structure, making it more difficult to adapt to new situations which challenge one's established viewpoint. The more rigid the ego, the sharper the break must be in the end. If a crucial phase of the Saturn-Uranus cycle coincides with some overwhelming emotional crisis, the cause will always be the rigid inertia of social customs, privileges, personal habits or assumed behavior patterns which resist the call of the creative spirit within.

A characteristic quality of this present century is precisely this Uranian challenge to everything for which Saturn stands. Everywhere, and in all societies, there is a gradual and sometimes violent break-down of social, religious and cultural forms and customs. This inevitably leads to a break-down of many egos which are unable to contain the energy of new, creative forces. For this reason, the current cycles of Uranus and Saturn often have a disruptive effect. The main problem facing each individual during the crucial phases of these cycles is, "How can he *constructively use* the creative Uranian power which is challenging the inertia and security of his ego?" As a corollary, one must also face the challenge to contribute wisely to this process of social change which these crucial phases of the Saturn-Uranus cycle measure. It will be important, in either case, to avoid the twin evils of either a dependence on or a return to the past, or an over-radical transformation which would destroy that part of the past which is essential to the future.

The Saturn-Uranus cycle spans approximately 45 1/2 years. There was a triple conjunction in 1897 at 30 degrees Taurus (conjunct the Pleiades). A third triple conjunction will occur in 1988 affecting 29-30 degrees Sagittarius. The present cycle, which began in May, 1942, is the one affecting people today. Its *waxing square* was reached on December 8, 1952, at 14 degrees Libra-Cancer; on April 18, 1952, at 11 degrees Libra-Cancer; and for a third time on October 15, 1952, at 18 degrees Libra-Cancer. The *opposition* phase occurred on April 1, 1965, at 12 Pisces-Virgo; August 29, 1965, at 15 Pisces-Virgo; and a third time on February 24, 1966, at 19 Pisces-Virgo. The *waning square* was exact twice during October, 1975 — on the 4th at 2 degrees Leo-Scorpio and on the 17th at 3 degrees Leo-Scorpio. A third waning square followed on July 2, 1976, at 4 degrees Leo-Scorpio. At the conjunction Uranus, the rebel, the projector of images and force of divine discontent, will tend to break barriers and pierce wide windows in the fortified walls of an individual's Saturn ego. It arouses a yearning for that which is beyond *anything* connected with

Saturn, and it brings restlessness to those who are inclined to conform to normal social behavior. Complacency will be upset, as will the feeling that one is living rightly only if and when he conforms to the socially established rules of the game.

The basic challenge of the Saturn-Uranus conjunction of 1942 to an individual's social status and personal philosophy reached a climax in 1951-52 at the time of the waxing square and a final consummation at the opposition in 1965-66. Great things can happen at these turning-points, although perhaps through disturbing or cathartic challenges. At the time of this writing, the waning square phase of this cycle has just passed. The Uranus transformation of personal egos and social class identification, and of habitual and heretofore presumed logical patterns of thought and action, should produce a crisis in consciousness leading to a revision of values and motives. This is the time to correct past mistakes and focus on the future. Thus, one may be better prepared to meet the new creative forces which will be released at the conjunction in 1988. The only way to prepare oneself for the challenges of the Saturn-Uranus cycle is by total acceptance of the fact that resistance to change is always useless in the final analysis and represents a simple refusal to grow psychologically and spiritually. This must not, however, be interpreted to mean that one must accept any and all changes which present themselves. A sense of discrimination must be used. At the same time, however, a person must keep himself open to any challenge which may lead to a greater maturity by opening the Saturnian ego-structure to the inflow of new and creative energies.

THE SATURN-URANUS CYCLE IN THE HOUSES. The natal (or solar) House in which the transiting Saturn-Uranus conjunction falls will indicate the field of experience where one might expect upsets, and where much of what a person previously thought settled and firm is questioned. The House position also indicates where an individual is most open to and in need of social, spiritual or psychological transformation. For the duration of the cycle, that particular natal or solar House will be the focal point for the challenges which life presents to one's ego-inertia and conservatism. The experiences of that House will present both the basic problem and the opportunity for its solution.

In the 1st House, the current challenge to one's habits and attitude has a personal significance and can lead to restlessness and nervous indecision. There is an impatience with present conditions and a general dissatisfaction with oneself. One wants to feel different, to be another person. Inconsistencies appear in one's behavior, and people may say that he is not himself. At this time a person must not lose touch with his personal integrity, no matter what change he wishes to introduce into his life. The challenge is to remain firm and centered, even while opening the consciousness to the new, and this can lead to a larger sense of integration and harmony.

In the 2nd House, this conjunction can indicate impatience with one's habitual patterns of giving substance and form to his individuality. A person may no longer be satisfied with his present use of mental abilities or other inherited gifts. Yet a restless search for a new mode of expressing thoughts and feelings can lead to a hasty repudiation of something one has depended on for spiritual, personal, financial or social substance. The danger here is of casting aside something which will be necessary later as a foundation for a new departure.

In the 3rd House, it may be necessary to learn that logic and know-how are a means rather than an end in themselves. It is advantageous to have a well-ordered daily schedule and relate to the environment in an organized manner, provided one's mind remains daring enough to create. Unsure egos and literal minds, people who cling to social and traditional standards, may find this transit upsetting. Any current feeling of mal-adjustment to the environment means that one must now get out of a rut to avoid battering circumstances.

In the 4th House, this conjunction will be experienced on the level where a person feels most comfortably secure, either in his home or in his strongest convictions. That is the place to begin one's self-renewal. Challenges will enable one to grow stronger provided he is willing to doubt the absolute certainty of his present foundations. What happens will often unsettle everything which is firmly established. There may be a change of residence or the desire to modernize one's home. Young people may break away from the security and influence of their parents, hopefully without repudiating them too violently.

In the 5th House, a personal crisis involving the development of one's creative capacities can arise at this time. One's pride in past accomplishments may be rudely shocked. If the ego is open to inspiration and ready to allow the greater life to act *through* him, then one's creative self-expression will gain in meaning. It will be better to risk all and lose than to stagnate in fear.

In the 6th House, a stimulation of the will to be renewed and of the power to accomplish reforms will be felt. What one sets in motion now can enable him to achieve real personal maturity. He should learn new ways of doing things or circumstances may oblige him to do so. The more ready one is to welcome change — on the job, in one's daily routine, in his diet, or in some other manifestation of self-discipline — the more likely he will be to avoid ill health or some unnecessary psychological crisis. A person should not be afraid to experiment and to seek new techniques of living.

In the 7th House, there is a call for a love which will transfigure the narrow and petty limitations of one's purely egocentric attitudes. This is the time to forget one's habitual patterns of relating to others. A person should break out of his narrow circle of acquaintances, meet new people, and overcome the fear which has formed a barrier to accepting the social opportunities which arise. Personal security should not be placed above one's interpersonal relationships. On the other hand, it would be unwise to throw all convention to the winds or try to overcome one's fear of others by aggressively breaking in where angels fear to tread.

In the 8th House, one's individualistic and perhaps ego-centric use of social power or inherited wealth may receive a rude shock following this conjunction. It is no longer possible to feel the same way about the fruits of one's business activities or intimate relationships. Although one need not break relationships or leave his business, his *attitude* toward them is in need of revision, as are his expectations of the value he anticipates they will produce.

In the 9th House, the Saturn-Uranus conjunction can indicate a time when conditions are ripe for a clean break with religious or social traditions. Uranus offers the opportunity for religious conversion, calling one to wider horizons and helping him see the value of his relationships in a new light. A person should heed this call if he wants to avoid upsets. A long journey may be at the center of the situation.

In the 10th House, one arrives at a critical turning-point in his career, often brought on by a restless dissatisfaction and yearning for change. One should act not on sudden impulse, but only after having weighed the objective *needs* of the situation or of the people involved in a dispassionate manner. A person must clearly understand the relationship which exists between the objective situation and his own past actions. This applies equally to his contacts with individuals and with society at large. Only through an understanding of this relationship of past to present will the future trend be determined.

In the 11th House, one should question his cherished ideals and social connections and consider inaugurating a new way of life. This is the time to grow beyond conventional patterns of behavior and stress individual qualities rather than class standards. On the other hand, there is no point in forcing issues or rushing into projects which are too risky or impractical. If conventional friendships are holding one back, he should not be afraid to break them if such a decision might lead to a participation in a spiritually and socially more significant type of life.

In the 12th House, the desire to make a break with some karmic condition which seems excessively binding, or to free oneself from the set of conditions which holds one to an established social or spiritual pattern may be very compelling and can lead to explosive behavior. Yet, making a sudden and forceful break without understanding the meaning of past experiences will not enable one to start a new cycle in a constructive manner. A synthesis of the past, of the results of one's social and professional success and failure, and also the methods employed to attain those results, must now be built into a seed for the future cycle. A person must seek the inspiration and the vision necessary to shape all these conditions inherited from the past into new ends, ideally at a higher level of activity.

The Jupiter-Uranus Cycle

The division of the 84-year Uranus cycle into seven 12-year periods establishes a correspondence with the 11.8 year cycle of Jupiter. This relationship of Jupiter to Uranus also manifests in what Rudhyar calls the "Great Cycle of Uranus" which lasts approximately 1004 years (12 revolutions of Uranus around the Sun). If one multiplies the Jupiter cycle by the Uranus cycle (11.8 x 84) the total is 991. In Rudhyar's view, this Great Cycle of Uranus, which is very close to a millenium, is the archetypal cycle of the process of Civilization as it affects the entire human species. Multiples of several of the cycles linking the outer planets add up to a number close to a millenium. Two Neptune-Pluto cycles total approximately 984 2/3 years; twenty-two Saturn-Uranus cycles comprise 998 years; and fifty Jupiter-Saturn cycles add up to 983 years. Every time Uranus conjoins Jupiter, a new trend toward social, cultural, religious and psychological transformation begins in the world. The challenge is, of course, worldwide and addressed to all nations and all forms of social organization. At that time, changes in world conditions become *necessary* and everyone must participate in them. The House in which these conjunctions fall identifies the circumstances or experiences in which it will be most necessary to introduce changes in behavior, feeling and thought. Also, the House position indicates how one may be able to play a significant part in the impending transformation.

In other words, the natal (or solar) House in which the conjunction of Jupiter and Uranus falls determines the principal focus of those challenges to the accepted cultural values for the next fourteen years (the duration of the cycle). However much the challenges appear to be external, and however much physical energy may be demanded to meet them, what the conjunctions actually instigate is a rebellion against *one's own bondage* to the values which condition one's personal behavior and viewpoint. The challenge will not be met if one simply tries to adapt *outwardly* to the new circumstances. There must also be an *inner* change in order to grow as an individual. The impact of these opportunities for growth will reach a critical phase at the time of the waxing square, and will culminate at the opposition, when the full meaning of what was at stake can finally become clear. At that time one may simply discover that he has not been able to orient himself properly to the challenging events or inner realizations born at the conjunction. At the opposition an attempt must be made to view the confrontation and experiences which have developed in a truly objective light, unemotionally and with complete intellectual honesty. Then in the waning half of the cycle, a critical re-evaluation of purpose will occur at the "last quarter" square. It will unfold on the basis of what one has understood, evaluated, and fully accepted at the opposition.

THE JUPITER-URANUS CYCLE IN THE HOUSES. The natal or solar House in which this conjunction falls every fourteen years will indicate the area of life in which one may expect to find Uranian transformation of one's Jupiter social sense. In this individualized application of the cycle, one should also note the Houses in which the opposition and the waxing and waning squares fall.

> **In the 1st House,** this conjunction indicates that the new trend toward social and psychological transformation can find a channel for expression in a personal way. One will be challenged to change some aspect of the social, cultural or religious fields which particularly interest one and in which he can play a significant role. New social or religious trends or economic opportunities (perhaps even political openings) can now radically transform the quality and the implications of the personality. A new popularity can lead to personal expansion, provided one does not set out too recklessly on some revolutionary path. The personality should radiate a

dynamic enthusiasm, although fanaticism should be avoided. The creative forces of spirit are seeking expressions and one should be prepared to overcome the conservative limitations of his habitual conscious attitude and allow these forces to reorient the ego.

In the 2nd House, new trends in the social and economic fields can stir a person to develop latent resources. The conjunction will signal a revision of ancestral and inherited prejudices or traditions. One should not burn old bridges too ruthlessly, however, because the matter confronting him now is not as simple as he may have thought. Important financial developments, which may be unexpected if not actually unfavorable, are likely. A person should take a fresh look at what he has inherited, both materially and psychologically, discovering new ways to use what he has in order to affirm his personal uniqueness of being.

In the 3rd House, experiences can test one's willingness to meet the trials of daily life with more expansiveness and enthusiasm. One should be open to inspirations which could lead to a better adjustment to circumstances. Some relative or influential neighbor can be responsible for an important change. The strong personality may release a compelling and regenerative vision capable of transforming the environment. Any kind of writing and intellectual activity is favoured. The more one is dedicated to a work transcending one's own personality, the more brilliance and originality the mind should have.

In the 4th House, important developments can take place in one's home life, or in one's manner of emotional expression. He feels better able to establish himself on broader foundations, provided he is able to break with family traditions and personal fears. Experiences at this time can move one to the very depths of his being and can force a person to exteriorize feelings long held within the subconscious. Real estate matters may prove particularly exciting.

In the 5th House, great speculative vision can enable one to take a more creative and inspiring approach to anything dealing with self-expression, education or love. Some people, however, will have to watch their emotional impulses lest they become carried away. Events may be thrilling; romance and speculation can captivate; however, there is also a danger of losing all sense of perspective. One can take a chance, but only if his foundations are good. Rich experiences, and especially an intensification of one's deepest psychological and spiritual nature, can bring revelations to the artist, the true mystic, and also to the humanistic astrologer.

In the 6th House, unusual work opportunities may appeal. One may be exceptionally enthusiastic about one's job or the cause he serves. One should apply himself with zeal and not be afraid to learn new techniques or to change his established line of work or daily routine. What is needed most is an eagerness to learn new things, to improve oneself technically and psychologically, even if this entails a crisis. A powerful social or religious influence can bring great inspiration, if a person is not afraid of the unusual. At this time a person should act with the greatest sense of spiritual dedication he can muster.

In the 7th House, interpersonal relationships of an intimate character or of great importance to one's social progress can exert an inspirational influence. One must be willing to learn new lessons in cooperation and sharing which should take the place of personal ambition and possessiveness. In some cases, an influential partner may push one to expand, perhaps too forcibly and hastily. One should not be afraid to change his relationships if the opportunity arises, since what now comes through others may be highly stimulating. The strong personality can now act truly as a reformer in his relationships and set in motion activities of a socially and spiritually significant nature. Traditional attitudes and crystallized habits must be questioned and nothing taken for granted, in oneself or in others, if one would progress constructively.

In the 8th House, the challenge of Jupiter-Uranus is to approach one's business life and everything that results from one's relationships (especially marriage) in a freer and more imaginative manner. There may be a need for changes or new partnerships, or else present circumstances bring one in touch with unusual social conditions or groups working along untried paths. One's career can benefit from such unfamiliar contacts. In some cases, there may be the possibility of unexpectedly large gains through inheritance which might enable one to enlarge the scope of his social or business activities.

In the 9th House, the time has come to widen one's interest through travel, philosophical or religious study, and to develop new mental or spiritual faculties. One might meet people of importance during a long journey who bring a great deal of inspiration to his life. Stirring messages may arrive either through the mail or from within one's own awakened consciousness. They can compel him to dissolve many of his inhibitions and to develop a new form of social expression. A person should try to achieve the most universal view-point possible without setting off too recklessly upon revolutionary paths. He should keep himself in contact with his real and concrete base of operations, as he can now be easily overwhelmed by thoughts or ideals which are essentially foreign to his nature. Constructive expansion — spiritually, psychologically or socially — will depend on how objectively one views his true place and capacity. In this way a person's desires for achievement may be based on reality instead of dreams.

In the 10th House, this transit may signal a high tide period in one's career or public life. He may receive some striking spiritual or professional inspiration which can lead to new authority and responsibilities. Strong regenerative urges bring radical changes in one's social or professional environment. This can be a time of public consecration of all one has worked for both socially and spiritually. Society may at last recognize the value of his individual contributions. Grandiloquent gestures, however, are to be avoided. A uniquely personal ambition to increase one's public standing can put one on the spot. On the other hand, the socially or politically oriented individual could now use his public prestige and position in order to further the social transformations revealed necessary at this time.

In the 11th House, a revolutionary trend requires changes on social, political and economic levels. When this conjunction falls in the 11th House, a person is asked to align himself with new ideals and aspirations affecting the larger social issues of the times. He is called to support those people or groups who are actively working toward the needed transformations. An expanded social consciousness can result from the company of a friend of wealth or social accomplishment who urges one on.

In the 12th House, the challenge is to develop a more creative and imaginative attitude toward one's past and one's community. Psychologically, social or religious complexes may now come to the surface and dominate one's behavior. Such an occurrence will undoubtedly be strenuous; however it can also give one an opportunity to see what is really happening in his innermost nature and thereby to transform it consciously. A person should open himself to the inner voice, trying to expand his consciousness through introspection or meditation. Important messages may come through people who have spiritual gifts, or through one's own awakened psychic faculties. On material levels, a person may receive unexpected rewards for services rendered in the past. Anyone able to divorce the past and break through his traditional, racial molds of consciousness can now take an important step forward.

IX

The Neptune Cycle

Neptune is the complement of Uranus and together they show how the Saturn-conditioned personality, influenced by a *particular* geographical and social environment, can become a spirit-conditioned individual able to organize his life according to a universal reality. These two planets refer to more-than-individual factors in the life: Uranus represents the vision of the greater whole of which each of us is a part; Neptune refers to the effort at collective organization on the basis of maximum inclusiveness. Neptune substantiates what Uranus envisions. Neither Uranus nor Neptune may be classed as fortunate or unfortunate, good or bad. They simply reveal the challenge which forever directs the individual to grow in inclusiveness and harmony. Uranus and Neptune cannot function positively in a life unless that person is consciously aware of the larger frame of reference which they identify and feels himself an essential part of that greater whole. The negative interpretation given to Neptune by so many astrologers will be true in all those cases in which the Saturn-ego is incapable of recognizing and living by the universal values which Neptune symbolizes. Thus, according to Rudhyar, negative Neptune is a compensation for unwholesome and frustrated living. This occurs when a person becomes a slave to collective enthusiasms, demands, or standards of morality.

The myriad of artificial paradises symbolized by the negative aspect of Neptune — the confusion, glamour, self-deception, illusion, and the various escapes into drugs and alcohol — are all due to an individual's refusal to face the totality of his life situation. There is always a tendency to isolate desired elements out of one's total experience of life, and then to exaggerate their importance in relation to elements that are considered undesirable but which are, nonetheless, part of the total experience. In such cases, when one surrenders his will through fear of having to confront something undesirable, he becomes incapable of acting as an integrated whole. While negative Neptune will always strive to *exclude* some part of total reality, positive Neptune will endeavor to *include* EVERYTHING. This is why Marc Jones saw Neptune as representing the individual's responsibility or obligation to society, or to any group he belongs to. Rudhyar interpreted this effort toward total inclusiveness as a person's ability to participate or lead in the building of physical, psychological and social structures through which the largest number of possible elements are integrated.

NEPTUNE AND THE COLLECTIVE DESTINY. There are two approaches to the interpretation of the three trans-Saturnian planets: from the individual to the collective, and from the universal to the particular. These parallel the involutionary and evolutionary tides described in Chapter 4, "The Personal Planets." In terms of an individual destiny, this tide flows from the Sun outward to Pluto and beyond, while in terms of man's collective destiny the tide flows in the opposite direction. Thus, when working from the universal to the particular, we find new factors are introduced to humanity as a whole through Pluto, the most remote of the three universal planets. This energy is then stepped down through Neptune and Uranus.*

These three planets refer then to the form which the destiny of the collective will take at a given time in history. That form will impose itself on the individual destiny of each person living at that time. The "Hippie" generation offers a good illustration of this process. Their rebellion against the Establishment was not a rebellion of individuals, but the rebellion of an age-group. The members of that group organized themselves into a caste of non-conformists, while at the same time conforming quite strictly to rigid group-patterns of behavior, dress and even language. They felt compelled, in their search for something stable and secure to adhere to, to group themselves together in conformity to their self-imposed "non-conforming" rules. Where this revolt against the established society mentality did not succeed or became overwhelmingly futile, there was a general escape from reality through drugs. Thus an entire generation sought to lose itself in an artificial, chemically induced paradise. Astrologically, this trend is linked to the conjunction of Uranus and Pluto in Virgo sextile Neptune in Scorpio which remained in orb from 1963 through 1968.

To approach these three universal planets from an individual point of view, the astrologer must see them as the three basic steps on the path of transformation. Together they enable each person to emerge from the level of purely egocentric behavior and to reach an identification with his true Self. They describe the evolutionary tide of individual manifestation beginning with Uranus and reaching toward Pluto and beyond. The first step on this path of transformation is the feeling of complete dissatisfaction with things as they are. This dissatisfaction, however, must not exist because of a desire for self-aggrandizement, which is the Jupiterian urge to possess more in the way of material goods and to become a more powerful ego. It must be a dissatisfaction with the *quality* of one's life and the personal aims and goals which one has set himself. It is a "divine discontent" born of a desire to become "more than man" on one's normal level of functioning. This is the Uranian dis-

---

*Cf. Rudhyar's *The Sun Is Also a Star*, Dutton, N.Y. p.87.

satisfaction which can lead one to try to transcend the habitual and the traditional, and to reach toward some "beyond", toward some greater realm of consciousness and being. If an individual acts as a result of Uranian dissatisfaction, a crisis is bound to occur, because everything established under Saturn will resist the necessary change. As Uranus indicates the desire to change as a result of one's vision of new possibilities of a transcendent nature, it "influences" a person especially on mental levels, through radically new and challenging ideas.

Neptune, on the other hand, is the pole of the transformation process which more particularly affects one's basic feelings, one's sense of value in what he does and thinks. A person can suddenly open himself to a new Uranian vision and yet be unable to act out that vision because of fear and insecurity. In such a case, Neptune will have to act on Saturn, dissolving those Saturnian limitations and fears by exposing one to the glamourous dreams and visions of some sort of mystical transmutation. One must not only *think* that the new step envisioned by Uranus is the right thing for him to do, he must also *feel* that it is necessary. He must yearn for the new state and have complete faith in his capacity to reach it. Then Pluto can reveal the third step, the need to *act*. That action will be grounded in Uranian vision and Neptunian faith. Thus, with the determination to dedicate oneself, as an individual rather than a conforming member of a group, one may come to a full participation in the life of his society or, religiously speaking, to an accordance with the "will of God".

Such an individualized use of the universal planets only applies in those cases where the Saturnian ego is ready to open itself to a greater all-encompassing reality. For the majority of people, these planets refer primarily to a collective destiny, indicating by their position in the birth-chart the way in which one can or will react to collective fate. With regard to these planets, only a few individuals *act*, while the rest merely *react*. In this respect, the astrologer must not think of collective fate only in spectacular terms such as wars, revolutions, political violence, epidemics, earthquakes and the like. The mundane conditions of one's social environment are also an expression of collective destiny. The danger inherent in automobile traffic is just as much a collective phenomenon as a tidal wave. The pollution of our waters, the contamination of our food, the poisoning of the air we breathe and the constant danger from radio-active contamination are the conditions of life into which we were all born. The endemic famine so prevalent in the under-developed countries, as well as the slum conditions existing in cities throughout the affluent world, are also expressions of collective fate. Everywhere today societies force collective tragedies upon a large number of individuals for social, religious or political reasons. People are tortured, either psychologically or physically, for their beliefs and convictions. This, too, is a form of collective fate.

All of these expressions of Man's collective fate influence each individual even if he is not personally suffering from it in an evident fashion. They establish a collective challenge to which each person has the responsibility to contribute what he can toward the solution. The problems which humanity has are the result of the world-view which humanity has adopted, either consciously or unconsciously. Neptune is the clearest indicator of the manner in which the individual feels the power of collective destiny. It is the planet of social obligation in Marc Jones' terms. Thus, when Neptune is prominent in a birth-chart, the fulfillment of the individual destiny will depend in large measure on the way in which that individual reacts, either physically or psychologically, to the pressures of collective fate. This reaction, however, need not necessarily result in negative experiences. That person can become a hero or a leader just as easily as a victim or a martyr.

More specifically, in a birth-chart or by transit, Neptune tends to *unfocus whatever function of the body or the psyche is represented by the Sign and the planets* involved. Neptune unfocuses because its task is to dissolve the well-defined boundaries established by Jupiter and Saturn. Thus, whatever Neptune touches can no longer have the value it had before the contact. Security and self-assuredness are undermined; irrational and unconscious elements in the personality invade the conscious ego, dissolving everything that was previously thought and felt to be solid, reliable and valid in one's life. The result of this dissolving process will depend on what unconscious, universal or collective elements invade the conscious ego. This "what" cannot be foreseen by astrological means, although the individual's level of consciousness will make or break the total personality.

Psychologically, Neptune replaces what is familiar, secure and limited with unfamiliar and vaster values to which the person may be inclined to surrender himself. The feelings are stirred by a deep yearning for what is beyond the familiar, and one dreams great dreams of a more perfect world, and of greater joy in human relationships based on compassion and universal love. If an individual reacts to Neptune in a negative way, then the planet will indicate the attempt to escape from the boredom and limitations of the Saturnian world through drugs, alcohol, sex, or by dreaming one's life away. It can also indicate the escape from personal responsibility through the loss of Self in some collective movement or religious group which makes all the decisions for the individual. Many contemporary political and religious movements currently popular with the younger generation — Marxism-Leninism, Maoism, the myriad of terrorist groups, such religious groups as the Unification Church (Reverend Sun Yung Moon) and the Hari-Krishna movement — are primarily a negative reaction to Neptune; they seek a leveling of social distinctions, a loss of the individual in the collective, or they recognize the use of violence or deceit to attain their ends. Mediumship is also a negative Neptune phenomenon in that the individual gives himself up to unconscious forces instead of being a *conscious* intermediary.

The Neptune Generations

Every age group approaches the solution to personal and social problems in a particular way. The approach is conditioned principally by cultural and social influences in the environment when one was born and is reflected in one's parents' behavior, and in the socio-economic and political pressures which mold one's early life. Neptune and Pluto, through their transit of the Signs, indicate the type of approach which will be adopted by a given age group in order to solve its life problems. Thus, the passage of Pluto through a Sign and of Neptune through two consecutive Signs (positive and negative) astrologically describe the phenomenon of generations. The *conscious* approach taken collectively by a generation to solve the problems with which it is confronted is shown by the Signs through which these two planets are passing *at the time the problem arises*. The natal Sign positions of Neptune and Pluto, on the other hand, show the sort of irrational energies within the collective unconscious which are being activated. In other words, the *root* of a problem or crisis (which takes on the characteristics of the Sign through which Neptune is transiting) is to be found in the meaning of *natal* Neptune's Sign.

Neptune in Gemini — 1888-89 to 1901-02. The collective trend of this transit is also the foundation for the current 500-year Neptune-Pluto cycle which began with the conjunction of those two planets in 1891-92 at 9 Gemini. In this Sign, Neptune exerted its dissolving influence within the minds of human beings. Slowly it broke down many of the ideas concerning the universe and human nature which had been the accepted foundation for 19th century thought. The mental concepts which were to dominate and shape the 20th century were offered principally through people born during the transit of Neptune through Gemini. Our present electronic society is due to many discoveries and inventions made at this time, and to the establishment of Planck's quantum theory and Einstein's formula, which led to atomic fission and then atomic fusion. Freudian psychoanalysis opened a new era in the understanding of the human personality. Neptune in Gemini also described a fundamental collective tendency to become enslaved by the glamour of the intellect, the cult of scientific knowledge and "reason" as a means to solve all problems and to separate the "true" from the "false." It stimulated the avid and restless search for knowledge about particulars and the trend toward establishing categories for facts and statistics.

Neptune in Cancer — 1902 to 1914-15. In this Sign Neptune worked to dissolve all walls and protective shells in men and nations. Old patterns of living, family pride, over-emphasis on national, social and personal differences, and class distinctions had to disappear. All established boundaries were threatened, as were traditional forms of imperialism. Traditional values had to be seen in a new light, and in terms of some greater encompassing reality.

Neptune in Leo — 1914-15 to 1928-29. As Neptune's North node (heliocentric) was in 12 Leo, a new Neptune cycle began when Neptune reached this degree by transit in October 1919. Neptune here dissolved the will and the sense of ego-pride or national pride with the aim of making people and nations realize that they belonged to an entity greater than themselves. Autocratic ways of living had to give way to a feeling of greater inter-dependence. Jung's process of individuation, achieved by opening the conscious ego to the collective unconscious, could be called a Neptune in Leo phenomenon. His ideas, along with those of Freud and Adler, influenced the collective mentality more and more during the period of this transit. The Neptunian escapist tendencies manifested in all the excesses of the "Jazz age". All established values were questioned, and life seemed to lack purpose and direction. World War I almost totally destroyed the social class structure, as well as entire nations in some cases. Europe's erstwhile domination of the world economy collapsed, and other continents were forced to produce for themselves what they had formerly bought from Europe. Socialist, Communist and Anarchist movements gained power as did the labor movement. The veterans of the "Great War" were not content to return to their sweat-shops and slave wages. Their horizons had been broadened and could never again be brought back to the narrow rut in which the social and economic barons had kept them for centuries. The traditional codes of behavior of the Victorian Age collapsed, and in sexual morality, politics and art, the keynote became "Anything goes." Women demanded and finally received the right to vote. Prohibition in the United States began a wave of organized crime whose power today reaches every part of the non-Communist world.

Neptune in Virgo — 1929 to 1942. The unprecedented wave of prosperity of the 1920s finally led to the Wall Street crash in 1929 and then the Great Depression. This depression colored most of the transit of Neptune through Virgo and eventually led to the Second World War. The dissolution of the will to power in individuals and nations begun while Neptune transited Leo was carried a step further. Virgo is the symbol of man's critical and analytical faculty. The transit of Neptune through this Sign attempted to spiritualize and universalize this faculty, to open the mind to more global truths in all spheres. For this reason there was a trend to criticize rationalism and to integrate particular things into a greater whole. The negative manifestations of this transit introduced mass propaganda and deception on a grand scale, especially in Germany. Specious arguments for the superiority of one race above all others poisoned the mind of the nation which, above all others, had always prided itself on its rationalism. All the technology of modern man was focused on the single purpose of destruction. With the greatest efficiency, millions of people were exterminated in the name of racial purity. This transit saw the rise of dictatorship, both fascist and communist, and the growth of fanatical nationalism

Neptune in Libra — 1942 to 1956-57. This was an important transit in terms of man's attempt to relate in new and more universal ways with his fellow creatures. What is currently happening in the United Nations clearly shows how far men have come in the actual *achievement* of their Neptunian ideal of a global society. Born out of the ashes of World War II, this organization is truly a Neptune in Libra phenomenon. The Libra accent on cooperation, and on a full and conscious participation of individuals and nations in some greater Whole, is still a Neptunian dream. The vision of Dumbarton Oaks to unite nations and continents, races and cultures — to bring them together working toward a common aim of peaceful co-operation — is still essentially that, merely a vision. During this period the first atomic bomb was exploded over Hiroshima and nuclear weapons proliferated. The power of international cartels became firmly established. The world divided into two armed camps — NATO and SEATO on the one side, and the communist bloc on the other. The European Common Market was established, ostensibly to join that continent and prevent further wars, and actually as a trading bloc to compete with the American hold on world markets which Europe lost after World War I. Many positive things happened during this transit to bring people closer together. Most notable among these was the civil rights movement. Group psychology became an important method for the attainment of personal fulfillment, primarily in the United States. The establishment of the World Council of Churches in 1948 laid the groundwork for the ecumenical movement to follow.

Neptune in Scorpio — 1957 to 1970. This transit stressed the emotional yearning of individuals to unite in special groups, whether on spiritual levels or in terms of business. Man's common humanity was stirred to the roots, and the common passions took on mystical or "religious" overtones. This transit began with sit-ins and peaceful demonstrations, and ended with race riots. Many goals of racial equality were, however, achieved. Riots, violence and assassinations became a common method of political change, as did terrorist bombings and hijackings. Young people dropped out of society and into a world of drugs.

Pornography gained in popularity, and indiscriminate sex became the norm. Black magic and many "occult arts" also became popular. As the protest against war (especially the United States involvement in Vietnam) grew, the protest itself became increasingly more violent. This paralleled a tremendous increase in street crime, especially drug related. Thousands of young men went into voluntary exile rather than serve in Vietnam, while at home people barricaded themselves in their houses and ignored the violence on their doorsteps.

Neptune in Sagittarius — 1970 to 1984. This transit of Neptune through the Sign of expansion of relationships, large-scale management and of the broadest possible use of mental and social power may herald many changes in those areas. Whereas the Jupiter-Saturn level of mentality uses Sagittarius energies in order to increase the scope of the personal ego or the individual nation, Neptune here suggests to human beings that the time has come to settle their problems on a world-wide basis. The frame of reference for all new social, cultural, ethical or political plans must be humanity as a whole. National and personal greed, whether for power or possessions, must give way to an ideal of abundance for all people on this planet. The blind increase in production and the concomitant waste of energy and natural resources must now be controlled. Consideration for the quality of life must outweigh the emphasis on quantity. There must be an attempt to formulate systems of organizations in which all points of view, every racial or socio-economic system can eventually find its place. There is a danger here that practical considerations may be lost in the utopian dreams of social reformers and their unrealistic panaceas for present-day social and economic problems. One must beware of glamour, self-deceit and over-idealization in the spiritual-religious realms. Already many new religious movements have sprung up and gathered a host of followers, especially among the young. Such evangelical movements, although a positive alternative to the drug-oriented escapes of the Neptune in Scorpio transit, may prove equally dangerous.

Neptune in Capricorn — 1984 to 1998. During this period universal movements and tendencies which began when Neptune entered Aries in 1861, and more particularly since Neptune entered Libra in 1942, should reach a more concrete and organized condition. There may be political attempts to set up a world government. In some way, Neptune will give a mystic tonality to forms of social, national or international organizations. In 1992, Uranus and Neptune will conjoin in Capricorn 16. One hundred and seventy-one years earlier they were also in conjunction in Capricorn 3. Since the waning quarter phase of the Uranus-Neptune cycle (heliocentrically exact in April 1955), individuals and nations should have realized progressively the real value of their way of life and have been prepared to introduce the necessary changes which would make possible a freer and more creative relationship between the individual and society. What will evolve during the new cycle (1992-2163) will depend on what is done toward this end between 1955 and 1992. In one sense, it can be said that Neptune in Capricorn relates to attempts to spiritualize matter and materialism, or to materialize spirit in some way. Rudhyar wrote once that Capricorn has two faces: Christ and Caesar. A lot will depend on how people interpret the Neptune challenge — as a call to a new Christ birth, or as the establishment of some authoritarian State.

The Personal Cycle of Neptune

In any personalized consideration of Neptune, the astrologer must always take into account its sidereal period, which is about twice that of Uranus. This means that most people will never experience more than half a complete Neptune cycle in the course of their lives. Thus the personal cycle cannot begin when Neptune crosses the Ascendant, since many people will not experience this transit in a lifetime. The House position of Neptune in the birth-chart will reveal the type of experiences and confrontations which will potentially be able to free the individual from his personal ego-limitations and change the nature of his personality. Through such experiences or confrontations, Neptune will slowly *dissolve* all that once seemed solid, secure, and objective from the viewpoint of Saturnian logic. There will be a call to what is "beyond" the familiar in the sphere of Neptune's natal House, a call to discover a vaster, more inclusive and universal form for the characteristic experiences of that House. The quadrant in which natal Neptune is found will indicate the type of growth which society will ask of an individual with great insistence. Secondary accents will be revealed by transiting Neptune's change of quadrant.

When Neptune Crosses the Ascendant and Transits the 1st House, one may either express some collective purpose, or else succumb to the pressure of society and attempt to escape into some kind of "artificial paradise". This transit will inevitably emphasize the development of a social kind of consciousness, and the person will be more receptive than before to those standards and values accepted by his community, religion or culture. This means that there will be the constant danger of self-loss in misunderstood issues of a collective nature. Everything that is remote will attract the attention, and there may be a mystical or humanitarian approach to life and its problems. The more idealistic side of the nature should be stressed, but there is a danger here of losing one's sense of objective reality and practical considerations. The positive aspects of this transit emphasize one's longing for a new state of consciousness. New feelings or doubts as to who or what one really is surge into the mind, and this can signal the beginning of a gradual process of ego-metamorphosis. Whatever form this process takes, endless questions as to the nature of the Self are raised which will challenge the integrity of one's sense of identity.

On negative levels, a Neptune transit of the 1st House can bring anxieties into one's life the root-cause of which will be difficult to fathom. There is a tendency to build up fantasies, to lead a dream-like existence or to become lost in a perpetual fog. Peculiar conditions may arise which may make one secretive about personal affairs. These may be based on misconceptions concerning everything that touches one's personal life and attitudes. Values can become distorted by the glamour of some cherished illusion, and a person can become enamoured with a completely false idea of his or her own worth. This can result in a superiority or an inferiority complex; and in either case it can lead to uncertainty and a distrust of other people. Discontent with the world and oneself can be aggravated by the fact that one does not really know what is wrong or how one could change it. This can be a time of general indecisiveness and dissatisfaction. Opportunities may be either magnified out of all proportion, or by-passed through short-sightedness. The most important challenge at this time is to pierce through the illusion and the glamour which one is inclined to build around oneself, and to be as self-critical as possible.

When Neptune Transits the 2nd House there will be a real necessity to keep one's feet firmly planted in reality, especially in so far as money and material possessions are concerned. An over-sensitivity toward possessions may tend to make one over-conscientious at that time, or one may refuse to give any worth or significance to material values. A person can become parasitical, feeling that society owes him a living. At the other extreme, he may have a strong desire to make money the easiest possible way, without regard for the ethics of the means employed. Social obligations can drain one's resources; therefore, one should carefully consider whether it is really necessary to keep up with the Joneses. It often happens that one's financial situation is not what it seemed during this transit. Confused conditions can arise, and therefore one may have to learn the necessity of keeping his material affairs in an orderly fashion. Fraud, deception, and an over-estimation of one's potential can all cause loss. A lack of definite purpose can also hinder the best use of one's assets. What happens at this time will depend on a person's reaction to the Neptune transit of the 1st House. If Neptune's passage over the Ascendant imposed a new collective destiny on that individual, the problem of the 2nd House transit will be how to use his resources — material and psychological — in order to fulfill the mission he has accepted.

When Neptune Transits the 3rd House, social, humanitarian or mystical values tend to influence the intellectual life. One can become the mouthpiece for collective values; however, although this contact with collective issues can be very positive, it can also create intellectual delusions and bring everyday life activities out of focus. One's thinking can be inspired or muddled, and one can become prey to strange mental conditions — fear, anxieties or disturbing dreams or hallucinations. From another point of view, this transit asks one to bring a broad perspective to bear on the petty problems of mundane existence. As Neptune is the planet of social obligation, this transit may impose many new duties and responsibilities in one's everyday relationships. It may become necessary to distinguish between obligation and imposition as relatives, neighbors and co-workers may impose their demands and yet give no credit for the help they received. During this transit it will be important to keep good order in one's environment, for Neptune does not like order, and objects in daily use can mysteriously disappear. Letters or other papers can be mislaid, lost, or be deceptive in content. Messages can be forgotten or distorted. Travel in the immediate environment can be hampered by detours or incorrect directions. One can be short-changed or receive the wrong merchandise while shopping. To offset such tendencies, one should try to seek the larger meanings behind the petty upsets of daily life, respect orderly thinking and accuracy, and be as tolerant as possible in one's everyday contacts.

When Neptune Crosses the Nadir and Transits the 4th House, the influence of collective or social forces tends to dissolve the normal and ancestral boundaries of the home or of the concrete personality. One's search for a more universal center may begin at this time, perhaps under the influence of some glamourous ideal or person. This may manifest as a yearning to find a broader meaning to one's existence. The feelings (or the home) open up to a great variety of influences, and a person may have to fight against continual inner uncertainties as well as the tendency to give in to insidious fears, imaginings or anxieties. On psychological levels, one's habitual feelings can now be modified by images or dreams surging up from the collective unconscious. During this transit one should try to open himself (and his home) to ideas and people that embody Neptunian values, values related to a more universal, inclusive and compassionate way of living. Astrology, spiritualism, mystic experiences, or people interested in such matters can help the individual to stop unhealthy brooding and to overcome the tendency to shut himself up in either his home or himself. In some cases, things may happen which will create or reveal "skeletons" in the closet, things which for various reasons one feels should be concealed from the public eye. In all events, this transit calls for the establishment of a wider and more inclusive foundation for the personality and for the home. It is this subtle trend which often makes one feel that the roots of his self-confidence (based on a narrower conception of self) are slowly being eaten away, and that the established foundations of his life are built on sand.

When Neptune Transits the 5th House, there is a tendency to glamourize one's emotional entanglements and romantic experiences. Subtly, one is compelled to reconsider his attitude toward his dreams, love affairs, and habitual outlets of creative self-expression. One can be attracted by Neptunian things such as music, theatre, motion pictures, astrology, mysticism, depth psychology or perhaps alcohol and drugs at this time. Peculiar circumstances can surround one's love affairs and sexual adventures. Neptune dissolves one's overly-personal attitudes and opens one's emotions to more-than-personal spiritual values as a source of creative self-expression. A quality of harmlessness must pervade one's actions. This expression of true love must take the place of the usual possessive and clinging forms of love that are the limiting expression of the personal ego. If, during this transit, an individual feels a vague sense of unrest and emotional dissatisfaction in his relationships, it will be due to the muddled condition of the feelings he wishes to express. Sometimes one yearns for the unattainable, an unattainable which is not very clear even in his own mind. He is tempted to depreciate what he has and to long for the love that is denied, to give to the undeserving and to withold from the worthy. The need for love is great during this transit; however, one is usually afraid to give completely of himself before being sure his love will be received. Nevertheless, Neptune in the 5th House states that one's greatest happiness will come only in giving himself wholly and without counting the cost or expecting a return. Only an unselfish, undemanding love can provide that for which one vaguely yearns. Only the love which measures up to one's highest ideals can bring satisfaction at this time, and any love which does not meet this standard is likely to bring suffering to the personal ego.

When Neptune Transits the 6th House, one reaps the fruits of his 5th House efforts to express his highest ideals. Personal pride must be dissolved in order that the experiences of this transit may bring about a very thorough and far-reaching emotional transformation. The planet of social obligation in the House of work and service does not allow one to forget his obligations to others. The necessity of caring for others — perhaps in illness, if one's own health does not suffer as a result of some unwise 5th House expression — or of performing thankless tasks either at home or on the job will put one's capacity for service to the test. Happiness will now lie in helping others whenever and wherever possible, in putting a willing shoulder to the wheel and plugging away at the task with perfect faith that the future will bring just rewards. In this way a truly compassionate and humanitarian Neptunian attitude can be developed.

When Neptune Crosses the Descendant and Transits the 7th House, the metamorphosis of the personal ego into a vaster consciousness of reality has to prove itself in the field of interpersonal relationships. The positive aspect of Neptune is inclusiveness and compassion; therefore, a person has to prove his capacity to be compassionate. This means to include within the field, not only of his consciousness, but also of one's love, all manner of people, potential enemies as well as friends, persecutors as well as intimates, and in some cases "disciples" whose unwise enthusiasm often creates more problems and greater anguish than the hatred of "open enemies." As Neptune's action is impersonal, there may be a tendency to stand apart from one's associates rather than experiencing them intimately and personally. In other words, with Neptune in the 7th House, the *quality and value of the relationship* one tries to establish in terms of certain ideals is more important than any particular person with particular needs. This can have drawbacks unless one is *really* capable of radiating universal love. On other levels of being, Neptune's transit of the 7th House can make one particularly vulnerable to the actions of one's associates. It is easy to succumb to the glamour of partners of either sex. One may be deceived or defrauded by them, the more so when a person has been caught in the glamour of their gifts, promises or pretenses. Anyone thus caught in the net of Neptune may have to pay dearly for it in one way or another — socially or psychologically. Of course, it is possible to see through the glamour and to accept it for what it is at the time, and this can be done early enough to avoid all but a temporary inconvenience.

One must also beware of becoming the slave of others through wanting to carry their burdens or help them in spite of themselves. Such behavior can be dangerous, for in doing so one accepts the responsibility for their acts and takes their karma onto one's own shoulders. Relationships based on pity can lead to one being exploited. When an individual's attitude toward relationships is too personal and therefore limited to the conscious ego-self, this transit can make one feel that he lives in a world of confusion. As one's impressions of other people, their motives and intentions are apt to be entirely wrong due to one's self-projection onto them, a person may feel that others do not understand him. He meets the outer world with an uneasiness which can develop into suspicion, and his own uncertainty leads others to misunderstand his motives or generous gestures. At this time one feels that something is changing, or should change in his relations with others and with the outer world. Still, if the opportunity for change presents itself, there may be indecision because a person is not clear of what he wants. It is therefore important during this transit to know first of all what one wants in order to know later whether this desire is purely personal or attuned to the unselfish service ideal of Neptune. As long as one assumes too much of other people, or associates with them because of ulterior personal motives, this transit can bring deception, anxiety, suspicion or fraud. Only the attitude which is based on giving rather than receiving and on service rather than selfishness will enable one to participate happily and significantly in both intimate and social relationships.

When Neptune Transits the 8th House, the emotional aspiration toward a "mystical" union with the beloved should become more definite. A humanitarian outlook, or the dedication to a more-than-personal work should now bear fruit, even if this poses problems of social organization. One must be careful of self-delusion about the potential results of one's relationships. Wishful thinking and an overly passive attitude can create such problems. One should beware of artificial paradises, and of saying "yes" or "no" simply because one's partners have asked for or refused something. A person must make sure that everything is aboveboard in all his business dealings, for disappointment or loss is possible now through some form of deception or trickery. There can also be treachery in law-suits at this time, especially in relation to inheritance. Neptune can create confusion and glamour so that one is obliged to clarify his ideas and values, especially in relation to business dealings and the productivity of all partnerships. In short, one must keep a clear head and not go to extremes of credulity, being gullible at one time and overly suspicious at others.

When Neptune Transits the 9th House it accomplishes its purpose by raising clouds of confusion in the mind and creating doubts about one's views of success, morality, religion, philosophy, law and abstract subjects in general. This planet is symbolically enlarging the boundaries of the mind by creating dissatisfaction with things as they are. Vague worries, conscience, discontent and confusing dreams may cause trouble. The understanding of the real meaning and value of one's life-relationships may be quite out of focus, whether with other people in general or with intimate partners in particular. The problem may be due to an extreme of idealism, or because abstract principles seem more important than real people. One's judgement can be too vacillating or too vague, or based on factors related to one's religious or spiritual faith. Absurd situations can arise because of superstition, fanaticism, religious or scientific prejudice. In the 9th House Neptune dissolves mental limitations through creating a yearning to lose oneself in vast theories, psychic phenomena and exotic ideas. Images from the collective unconscious may arise insistently through powerful dreams. The expansion of consciousness can also come through travel to foreign lands or contacts with strange people and ideas. These same things may also cause deceptive conditons and confusion.

When Neptune Crosses the Midheaven and Transits the 10th House, the growth in influence which is the general meaning of the fourth quadrant may correlate with a public or professional function which involves the interests of a community. If the scope of one's destiny permits it, this transit can coincide with a public stand in defense of international, humanitarian or transcendent values and activities. One may become the spokesman for his community's ideals. If, on the other hand, the transit of the third quadrant has built up illusions concerning one's true worth, then the transit of the 10th House can lead to a showdown. Many people in fact do not know the *real* value of their contribution to society and often think that they possess greater abilities and knowledge than is actually the case. Conversely, it can happen that one's real worth may go unnoticed and unrecognized, perhaps through self-depreciation. In either case, during this 10th House transit, the exaggerated situation is likely to be unmasked. Indiscretions can open one to attack, and therefore one should watch out for slander or scandal. It is important not to let a dreamy idealism obscure the present need for an effort to attain more worth in the eyes of the world. One must be above suspicion at all times and thoroughly capable of performing any task he undertakes, for with one mis-step the whole structure can collapse.

When Neptune Transits the 11th House a person is attracted by the glamour of the social life, parties, club activities, or participation in some idealistic group. Those dreams tend to be unrealistic, and one may be drawn toward social fads of all kinds. At this time a person must be careful not to fall under the spell of false "Masters" or prophets, or to become involved in social intrigues. He must be the master of his fate rather than dependent on other people. Contacts with friends or groups may become more confused and uncertain, and this state of affairs can make a person doubt his social capacities and the worth of his established objectives. One may even neglect to maintain contacts under the illusion that he is not wanted by his friends. Instead of brooding over such a situation, one should realize that Neptune is dissolving one form of social participation in the hope that he will open himself to something more worthwhile, more encompassing in value and more spiritual in quality. In these terms, the breaking of ties with unworthy people and discontinuing to participate in selfish and limiting social activities will be all to the good. The world has need of crusading zeal, and of people capable of focusing through their minds and public activities a vision of the next step ahead in terms of society's needs. One should therefore prepare himself, if possible, to assume such a responsibility or, if he is not ready, at least to seek friends and companions among those who are fired by a similar desire to create the conditions for social or religious change.

When Neptune Transits the 12th House it is in its element, for both factors dissolve the refuse of the past. Here one may cleanse the subconscious of its limiting ghosts, and work toward the realization of the great dreams one had in the 11th House. The less a person remains a slave to outworn ideals and social activities, the less likely this transit is to bring on troublesome psychological states. In the 12th House, one must avoid building up doubts and fears concerning his personal and social worth. He must weed out all false conceptions and look reality in the face without self-pity. There may be a tendency to withdraw from one's social life and to dwell on one's dreams or delusions. A person may become the target for gossip or underhanded attacks; however, if he maintains a true self-respect, slander will not hurt him. For those who have psychic gifts, this transit can strengthen contact with more subtle realms of reality and bring enlightenment; for true mystic experiences are possible.

The results of one's past experiences in social and interpersonal living, and the images built up in the psyche as a result of those experiences, are likely to precipitate crises. If one has failed or been frustrated, or if laziness and a conforming spirit have kept him in a rut, he may now become prey to feelings of guilt and remorse, feeling even less capable than before of taking a step forward toward his greater destiny. The challenge here is to accept one's failures for what they are and to have the courage to go on from there in terms of the actual situation in which one finds himself. There is no need to brood over the past or to feel that, because one has failed once, it is necessary to fail again. Until an individual becomes perfect, every cycle will leave some "unfinished business" which will condition the new phase. This is inevitable. What matters is the will to accept that unfinished business in all lucidity and as well as one can. Then a person must prepare himself to go forward and to do better in the new cycle. Whatever is done or not done during this 12th House transit will, in any case, condition the future. One must therefore permit Neptune to dissolve the memory of all that one has left undone so that he may create a seed out of what *has* been done. That seed will germinate when Neptune comes to the Ascendant with a new call to the life of the spirit.

INDIVIDUAL NEPTUNE CRISES. Apart from the general trends just discussed, individual Neptunian crises, like Uranian crises, can coincide with aspects of transiting Neptune. How such a crisis will manifest is contingent on so many variables that accurate prediction is precluded. It is very difficult to time such crises with any precision, for Neptune moves very slowly. Thus, a Neptune transit to the natal Sun, for example, will more likely refer to an entire period in the native's life than a specifically timed event. Such timing, however, is not the principal concern of the humanistic astrologer; nor is it his task to determine the intensity of a crisis before it actually takes place. The intensity of such crises will necessarily vary according to social conditions. Additionally, no one, and especially not the humanistic astrologer, has the right to decide beforehand whether the results of a crisis will be positive or negative. The crisis may be internal or external or both. How is the astrologer to know? Furthermore, in the case of an inner crisis, the external results may come much later than the time measured by an exact aspect of transiting Neptune to a natal planet. Neptunian crises differ from Uranian crises in the sense that, instead of changing the form, implications or meaning of life in some sudden or drastic way, the person *slowly* begins to relate to people and events in an elusively unfamiliar way. Irrational ideas begin to influence the conscious behavior, and especially the emotional responses or feeling reactions. There can be a sense of identification with downtrodden or suffering people. Negatively, however, there can also be a tendency to lose one's sense of Self in various forms of intoxication or artificial paradises, to feel incapable of standing up to outside social or inner psychological pressures.

The Uranus-Neptune Cycle

The Uranus-Neptune cycle has a duration of 171 years, and therefore it surpasses the scope of an individual's life. The present cycle of those two planets began with their conjunction on 3 degrees of Capricorn in the Spring of 1821. The waxing square was repeated several times between 1867 and 1871. The opposition phase lasted from February 28, 1906 to December 2, 1909 and was repeated nine times. The waning square was exact for the first time on July 15, 1954, and repeated on December 2, 1954, June 11, 1955 and again on January 19 and May 5, 1956. It remained within a one degree orb from September 1953 to March 1957 — three and a half years. The next conjunction will take place in 1992 near Capricorn 16. The phases of the Uranus-Neptune cycle are related to the historical events which have conditioned the type of society in which we are living today. Astrologers do not usually take into account the fact that many of the problems which confront an individual in his personal life are largely determined by important national and international events of the past. The present Uranus-Neptune cycle began shortly before the death of Napoleon, and the image of what he stood for is still very much alive today. Not only are the Napoleonic laws still applied in France, but in many countries throughout the world. European astrologers are indebted to him for the obligatory mention of the birth time on birth certificates in all countries which were part of his empire. The Napoleonic image undoubtedly influenced Mussolini and Hitler, as well as the many dictators in Africa and Latin America. The single-minded way in which Napoleon sought and used social power is currently reflected in the way in which industrial barons have seized on the inventions and discoveries of scientific technology and built up international cartels. The personal and social power which they command today is even greater than that which Napoleon himself once had.

The enormous power of the military-industrial complex reflects a concentration of the power made available by the industrial, techno-logical and socio-political revolutions since the beginning of the 19th century. For better or worse, the economic, political and social lives of over half the world's population are in the hands of a few powerful individuals. The present Uranus-Neptune cycle, which began with the conjunction in Capricorn, is a fitting astrological symbol for the use of social power for self-glorification. Capricorn refers to the domination of all social activity by the State, the corporation or the bank, or by some dominant personage — the dictator or political "boss", the baron of industry, or the leader of an underworld syndicate. As the next two conjunctions of Uranus and Neptune in 1992 and 2163 will also be in Capricorn, it would seem that the accent on the use and misuse of social power will affect humanity for some time to come. What must be learned from this cycle is how to use the power born of Uranian changes and inventions for the good of all people, and not only for the benefit of a small group of "rugged individualists". Worthy attempts at building various kinds of humanitarian organizations have been made, notably by some of the greatest of the robber-barons, such as Henry Ford, John D. Rockefeller and Andrew Carnegie. By and large, however, industrialists are interested in their personal welfare, and statesmen are interested in their own national interests. The urge to acquire money and power even at the expense of moral values remains the rule rather than the exception.

The opposition aspect between these two planets at the beginning of this century brought to a climax all that humanity has tried to achieve in the way of a global metamorphosis since 1821. Unfortunately, because humanity did not succeed in achieving a wise, ethical and spiritual control of the tremendous new energies put at its disposal since the time of the conjunction, the opposition aspect has led to the world-wide cleavages and destruction through which we have had to live — world wars, nuclear arms proliferation, global pollution, destruction to the point of extinction of many species of animals, and a world-wide climate of hostility and fear. Uranus and Neptune have not yet succeeded in overcoming Saturn, symbol of imperialism and absolute national sovereignty. The obsolete institutions and ideologies of Saturn, as well as man's social and religious biases, remained. Then came the waning square of the fifties. This was a final challenge to humanity to orient itself in a better way to the pressures and confrontations of international politics. The ultimate results of all that was done, or left undone since the beginning of the century (the opposition aspect), should have been faced squarely at that time.

Those born around 1956 with this Uranus-Neptune square in their birth-charts may provide the means to set right the errors committed by their elders during the earlier phases of this cycle. Such a square brings to the fore both self-criticism and the criticism of society, of the established way of life, and of one's religious heritage insofar as these seem to stand in the way of an individual's desire for freedom of self-expression. Uranus always stands for the individual, Neptune for the community. The square pits what is unique and original against what is common, shared by all and universal. The lesson to be learned from this square is that the individual can grow and fulfill himself only in relation to the collectivity. In time the collectivity always becomes what its leading individuals have made it. For this reason, those born around the time of the waning square in 1956 have a particular problem concerning the value of their way of relating and adjusting themselves to society as individuals. The nature of the particular problem will be indicated by the House positions of the Uranus-Neptune square in the individual birth-chart, or the solar-chart if the birth time is unknown. Uranus' House position will show the unique conditions in which one will seek to express himself as an individual. Neptune's House position will indicate where society and tradition, the past, and one's subconscious memories may stop or delay his progress.

THE WANING URANUS-NEPTUNE SQUARE IN THE HOUSES. This waning square provided the general possibility for the individual to orient himself more appropriately to the pressures and confrontations of society. Its specific meaning and value must be found in looking at one's own birth-chart. The suggestions made below are thus only general guidelines, and I am obliged to interpret this aspect in terms of equal Houses, as the possible variations in a birth-chart are far too numerous to include.*

Uranus in the 1st House — Neptune in the 4th House. The challenge here is to be a true individual, and to be so with distinction. A crisis may challenge one to face in a new way his parents, his hereditary foundations, or the basic values and feelings on which he relies. One should decide now what his attitude toward life and his real goals should be. This may mean breaking away from conditions which seemed well-established. Uranus in the 2nd House — Neptune in the 5th House. The challenge here may come from one's desire for financial independence, or

---

*This square was **exact** at the following dates and zodiacal positions: 7/15/54 (23° 19′ Cancer-Libra); 12/2/54 (27° 20′ Cancer-Libra); 6/11/55 (25° 39′ Cancer-Libra); 1/19/56 (0° 23′ Leo-Scorpio); and 5/5/56 (28° 37′ Cancer-Libra).

from the need to acquire money. A person may wish to prove his individual worth according to his own conception of his destiny by developing his inherited faculties or building his personal assets. One must be careful of glamorous adventures and unsound risks, however. The key is to be true to oneself instead of following collective trends in Self-expression. Theatre, music or romantic involvements may hold one enthralled at this time. **Uranus in the 3rd House — Neptune in the 6th House.** The mind will be very restless at this time, as a person is eager for new experiences with both ideas and people. One is challenged to learn more and to perfect his techniques of work and self-expression. There may be health problems which oblige one to make certain changes either in his routine or in his environment. If one can overcome pride and develop true compassion, he could become a healer.

   Uranus in the 4th House — Neptune in the 7th House. Here one is challenged to overcome static conditions in the home. Psychologically, the desire for ego-security and stability will need to be revised in order for one to become a more complete personality. New ideals of interpersonal relationship may stimulate one emotionally, and one should beware of self-deception in those areas. **Uranus in the 5th House — Neptune in the 8th House.** The challenge at this time is to be creative, and to prove one's worth in some form of self-expression. One must be willing to take certain risks. One should not be surprised, however, if his partners refuse to back him in his efforts through fear of the consequences. At this time one should try to become more considerate of other people. Speculation should be carefully watched, and one must beware of deceptive clauses in contracts or agreements. **Uranus in the 6th House — Neptune in the 9th House.** Something must be changed here in one's life-routine. The service of a new cause or institution may oblige one to acquire some new technique necessary to his social or spiritual development. In some cases, there may be difficulties with employers or employees. A narrow, traditional way of approaching problems may hinder one's search for new paths of accomplishment. At this time it is wise to keep clear of glamorous promoters of mystical or drug-related experiences. When traveling long distances, especially by ship or plane, one should watch one's health.

   Uranus in the 7th House — Neptune in the 10th House. It may become necessary to introduce changes into one's interpersonal relationships, whether private or business, at this time. Such changes, however, even if worthwhile, may have unexpected social or professional consequences. There may be scandal or domestic conflicts which should be met with a bold and united front. **Uranus in the 8th House — Neptune in the 11th House.** The products and results of one's interpersonal relationships can pose problems. They may awaken enmity or stronger competition. It would be unwise to rely too blindly on the advice of friends or lawyers. Social glamour or the desire for public prestige can be an individual's downfall. He should, instead, broaden his ideals in business and social activities, follow new trends and not be afraid of change. **Uranus in the 9th House — Neptune in the 12th House.** At this time Uranus challenges one to develop a new and broader life philosophy, to become unconventional in his thinking and to seek new horizons either physically or spiritually. Only a new realization of the purpose of one's life can overcome the obstacles to personal expansion. At this time the main obstacles are the ghosts of the past.

Uranus in the 10th House — Neptune in the 1st House. Public and professional matters may force one to re-examine his feelings about himself. This is no time for a person to emphasize his own uniqueness. Rather, one should try to fit himself into a larger frame of reference which would give him a more-than-personal significance. One should try to dissolve those things within him which hinder this experience of being part of some greater reality. Mediumistic influences, drugs and wishful thinking should be avoided. This is a time to live up to the highest within oneself. **Uranus in the 11th House — Neptune in the 2nd House.** This is the time to seek new friends and to transform one's ideals so that they may be better adapted to one's real capacities and financial means. One should assert oneself rigorously and without wishful thinking in order that he neither overvalue nor undervalue his material and psychological assets. Dreams must be kept within the limits of what one can afford. **Uranus in the 12th House — Neptune in the 3rd House.** The challenge here is to meet the past, one's personal ghosts and unfinished business, and so bring a chapter of one's life to a close. In this way, a person will be able to give a broader meaning to his environment and his daily activities, thereby orienting his life more freely toward a greater tomorrow. The fruits of one's past efforts in relationships, business, and public participation can now enable one to transform many habitual patterns.

The tests implied in the last-quarter square of Uranus to Neptune came to a focus between 1953 and 1957, particularly in the birth-patterns of people born during that period. It was a phase implying the breakdown of old structures no longer useful to life either on the personal or the social level. From the 1950s to 1992 we are all challenged to face those inhibitions created by racial, cultural and religious traditions. Those born during this period will be particularly sensitive to such subconscious influences, and will make conscious efforts to free themselves from them. The frustrations which these energies imposed, especially during the younger years, and also the social or psychic compulsions which produce in so many people a sense of guilt or a subtle defeatism, must be purged. Whether the efforts of this group of young people now entering adulthood will be positive or self-defeating cannot be foretold. Those who succeed in facing up to the crisis, however, will be forming the seed which will be the foundation of the future cycle due to begin in 1992. This seed will grow during the period which separates the waning square from the conjunction: 1957 to 1992.

The Saturn-Neptune Cycle

At the level of the individual personality, Saturn represents the ego and a person's place in society. More generally speaking, Saturn is the principle of form, structure and limitation. It deals with everything which brings human experience to a precise and clear-cut (but narrow) focus of integration. Neptune, on the other hand, symbolizes the pressure of the collective — the group, nation or religion — upon the individual. It deals with everything that seeks to include a large variety of factors, and to universalize the particular, narrow, and personal point-of-view. It is the principle of federalism in politics, the desire to bring all people together on a basis of equality and idealism. Neptune is the mysticism and also the glamour of everything that is big, remote, mysterious and unapproachable. What Saturn forms, Neptune wants to un-focus. Slowly, subtly Neptune dissolves all the rigid insulating walls that Saturn erects. It repudiates all boundaries, classes and castes. Saturn sees things here and now, while Neptune lives in the timeless realms of the universal. Saturn always strives to *exclude* what does not fit into rigid categories or aristocratic and traditional standards. Neptune wants to *include* everything, even if this would mean levelling everyone and everything down to a common denominator and unifying or equalizing all differences. Thus Saturn and Neptune can be seen to work in almost completely opposite directions, whether it be within the individual or in society. Their cycle lasts approximately 35 years. These two planets were conjunct in August 1917 at Leo 5. This was followed, between November 1952 and July 1953, by three repeated conjunctions at Libra 22 and 23. The next conjunction will take place in 1989 at Capricorn 9.

The current cycle, which began in 1952, came to its waxing square phase in February 1963 with Saturn at Aquarius 16 and Neptune at Scorpio 16. Its opposition phase, the climax of the cycle, occurred three times between 1971 and 1972 at Gemini-Sagittarius 1, 3, and 5. The waning square will take place in 1979-80 around 16 and 20 of Virgo-Sagittarius. The important thing to understand in this cycle is what the *entire* period of 35 years brings forth. On the basis of such an historical understanding, the astrologer may then evaluate what *new approach* to the combining of Saturn and Neptune elements in human experience the new cycle may be expected to develop. During the thirty-five years following the conjunction, individuals *must* find a new solution to the problem of combining the principle of traditional form and exclusivism (Saturn) with the principle of universality and maximum inclusiveness (Neptune). The new cycle will challenge each person — particularly according to the House position in which the conjunction falls — to find a new way of integrating the concrete and the transcendent, the practical and the ideal, the need for selectiveness and the ideal of all-embracing compassion, aristocratic values and egalitarianism, egocentric individualism and humanitarian socialism. A new kind of balance between all these pairs of opposites becomes imperative as a result of the experiences of the preceding 35-year cycle.

Thus, between 1952-53 and 1971-72 (the waxing half of the present cycle) people must discover, both socially and individually, some new principle on which a truly constructive Saturn-Neptune balance can be based. The discovery of such a new principle has become imperative because of the inability of society to constructively balance those two energies during the preceding cycle which began in 1917. That was the cycle which began with the communist revolution in Russia and ended with the entire world divided into two armed camps with an iron curtain between them. The balance between Saturn and Neptune must be found not only on a global level, but also within individual nations and persons. From the psychological, humanistic point of view emphasized in this book, the critical phases in this cycle will accentuate man's need to find a new way of being broad, idealistic and inclusive (Neptune), while remaining at the same time clearly focused, definite and efficient (Saturn). People must learn to be warm with compassion and love, and yet retain their distinct and solid strength as individual egos. The problem lies in how to be *both* of these opposites and yet not be torn in inner psychological and outer social conflicts. It *is* possible to find convincing, dynamic, effective solutions capable of transforming society as well as its individual members.

SATURN-NEPTUNE CONJUNCTION IN THE HOUSES. The problem of integrating these two factors will affect each person differently according to his individual natal chart. A general meaning, however, can be found by considering the natal (or Solar) Houses involved with the conjunction and the following critical phases of this cycle. The conjunction's House position indicates the field of experience in which each person particularly needs to find a balance between Saturn and Neptune factors in his life.

In the 1st House the conjunction reveals the necessity to find a new definition for the type of relationship a person can establish between his individual uniqueness of being and the social or spiritual whole. One may become a concrete and personal focus for certain universal values, provided that he is willing to look in a new way at those things which he may previously have taken for granted, both within himself and within society. What is at stake in this Saturn-Neptune cycle is one's individual capacity to respond creatively and joyously to the present need for integration of the concrete and the universal. **In the 2nd House** the new cycle asks an individual to overcome the inertia of his habitual patterns of using both his material and psychological possessions. He should face life and society more openly and with greater confidence. If one has a strong ego, he may be able to give a concrete expression to the desires of the masses and become a focal point for the expression of those accumulated subconscious racial impulses with which he has identified himself in the past. A conservative outlook should give way to an attempt to use one's resources to fulfill the social and economic needs of the present day.

In the 3rd House this conjunction may indicate a strong influence of social factors in one's surroundings, and peculiar things may happen through one's neighbors or relatives. One should hold his mental energies well under control, as there is danger of becoming submerged in the tides of one's own subconscious mind. The opportunity is present to establish a new relationship between one's conscious mind and collective or mystical forces, if one will allow this to happen. This could bring illumination, provided one takes care not to shrink too much into his own shell. **In the 4th House** the Saturn-Neptune conjunction presents a challenge to give up one's past reliance on traditions or family patterns in order to establish himself on a broader foundation. Out of a feeling of dissatisfaction, an individual may realize that he must function better and more radiantly as a personality. This is the time to change one's habits and to broaden one's outlook, in general to pull oneself out of a rut. One might try to become more sociable at home. The solution to one's problems at this time lies inside oneself.

In the 5th House this conjunction presents especially great possibilities for the musician, the artist, the teacher or the psychologist if he accepts the challenge of transpersonal creativity. One must overcome shy and withdrawn behaviour and try to find a particular sphere in which he can link his personal creative capacity to a collective need. In some cases there may be a struggle between one's innate fear of the consequences and the glamour of risky adventures, especially in romantic involvements. It is important not to liberate oneself too explosively from one's inhibitions. **In the 6th House** problems can arise concerning one's work or health. This transit may precipitate a crisis aimed at dissolving one's ego-pride in order to prepare him for some form of disinterested service to a social or spiritual cause. One must maintain a straightforward relationship with one's boss and employees and be ready to discipline himself, to seek out more efficient techniques in his work, while at the same time adapting his action to the real needs of his community.

In the 7th House the new Saturn-Neptune cycle demands a deep transformation of one's attitude toward his interpersonal relationships. There is a call here to a larger and more impersonal life, to the development of compassion and idealism in all one's personal contacts. Fear, shyness, or a compensatory aggressiveness all must be avoided. One must be purposeful and efficient, but with the aim of making one's *relationships* with individuals or groups a concrete expression of some ideal cause. In the 8th House business activities have reached a turning point wherein it will be necessary to leave behind some old condition and tentatively enter into new activity. One will need to exercise his best judgement, as the situation may be somewhat confusing due to the dominance of social or collective factors. Close cooperation with large organizations may become necessary; however, one must keep his own purpose clearly defined. One's fears for his personal and social security should not stop him from linking his destiny to that of a larger enterprise.

In the 9th House this conjunction may indicate the potential for travel or a sojourn abroad, providing one has made clear-cut plans. Although the time has come to heed the call of greater, more spiritual or mystical values, it is important not to become swamped by issues too large for one's present capacity for understanding and assimilation. One should allow his imagination to carry him beyond everyday realities, but to come back to earth afterwards! Overly intense devotionalism or fanaticism must be avoided. On the other hand, metaphysical, religious or philosophical issues are likely to take on a definite form in the life. Even one's dreams may take insistent shape, and they could deeply affect the person at this time. This 9th House conjunction is particularly crucial in terms of the balance between the concrete and the transcendent, between one's personal, Saturnian ambition and Neptunian ideals of sharing. In the 10th House the call to a new way of balancing the individual and collective factors in one's life pits one's ambition for social or public power against an attitude which must take into consideration the interests of the community. It is possible that this transit will coincide with circumstances dominated by some kind of collective fate in which an individual is asked to play the part of a public symbol. One's destiny can be irrevocably linked to that of his community.

In the 11th House an individual should dedicate himself to some social or spiritual cause which could give a broader meaning to his personal activities. If one persists in clinging to old ideals and traditions, however, the new trend can create a condition of utter confusion. It is important not to allow conventionalism or moral taboos to prevent a person from linking his life to idealistic or socially conscious groups or friends. One must be neither too pessimistic nor too egocentric in sizing up the value of new social or spiritual trends, although one's practical sense could be useful in separating utopian ideals from what is really possible in terms of social transformation. **In the 12th House** this conjunction can indicate a tendency to become easily confused and distracted from one's chosen path by peculiar and unconscious psychological reactions. Old repressions and complexes are likely to be very active, and a person can lose himself in dreams, fantasies and introverted escapes. The results of one's past social or business activities may become depressing; if so, it would be more worthwhile to discover the reasons for these results and to work on the necessary changes in order to make a positive, new start than to brood over them. It may be necessary at this time to find a larger frame of reference for one's life, some more-than-personal ideal which can give meaning to what has previously seemed meaningless.

THE SATURN-NEPTUNE OPPOSITION IN THE HOUSES. As we are now experiencing the waning half of this cycle which began in 1972 with the opposition of Saturn and Neptune, an integration of these two energies is especially important at this time. The opposition signaled a culmination of the trend which began at the conjunction. It forms for many years hence a continuous background in both the individual and collective aspects in one's life.

Saturn in the 1st House — Neptune in the 7th House. Old man gloom may seem to be sitting on one's doorstep at this time, and a person may feel that he is walking around carrying the lid to his own coffin. Yet, if one can only see it, this is the supreme test of one's capacity to master life-conditions. It *seems* that the problem lies in one's marriage or close partnership, which seems to be dissolving into a mist as one stubbornly clings to his own personal viewpoint or his own selfish ego needs. It is important now to understand the other's point of view and to remain pliable and open-minded. Let go, relax, and be more receptive. It is pointless to give in to a sense of hopelessness and the worthlessness of all love. It is one's *approach* to the world and other people which is mainly at fault. **Saturn in the 2nd House — Neptune in the 8th House.** Business and financial affairs may seem in urgent need of a solution at this time; however, these are not new problems, but rather the result of past contacts with others and perhaps with one's own family background. In order to put one's business on a more collective, depersonalized basis (perhaps merging into a larger group concern), some sacrifice may be necessary. One should live up to the spirit of the times and not allow personal prejudice, excessive conservatism or selfishness to stand in the way. It would be foolish to cling too tenaciously to one's *own* possessions at a time when it is essential to enter *joint* enterprises. On the other hand, it is possible that one's business associates may have involved him in some very unpleasant and not altogether straightforward transactions. Whatever happens, the results may be depressing; however, in every case, much of this is due to one's own obstinacy or to an inherently conservative outlook which has refused to mold itself to the present-day economic and social realities.

Saturn in the 3rd House — Neptune in the 9th House. At this time a person may feel hampered by his environment and may long to escape by traveling somewhere far away. Extreme caution is advised, however, for the situation is confusing. One's best policy may be a quiet watchfulness. It is best not to become lost in narrow issues or despondent over them. Instead, one should try to grasp the larger issues, the ones which deal with social and national factors. The mail may bring peculiar news, perhaps false or scandalous reports which may cause one to feel quite gloomy. If the problems are insoluble, there is no point in brooding over them. Any form of despondency or nervous upset which one displays will only cause one's friends and relatives to become worried about him.

Saturn in the 4th House — Neptune in the 10th House. A strong hindrance producing uncertainty in one's life may emanate from the home. An old inferiority complex or psychological fear may also stand in the way of one's public activities. The latter may demand for their fulfillment an extreme development of a social sense, which a person may seem to lack just now. He may therefore hesitate to throw himself into some vast, communal enterprise or to adopt a social or mystical philosophy which would demand his giving up some part of his precious ego. There will be no point in sacrificing either one's home life in favor of career considerations, or one's career for the limitations of home. A climax of dissatisfaction with almost everything may at this time force a person to realize that the principal touble lies within himself, in his incapacity to display authority and firmness.

Saturn in the 5th House — Neptune in the 11th House. At this time a person may be torn by issues involving friends, groups, or social ideals. His sense of loyalty to a group which has embodied his ideals may now be tested. One can appear discouraged about his creativity and self-expression. On mundane levels, speculations can prove wrong, or one may lose possessions by fraudulent means. It seems unavoidable that some particular line of expression will now reach a dead-end. It may also be that what one has been striving for has lost its value, or perhaps a romantic entanglement has landed one in trouble. In any case, a person can find himself emotionally subject to a peculiar kind of discipline, most probably due to a strong dissatisfaction with oneself and one's inability to rouse himself to forceful action because of an inferiority complex. **Saturn in the 6th House — Neptune in the 12th House.** This is a time of conflict and strain, especially in one's inner life. There is danger of becoming absorbed in one's own subjective problems, so that the outer world is entirely colored by these considerations. Through inner discrimination and quiet meditation one may pull himself together and not be torn by the action of opposite forces. Matters of health are not favorable and may cause concern. Rest, even enforced rest, can be of great assistance and may also afford one the opportunity to solve his problems. Whatever happens, in some way one's impulses will be checked, and passionate motives and ideals of ruthless self-exertion will lose both strength and meaning. A change of consciousness is being brought about through a strong dissatisfaction with oneself. One may experience hidden enmity, and whatever social background one may have can vanish, leaving one with a sense of emptiness. This is not a time to remain static or dream idly, but a time to work hard and seriously.

Saturn in the 7th House — Neptune in the 1st House. A Neptunian condition is very insistent now, and all depends on the way one reacts to it. To some, this may mean the beginning of deep, mystical experiences; to others, it can be the start of a social career. In every case, however, an individual is likely to become absorbed in something larger than his personal ego. He can become the channel for energies transcending his normal consciousness. However, difficulties and tests are in evidence, above all difficulties involving one's life-partner. More general difficulties may also arise in meeting the outer world and its norm of behavior. It may be wise to heed the practical advice of associates, for they can bring common sense to one's presently diffused, idealistic attitudes. If a person is using *any* intoxicants or drugs, he should give them up. One can feel vague and diffuse, like a helpless cork floating on an angry sea. The solution will not be found in a bottle, but in cultivating a positive and firm ground-of-being in one's own Self. If a person is leading a purely social life, he should give up most of it and pay more attention to his partner, even if that partner seems old and dull. Others will not be so boring if a person himself becomes more positive, radiant and understanding. **Saturn in the 8th House — Neptune in the 2nd House.** Financial problems demand one's attention at this time. Money may be lacking and help may not easily be found in business partners or associates. The root of these problems may be one's personal attitude toward and his use of his own material assets. A person may be very generous and sympathetic by nature, ready to give up what he owns to his partners, and yet, this would be depriving oneself unwisely and at the same time would do no good to one's partners either. Conversely, one may tend toward wasteful self-indulgence in money matters and may therefore need all the firm power and wisdom of his associates in order to restrain his hand.

Saturn in the 9th House — Neptune in the 3rd House. A person may encounter notable difficulties within his own mind, and serious doubts or inhibiting mental complexes can stand in the way of expansion. One may find that somehow he is compelled to stand still. Correspondents seem partly responsible for the confused state of affairs in one's surroundings, or for the fact that objective reality and wishful thinking seem to be intermixed. All in all, one is dissatisfied with everything close at hand; yet things that are remote and perhaps even glamorous give little satisfaction. They may, in fact, lead to a realization of the apparent futility of one's past efforts and aspirations. One should not brood, even if difficulties come from abroad. Boring one's neighbors with a recital of one's problems will solve nothing. What is most needed is a better perspective on what is actually being done, and solitude can be useful at such a time. **Saturn in the 10th House — Neptune in the 4th House.** A stubborn protest may be made at this time either against one's social conditions, or against karmic necessities which are keeping a person bound to some peculiar psychological situation from which he is eager to escape. Something within one's soul, as much as in his outer environment, can hamper him. He will generally rebel against it and may feel himself the enemy of all traditional and established order. His own soul, moved by compassion or aroused by vast currents sweeping him onward, may seem lost in the influence of some group. One is therefore advised to use caution in extroverted, public actions. In other cases, the demands of one's career may outweigh those of his domestic life, drawing energy out of it and perhaps financial substance as well. A person may realize that he must now sacrifice his home life to his career. This will be all right, provided one is willing to accept his opportunities with courage and determination.

Saturn in the 11th House — Neptune in the 5th House. A possessive personal attitude, if such is noticeable in one's character, may be rudely challenged at this time. Life is trying to teach the value of trans-personal expression in which egocentric creativity must give way to a form of creation based on more-than-personal needs and values. One's friends may represent two different types of ideals or wishes, one of which may be very depressive and run counter to one's highest form of self-expression. Yet, if a person can transform his impulses and desires for love and attention instead of losing himself in self-contemplation, then he will gain a most valuable perspective on life. In other cases, this will be the time to incorporate one's ideals into some concrete form of self-expression. One may find himself possessed of a wealth of spiritual power which may startle him. If he clings to out-worn ideals, however, the present situation will become confused and deceptive. **Saturn in the 12th House — Neptune in the 6th House.** One can feel weighed down by feelings of insecurity at this time. He may be out of work, or experiencing unfavorable health conditions. In any case, there is a peculiar diffidence in his personal attitude which must be overcome. These are days of personal testing which may involve a major psychological crisis. A phase of development is coming to a close; matters which have previously affected either one's personal life or his career are reaching a climax, a point of consummation or a dead stop. This can be confusing, and one must be careful not to be weighed down by a sense of hopelessness or frustration. Whatever happens, the root of one's problems comes from the fact that he has exhausted the possibilities of this phase of his life and is at the threshold of another. One is recapitulating his past, balancing his accounts prior to letting go. Pull everything together — and go.

The Jupiter-Neptune Cycle

Jupiter and Neptune are, in different ways, both symbols of collective action. The conjunctions of these two planets take place at 13-year intervals, and every thirteenth conjunction recurs at nearly the same zodiacal position. As Neptune's complete sidereal cycle averages approximately 165 years, these Jupiter-Neptune conjunctions divide the Neptune cycle into 13 sub-periods of a little less than 13 years each (13x13=169). Thus, it would seem then that the Jupiter-Neptune cycle is linked to the symbolism of the number 13. As Neptune moves from one Sign to the next, it meets Jupiter only once while transiting each Sign. For this reason, Rudhyar has formed the opinion that *the Jupiter-Neptune conjunction is the high-point of Neptune's stay in a given Sign.* The high-point of Neptune's current transit of Sagittarius, therefore, was the Jupiter-Neptune conjunction of 1971 which occurred at the first degree of that Sign. The number 12, symbol of perfection in Pythagorean philosophy, is not only a basic number in astrology, but may also be linked to Jupiter's cycle of nearly 12 years. Thus, it refers to the Jupiterian social function and to all forms of *organized* religion and brotherhood, including the 12 disciples of Jesus. The number 13 refers to the Christ principle and as such is the symbol of the power to overcome death and limitations on all planes. It reveals the urge to transcend all forms of social or religious consciousness as it is expressed in organized groups, cultural traditions and institutions. Therefore, in essence, the Jupiter-Neptune cycle gives mankind a basic rhythm of and describes its urge toward transcendence.

This urge can lead ultimately to positive results, although at first those results may be negative; for the Jupiter trend is always basically expansive, and the link to Neptune can over-stimulate this trend. For this reason, the Jupiter-Neptune cycle often relates to over-production, to an uncontrolled proliferation of goods and values on all levels, intellectual and psychological as well as social and economic. Neptune can add a great deal of confusion and intoxication, and may also introduce a tendency to over-idealization and self-deceit through the glamorous search for various dreamy beyonds. From Rudhyar's humanistic point of view, what is being "Neptunized" is the ego's normal Jupiterian urge to grow and expand. At the biological level, the Jupiterian process of cellular multiplication can be upset by Neptune, leading to various sorts of tumours, while at the socio-economic and political levels, Neptune brings to Jupiter's social action the great dreams of social reformers, panaceas which are supposed to do away with all economic and political evils. The tendency of those in public office to present new plans for social and economic reform is generally premature or deceptive at the time of the Jupiter-Neptune conjunction. The way this cycle works out always depends on the quality of the Jupiter function in the individual, which in turn depends on the level at which Saturn is operating. This problem is explained in detail in the Saturn-Uranus cycle. Neptune can universalize the Jupiterian consciousness only if the Saturn ego is open to a truly universalistic sense of human or cosmic existence.

The present Jupiter-Neptune cycle began in January, 1971 at Sagittarius 1 and reached the waxing square aspect in 1974. The present economic recession (1975-1977) is the result of the exaggerated trend of the present cycle, the over-production at all levels to which this cycle can refer when the Jupiter and Saturn functions in nations and individuals are not sufficiently universalized. This is why the only solution to modern problems lies in the development of a global consciousness which would permit a world-wide distribution of goods and products. Through Neptunian suffering, the world is being made to realize that solutions to the problems of hunger and deprivation must be sought on a planetary basis, even if this means relinquishing some degree of national sovereignty. The present financial and economic crisis will not be solved until individuals and nations are willing to introduce a totally new pattern of *global* circulation of wealth.

JUPITER-NEPTUNE CONJUNCTION IN THE HOUSES. These conjunctions which occur every 13 years introduce new trends of social or spiritual expansion. There is also a potential danger of inflation, either social, economic or personal. Human nature being what it is, it may be more useful to stress the dangers of these conjunctions in the following interpretations. These will indicate the *type of experiences* which could lead a person to overstep the boundaries of his life and personality, and to venture into unsound, inflationary paths.

In the 1st House this conjunction essentially affects the ego, one's sense of personal uniqueness and difference from others. It tends to arouse pride, self-intoxication and personal glamour. One must therefore strive to act on the basis of his true experience of Self, rather than relying on appearances. In some cases, the opportunity may arise to identify oneself personally with some vast social or religious trend which brings about a spiritual or inner conversion. In other cases, this tendency might manifest as an intoxication. Above all, it is important to learn detachment and develop a sense of perspective. **In the 2nd House** the accent is on the manner in which a person uses his financial resources, possessions and inherited gifts. There is a danger of financial over-expansion or the dissipation of one's physical and emotional energies. One must now learn to manage his possessions — and especially his savings — carefully and wisely. The tendency is to give in to a desire to make grandiose gestures or spend lavishly for idealistic ventures. **In the 3rd House** the stimulation of this conjunction may principally affect a trend toward changes in one's immediate environment. There may be a desire for increased comfort and luxury, and the pressures of social or religious groups may be felt in one's everyday life. At this time one is optimistic and should go ahead with enthusiasm whenever one is working to improve his mind or learn more about people or the social and economic forces which affect his life. One can also expand the range of his close contacts; however, he should constantly ask himself if he is operating within the limits of his real capacity to absorb and assimilate these new factors and to use them effectively in his life.

In the 4th House this inflationary trend tends to reach one through his home and his desire for personal ease and security. It may also manifest in terms of one's power over those dependent upon him. What is needed here is a quiet and steady readjustment to one's social and psychological conditions — a calm reevaluation of oneself, one's feelings and one's home. This conjunction provides an opportunity for a deep and significant realization of one's own power and worth, even though this may come through the results of exaggerated gestures. **In the 5th House** problems may arise through an unbridled use of the imagination, or conversely, from a suppressed desire for self-expression. Explosive inhibitions, a love of theatrical gestures, or a craving for self-perpetuation through one's progeny may also create difficulties at this time. One must be careful not to be over-generous or over-lenient toward his children; nor should he spend recklessly to feed his dreams of prosperity. There will be opportunities to increase one's capacity for self-expression along artistic, romantic, social or spiritual lines at this time, provided one does so with a conscious awareness of realistic limitations. **In the 6th House** the conjunction points to the possibility of congestive conditions of mind or body, problems of self-loss in work or devotion to some glamorous personality. There is also the possibility of problems arising due to an over-concern with one's health or self-development. At this time there is a need for a deeper psychological re-orientation of one's emotions and of one's sense of Self. It is wise to check up on one's health, avoid over-eating, and control any extreme tendency to better one's performance in any field of activity.

In the **7th House** the inflationary experiences deal mainly with intimate relationships, marriage and new social contacts. There may be a tendency to lose oneself in others. A person must be aware of the danger of over-expansion and exaggerated optimism. Certain people, on the other hand, may tend to over-react to this danger and become afraid to grasp the opportunities to enter into new and unusual partnerships. One may want to trust circumstances yet, at the same time, doubt the ultimate results. One must have faith both in his abilities and in others. **In the 8th House** the Jupiter-Neptune trend makes itself felt primarily in the sphere of business, and in all that touches the fruits of one's intimate or contractual associations. Legacies and new plans for self-regeneration, spiritualism or mystic experiences may also be involved. Here one may want to link his activity or his business to some large corporation, or the latter may exert pressure for one to do so. It is important not to be too trustful or to speculate, especially with others' money. This is not the time to gamble on the love or goodwill of others. Undoubtedly there is the possibility that one may reap a big harvest from his contracts or stock-market investments; however, the danger of losing it all is equally great. Moderation must be used in all things. **In the 9th House** the path to personal inflation is through unsound generalizations and glamorous dreams or visions. Escape into the remote and the transcendent, especially through religion or travel, may cause one to absorb more than he can healthfully assimilate. One must reflect carefully before he abandons the near-at-hand and concrete for the distant, the abstract and the transcendent. This is the time to learn that dreams, speculation, long journeys and even religion are no substitute for efficient living in the here-and-now.

In the **10th House** the inflationary trend of the Jupiter-Neptune conjunction principally affects one's professional life and public prestige. It is important not to seek more power over society or other individuals than one can effectively manage. The danger is being swept off one's feet by the glamour of what is being offered. **In the 11th House** one should beware of unsound plans for social or group reform, idle wishes, utopian ideals or fruitless day-dreams. It is, of course, quite in order for one to desire to change things and to adjust to some new social or economic condition. The danger lies in overdoing those revolutionary gestures, or in trusting one's friends, political party or community groups too much. In the 12th House the new Jupiter-Neptune cycle may produce social experiences or peculiar psychological compulsions which could lead one to entertain a false sense of the value in social or spiritual things and further, to a false sense of achievement. There will, in any case, be a great stirring up of unconscious forces in one's nature. If this results in a fuller self-absorption in some social work or community service, one must still be sure to carefully evaluate the worth of such activities. The demands of society must be weighed against one's own need for self-realization. If a strange upheaval is experienced in one's inner life, one should seek to discover its hidden causes. This may be a good time for psycho-analysis.

JUPITER-NEPTUNE OPPOSITION IN THE HOUSES. The opposition aspect describes the culmination or climax of the Jupiter-Neptune rhythm. In terms of the present cycle which began January, 1971, the opposition occurred in June 1977, at Gemini-Sagittarius 14. In order to derive an individualized meaning for this cycle of transcendence, this opposition should be examined from the natal (or Solar) Houses in which it fell.

Jupiter in the 1st House — Neptune in the 7th House. Jupiterian factors will now dominate one's personal life. Therefore, this is the time to relate oneself personally in a new way toward whatever activity will enable one to display his authority and to prove his personal worth in society. The situation holds definite promise of personal expansion, provided one has worked constructively and without exaggeration since the conjunction in 1971. If this is the case, then one may expect greater activity now in his social sphere. There may, however, be an uncertain or unfocalized trend in one's conjugal life or his contacts with the outer world in general. This can impede personal expansion, and, in some cases, a person may have to spend more than he can afford in order to cope with the demands of his partner or to maintain his social position.

Jupiter in the 2nd House — Neptune in the 8th House. Although one's financial position may seem very good and his credit-rating high, there may now be a dilemma relating to partnership funds. It may be that during these last years one has had to spend a great deal of money, time and energy in order to bolster a confused or uncertain business situation. It is important, therefore, to carefully survey one's financial agreements, and especially the details of any large contractual arrangement offered to one at this time. One may be asked to overcome the selfish enjoyment of personal privileges and possessions, and to use one's resources in a more cooperative and humanitarian manner.

Jupiter in the 3rd House — Neptune in the 9th House. The mind is curiously awake to inner realities at this time, and one may now stand out as a person of extraordinary perception. Conversely, one may also be facing some important mental dilemma in relation to one's expansive activities of the past years. A person may seem at times to be attracted toward distant realms and far-reaching goals, and at other times the attention may be turned toward one's near environment and the concrete problems of daily existence. It may be necessary to universalize the social, moral or religious ideas which one has been using in order to expand within one's community. **Jupiter in the 4th House — Neptune in the 10th House.** Events which occur at this time broaden and stimulate one's feelings and his home life, and build up a person's sense of his own individual worth. Against this, Neptune demands insistently that one recognize the importance of living for more impersonal social or spiritual ideals. There may be obscure problems to solve in relation to one's professional obligations. Things which might lead to scandal must be avoided. If a person suffers from inflated ego, this transit can deflate it.

Jupiter in the 5th House — Neptune in the 11th House. Problems can arise at this time which deeply affect one's social sense as well as his creative energies. A person may find himself confronted by a dilemma: on the one hand, he is eager to expand his ego by a great deal of showing-off or dramatic displays, while on the other hand he is acutely aware of social or spiritual considerations and the pressure of group activities and collective standards on his free will. As always with an opposition aspect, the problem which life presents here is one of the reconciliation of opposing factors. It is a problem of psychological and social integration. If one successfully solves this dilemma, he will come to a deeper realization of his own individuality and a keener appreciation of his associates. **Jupiter in the 6th House — Neptune in the 12th House.** An excess of psychological tension at this time can easily lead to ill-health. The cause of this condition may be some deep-seated confusion which casts a shadow over one's everyday work, or over any form of service which he may be trying to render to society. Strange events may crop up on one's surroundings. The pressure of new conditions may seem disconcerting to one's conservatism in matters of work and service, or else one's position among wealthy people or the patronage which influential people may give can be jeopardised by new public developments.

Jupiter in the 7th House — Neptune in the 1st House. Neptunian elements strongly overshadow one's personal life, and may bring either a good deal of glamour and social excitement, or a touch of the mystical or religious. Everything seems to dissolve one's rational ego into a sea of bliss or mirage-like appearances. It is important not to lose oneself too completely in the illusion of vast, collective ideals. At this time a dilemma may arise between such Neptunian tendencies and the more rigid and conservative trends of either religious orthodoxy or social well-being and respectability. One's marriage partner or other intimate associates are likely to stand for the latter, and thus psychological or social tensions may easily be generated. **Jupiter in the 8th House — Neptune in the 2nd House.** A condition of uncertainty and perhaps deception pervades one's business and financial life. There is the possibility that one may acquire wealth illegally, and that the ultimate results of the procedure may turn out to be deceptive as well. At any rate, one's activities are likely to be very much controlled by social and collective interests, and may depend on the moods of the public. One's personal effort to live up to the spirit of the times in the use of one's resources may meet opposition from partners. If possible, one should not allow prejudices or selfishness to stand in the way of greater social usefulness.

Jupiter in the 9th House — Neptune in the 3rd House. There can be a strong inclination to live in the clouds at this time and to give in to expansive dreams which take one away from the reality of his environment and mundane activities. An abstract or religious type of mental activity seems very favorable; however, the danger of illusion is also marked. Matters of correspondence, publication or printing may cause trouble. There can be a great deal of confusion between objective facts and subjective feelings, and this may be caused by relatives and neighbors that seem to surround a person at this time. In any case, vagueness and aimlessness must be avoided if one is to open himself to new realizations and new social concepts. **Jupiter in the 10th House — Neptune in the 4th House.** A strong dichotomy between one's home life and his public or professional affairs is described by this opposition. There may be a tendency to dissociate those two areas of life completely, and while thus living in two distinct and different spheres of life, to achieve a sense of strength and a better realization of one's destiny. Conditions in one's professional life should be very favorable, and one's prestige and authority should increase. There may, however, be conditions which stand in the way of reaping the fullest and most obvious advantages of this situation. Something within one's own soul, as much as in his outer, social or professional life, can be greatly confusing.

Jupiter in the 11th House — Neptune in the 5th House. There is a strong sense of glamour operating in one's life at this time, and especially in emotional matters. A person may wish to lead a life of social activity and cultivate friendships with the wealthy and prominent, and this prospect may turn one's head more than a little. Under any circumstance it is important to keep one's balance. Life may be trying to teach the value of impersonal service. This may be accomplished now through giving one's emotional expression a new direction. It is not enough to act impersonally; one must also feel impersonally and put those feelings into the form of self-expression which one has chosen. This means acting from the basis of social, collective or universal realities rather than from a strictly individualistic point of view. It is important not to let one's more orthodox friends and advisers cool his ardour, even though he might profitably take their counsel into consideration. **Jupiter in the 12th House — Neptune in the 6th House.** This present period may affect one's health, or it may lead to unusual social or mystical developments. A choice may be demanded, and the issue is likely to be based on psychological and spiritual factors. At this time a person should take things easy and try to remain as optimistic and secure in his own identity as he possibly can. Although one's job or health can be involved, what happens now is really a test of character. Through quiet meditation one can pull oneself together, and enforced rest may be of great assistance. Since one is approaching the end of a social cycle, he will now be able to reap the fruits, whether good or bad, of the type of relationship which he has established between himself and society. Whatever happens lends itself to the development of greater compassion and dedication in one's work, even if this must come through a crisis which dissolves one's pride.

THE WANING JUPITER-NEPTUNE CYCLE IN THE HOUSES. The last quarter square of these two planets will occur in September, 1980, at Virgo-Sagittarius 19. This is the aspect which refers to a crisis in consciousness, and it may signal a turning point in the general mentality toward over-production, inflation and waste. In order to see how this trend will apply to an individual, it must be viewed in relation to the natal (or Solar) Houses involved. The preceding sections on the conjunction and the opposition should give the reader sufficent familiarity with these planets' interrelationship to enable him or her to understand how this phase manifests in the individual life.

X

The Pluto Cycle

Although astronomers are now postulating the existence of another planet beyond the orbit of Pluto, at the time of this writing Pluto is still the furthest known planet from the Sun and describes the outer-most limits of human consciousness. Since its discovery in 1930, many of the original astronomical concepts about the planet have changed drastically. Originally, Pluto was thought to be only 3,700 miles in diameter, less than half that of the Earth. More recently, however, astronomical observations now suggest that it may be considerably larger than the Earth. Its small appearance, according to Jeff Mayo, is now believed to be an effect of specular reflection — its disc is brightest at the center and darkens toward the outer edges. Its apparent magnitude also varies regularly over a period of even a few days. Pluto's small size has therefore been an illusion.

Pluto remains from approximately 12 to 32 years in a zodiacal Sign, averaging 20 1/2 years. Along with Neptune its transit isolates quite accurately the successive waves which are loosely called "generations" or "age-groups". Each generation can be roughly characterized by the passage of Pluto through one Sign of the zodiac, or the passage of Neptune through two successive Signs, one positive and one negative. Rudhyar has suggested counting modern generations from the Neptune-Pluto conjunction of 1891-1893. Thus, the "first" generation was born as Neptune transited through Gemini and Cancer, from 1890 to 1915. The next generation was born between 1915 and 1942, as Neptune transited Leo and Virgo. The third generation of this cycle was born between 1942 and 1970, as Neptune was in Libra and Scorpio. Currently we are in the fourth generation of this modern Neptune-Pluto cycle. The Sign through which Pluto is transiting provides a general indication of what Rudhyar calls the "style of life" which typifies each generation or age-group. Pluto is thus a symbol of the collective mentality of that generation born during its passage through one particular Sign of the zodiac. In an individual birth-chart, therefore, Pluto indicates where the pressure of the collective mentality is concentrated. Its aspects to other natal planets show how the individual *should* orient himself toward this collective mentality.

The quality of the collective mind, which colors all the social, political, artistic, literary, scientific and industrial activities of a generation, sets up a particular bias in the way that generation approaches the universe and the practical problems of mundane existence. As long as a person is identified with this collective style of life and way of thinking, he will not as yet have become an independent individual, and Pluto would not be operating in an individualized manner in his birth-chart. Pluto will significantly "work" in a person's natal chart from the moment he begins to question the collective approach to life, or tries to find an individual solution to the problems generated by the collective mentality of his generation. As long as one remains identified with the collective mentality, there is no problem and therefore his *natal* Pluto will not "work". On the other hand, *Pluto always "works" as a transiting planet*, because it measures the *changing* pressures and demands of the collectivity at any given time. This is true even when a person accepts the collective way of seeing things automatically. Thus transiting Pluto measures the action of social fate, the pressure of collective conditions which appear inevitable by virtue of the fact that they are *impersonal*.

One of Rudhyar's key ideas is that each individual is born in answer to a problem or a need that seeks solution. This means, for example, that the people who were born when Pluto was in Virgo, a transit which awakened us to all the problems created by the collective faith in scientific technology, are the very people capable of finding solutions to those problems. This will only be true, however, IF they succeed in using their natal Pluto in a truly personalized manner. Because of this, Rudhyar has suggested that the natal position of Pluto is the indication of what an individual *can* best contribute toward the solution of the problems which modern society has produced. Natal Pluto indicates, according to its Sign, the nature of these problems and the general type of solution they will require. According to its House position, it shows the particular field of experience in which this solution should be sought. Knowing these things, a person may then attempt to commit himself *consciously and purposefully* to the type of social participation for which he is best fitted according to his individual birth-chart. Pluto will be, in Rudhyar's words, the certification of an individual's true selfhood, and in terms of social values, the symbol of his greatest contribution to life.

The Pluto Generations

Pluto in Taurus — 1852 to 1884. In this Sign of earth and matter, the "spirit of the times" emphasized man's attempt to conquer matter, to discover and use the energies which are the essence of matter. This period corresponds to the "Victorian Age", at which time the collective mentality emphasized the ideas of evolution, scientific materialism, possessiveness, a craving for security and a desire for concrete and tangible power. Scientists started to discover the secrets of material construction and destruction leading to the technological revolution of the 20th century. The trend was to give value to ideas and things according to the practical use to which they could be put.

Pluto in Gemini — 1884 to 1913. The social need revealed by the transit of Pluto through Gemini was the expansion of man's mental horizons. It signaled the building up of concrete knowledge and intellectual "know how", and the freedom from traditional, materialistic ways of thinking and social organization which evolved during the Taurean phase. Due to the development of rapid global communications of all kinds which occurred during this transit, the world began figuratively to shrink. The Gemini phase ended on the eve of the first global war.

Pluto in Cancer — 1913 to 1938. During this transit, the traditional foundations of national societies and of home and family life underwent profound modifications. Planets in the Sign Cancer can never have a truly universalizing influence because this Sign refers essentially to the need for *personal* integration within well-defined boundaries. The accent, therefore, was on partisan politics, nationalism and isolationism. That is why, in spite of the development of world communications and atomic energy, individuals and nations did not gain a universal spirit during this transit. Instead they tried to corner these new energies released by science for their personal or nationalistic use and aggrandisement. Perhaps this is not to be wondered at, since the widespread collective upheavals of the period threw individuals and nations back on themselves and obliged them to reorganize their personal and social foundations. This transit began on the eve of the first global war and ended as World War II began.

Pluto in Leo — 1938 to 1957. Pluto's entry into Leo is a basic signature of the second World War. This transit accentuated national and personal pride and the effort to express national and personal powers and abilities. Dictators came onto the political scene and industrial magnates created huge, multi-national business organizations. Rudhyar remarked that this period revealed a new feudalism, but now on a world-scale and reaching toward outer space. There was a glorification of ruthlessness, terrorism and totalitarian power. At the same time, however, the feudal devotion to some tyrannical leader or ideology started to crumble, as oppressed peoples began to fight against colonialism. Individuals in all fields tended to build up their personal power through the often selfish use of scientific technology. People born with Pluto in Leo often have problems in the use of their personal powers. They must control their Leo tendency toward pride, violent emotions, and the proclivity so magnified in Mussolini to compensate for over-sensitiveness in human relationships with a mask of arrogance and passionate superiority.

Pluto in Virgo — 1957 to 1971. This was a period of criticism and psychological crises, as individuals began to realize that they were obliged to live as slaves to the rhythm of a machine. Increasingly more and more people became aware that the scientific, technological trend was leading humanity to disaster and needed to be balanced by a sense of global purpose and a greater consideration for the basic quality of life. Those born during this transit have become the greatest critics of the deification of the computer, and during this time the public began to realize the dangers of chemical pollutants which are destroying the environment, land, sea and air.

Pluto in Libra — 1971 to 1983. During this transit the accent is on co-operation, as though a transformation of all the previous ways in which people and nations have related to each other is now possible. Individuals and nations will be obliged by circumstances to review the way in which they relate to the rest of the world. Whether this is on psychological or spiritual levels, or in terms of international economic relationships, the necessity for a global world-view should become clearer. The past has to be reviewed, and the worthwhile separated from the obsolete. Communism and world socialism have now reached a turning-point, having been born when Pluto was in the opposite Sign Aries. The stress on scientific technology and on synthetic materials has changed since Pluto entered Libra; there has been a new trend due to a growing concern over the pollution caused by chemical waste matter. People have begun to question the value of technological achievements based on quantitative analysis, and insist on the need for a *new quality of life,* symbolized by Libra. The Pluto in Leo people should now be able to make some practical and efficient contribution to the work of the world, since there is now a sextile between transiting and natal Pluto. The Pluto in Cancer people will pass through an actional crisis in terms of their possible contribution to life. Their partisan and separatist attitudes are being undermined. The Pluto in Gemini people will be more in tune with the new Libra trend and may suddenly find that the ideas for which they have been fighting for so long will now have a hearing.

Pluto in Scorpio — 1984 to 1995. During this transit, all values based on what Rudhyar has called "man's common humanity" will be emphasized. There will be an intense emotional yearning for deep union with others. Important mystical and spiritual experiences can be ahead for many people. Occult-oriented individuals or groups can come to the fore, and socialist or communist trends can become even stronger. Collective movements will gain power. During its transit of Scorpio Pluto will cut the orbit of Neptune, coming closer to the Earth than Neptune ever does. This may mean that there will be a new revolutionary force or impulse released into humanity at this time. Pluto will remain within Neptune's orbit for about twelve years, during the whole of its transit through Scorpio, and will be at its perihelion in 1988. While Pluto is in Libra and Scorpio, the call to men and nations will be to unite in brotherhood and love, and in a mutual understanding and tolerance of individual differences. If this is not possible, then perhaps once again, as has already happened in the two world wars of this century, individuals may be made to unite in death. Through the fire of man-made or planetary cataclysms, nuclear war or telluric upheaval, Pluto will teach people to know and feel (Scorpio) that we are all individually concerned with everything that happens to human beings everywhere on the globe.

Pluto in Sagittarius — 1995 to 2010. During this transit Pluto's speed begins to decrease. The collective mind should be occupied with the task of reorganizing the social life and building up a social consciousness related to those new values and powers made available since Pluto entered Libra in 1971. After the emotional crisis of the Scorpio transit, which will especially affect those born with Pluto in Leo, new ideologies will spring up with the purpose of building a more inclusive form of society and seeking to establish the laws and the means of inter-relationship necessary to make concrete what people have yearned for emotionally during the Scorpio phase. People born at this time will have to be careful of fanaticism, as the rights of individuals may be forgotten in the attempt to impose new laws, ideas and principles. The Pluto in Virgo people may find this to be a critical period in terms of their contribution to the work of the world.

Pluto in Capricorn — beginning 2010. The new social, national and international concepts which humanity has succeeded in mastering should be incorporated now into some concrete form. At the same time, Pluto will challenge in drastic fashion all forms of entrenched power. All forms of power which have been crystallized since Pluto was in Aries or Cancer will now be questioned. This is the critical phase for the Pluto in Libra people. There should be attempts at reorganization of political structures in terms of a new ideal of civilization, a global civilization within which nations and individuals may participate in freedom according to the new goals which humanity has set itself to accomplish.

The Personal Cycle of Pluto

Any discussion of a personalized "use" of Plutonian energies must be made with the strictures already mentioned regarding a conscious dissociation from the collective mentality. Since Pluto moves so slowly, there is usually one quadrant of the birth-chart which will be especially emphasized by Pluto's transit. The meaning of that quadrant, as it has been presented in the chapters on Saturn, Uranus and Neptune, will also apply in the case of Pluto. That quadrant will provide a basic indication of an individual's potential contribution to his times. Furthermore, whenever Pluto crosses an Angle of the natal or solar chart, there is usually a strong demand made on the individual to specify more clearly the nature of his essential destiny and social purpose. Any transit conjunction of Pluto with a natal planet will represent the call to a new order in one's use of that planetary function. It will force the personality into alignment with new ideals and new forms of social behavior, cutting one loose from past allegiances to collective or traditional values. Pluto always makes demands. Uranus inspires from the "outside," Neptune dissolves or absorbs, but Pluto demands rebirth, reintegration along new lines and deliberate self-sacrifice.

The natal (or solar) House in which Pluto is posited at birth will reveal how that individual will approach the collective mentality of his times, and how he can rise to meet the challenges of those collective needs. The House position will not indicate the *particular* responses of each person to such challenges, but rather, the *type of response* generally possible. This important distinction is never made in the cook-book variety of astrological text when meanings are given for planets in Signs and Houses. Analysis of Pluto's natal House position shows the basic contribution which an individual can potentially make to society. The transiting House position, on the other hand, will indicate how a person may best meet the social demands of the moment.

When Pluto Crosses the Ascendant and transits the 1st House, the individual will be strongly challenged to seek a deeper and more complete form of personal integration. A person may feel called upon to identify himself with, or to give an individual demonstration of, strongly established political trends or spiritual forces. At this time he should assert those qualities in his personality which single him out from the masses and express his unique abilities. There should be an uncompromising and fearless effort to free oneself from traditional thought patterns and become a personal example for others along the lines suggested by the Sign in which Pluto is found at birth. The personal tendency may be expressed positively as a desire to assume authority or, negatively, to become ruthless and stubborn in one's social contacts, wanting to boss other people and have one's own way regardless of the cost or obstacles. A person can be deeply affected by political occurrences and by strongly organized groups which claim his allegiance. Present developments can be far-reaching and disconcerting. There should be an eagerness to probe for deeper values in relation to spritual, social or political issues.

An attitude of self-righteousness and overweening pride must be avoided, and one should not become overly reliant on force in deciding the outcome of his arguments or in the furtherance of his desires. The danger of Pluto in the 1st House is too much power with little else to blend with it. Cooperation, understanding and compassion are virtues that need developing.

When Pluto transits the 2nd House one's best contribution to the present needs will be the inner or outer wealth that he has inherited at birth or acquired through his efforts. What is needed is efficient purposeful management and use of all that one owns: the energies and powers of his body; the facts, ideas and personal values he has assimilated through education and the example of his elders; the money he earns; and everything he has produced. One must dare to prove himself to the world. In some cases, this transit may indicate a challenge to renounce traditional ways of using one's possessions or energies in order to attain a spiritual ideal. In other cases, however, it may mean giving one's wealth, time or energy in order to sustain a worthwhile cause or outstanding personage. Extraordinary spiritual or creative gifts could be used to introduce new values to mankind. It is also possible that a person's capacities may be used in ways unbeknown to him to further some greater racial, national or social purpose.

When Pluto transits the 3rd House the intellectual and psychological way of life one has developed can become an example to others for solving relevant problems. A person should develop his intelligence and "know-how" in order to deal significantly with his environment. He may have to explain, either in speech or in writing, the new techniques of living which he has evolved for saner adaptation to the modern world. One must not be afraid to question or challenge what seem to be superficial or outmoded patterns of thought and action, even if what one says may severely upset the people with whom one is in daily contact. While bearing in mind that this planet always reveals the "naked truth", it is always well to control any tendency toward vindictiveness. In some cases, this transit can lead to one's being swept off his feet by collective forces or by an "act of God". The passing away of a relative or neighbor can be the means to break away from environmental limitations. There is a need to avoid extremist theories, fads and radical ideas related to one's routine of daily living. One must also take care not to become dictatorial with neighbors and relatives, especially one's brothers and sisters. By joining a local political group a person may be able to place himself in a position to influence collective opinion in a forward-looking manner; however, an overly radical expression of one's ideas or values can lead to social ostracism.

When Pluto reaches the Nadir and transits the 4th House, the challenge is to stand firmly by what one considers to be his own truth. He must be self-reliant and seek to build a new ground-of-being for his personal life and, if possible, for the social and political activities of his nation as well. A person should try to become a stout supporter of some new plan for world, national or social order, for in that way his *personal* stand may give courage to the fearful. In establishing a new foundation for one's life, it will be necessary to keep in tune with the times and be open to changes, however far-reaching they may be. One should bring new ideas into his home, and he should plumb the depths of his soul and examine his emotions for new power. This is an especially good time to work toward the fullest possible integration of one's personality. In seeking to establish all that one owns, materially and psychologically, in a new dimension of living, *inner* stability will be the reward.

When Pluto transits the 5th House there is a call to transpersonal creativity — what speaks *through* an individual becomes more universally significant than this person. This does not imply that one should become a medium, but rather a conscious intermediary. A person should not be afraid to take risks or to go beyond established limits and attitudes, for the opportunity is present to become a pioneer on cultural, scientific or artistic levels. At this time one should control his emotions and not indulge in a ruthless attempt to express himself at the cost of others, whether this be in love or in one's social life or career. It is also possible that a person may become the victim of another's ruthlessness. Such deep emotional experiences do, however, have the potential for opening the consciousness beyond the habitual level of personal desire. The time is ripe to create new values, purposes, forms and products made necessary by modern trends.

When Pluto transits the 6th House one should cultivate his ability to work unselfishly for a Cause, to serve some noble purpose or great personage. To this end, it will be necessary to demonstrate a capacity to overcome pain, discouragement, over-sensitivity and personal failings. Because Pluto lends itself to overzealous thoroughness, one must be careful not to be fanatical and exclusive, or to lose himself in needless self-sacrifice. The goal should be total dedication to a task enabling a person to reorient his interests and feelings away from self and toward a participation in the larger life of inter-personal relationships and global humanity. One must say yes to the goal of self-improvement; he must desire to change and grow. A person must also be ready to serve and obey, always with the conscious aim of outgrowing his personal egocentricity and selfishness so as to become a more integrated personality. An individual willingness to meet personal crises can be an inspiring example for others. On more mundane levels, problems may be provoked between employer and employees, especially involving labor unions. One can become a victim of reactionary or radical theories, or he may tend to become ruthless and dictatorial in his dealings while on the job. In health matters, one should beware of fads and single-minded adherence to this or that method of cure. It might be best to follow absolutely up-to-date methods in both labor situations and health problems.

When Pluto crosses the Descendant and transits the 7th House, the major contribution to the needs of the times will depend on the *social* consciousness of an individual rather than on the impact of personal example in some sphere. This transit points to the development of one's capacity to share and cooperate on a basis of equality, and to work together for a common social purpose. This means that one will make close contacts with others, not so much for who they are as individuals, but because they stand for the same spiritual truths or social purposes as oneself. Personal and emotional values take a secondary place. In some cases, one will have to watch out for fanaticism and ruthlessness. It may be fine to shake people out of their complacency and to destroy what one considers to be illusions or wrong ideas; however, there is with Pluto always a danger of overdoing it and thereby becoming a destroyer of other people's integrity, even with the best of intentions. One must realize that not everyone is ready to live and work in the spirit of total dedication that Pluto demands. During this transit, therefore, marriage and partnership can lead to far-reaching changes. Destiny can oblige one to cut himself free from past loyalties and to approach his outer life and relationships along totally new lines. One's associations with social, political or occult groups can present a challenge to rebirth and a deeper cooperation of efforts in a common cause.

When Pluto transits the 8th House, one's major contribution to society may be his capacity to make all his relationships produce value for everyone concerned. There should be a willingness to restructure one's habitual techniques both in business and in group encounters. The new demands of global responsibility can stimulate a person to reorient himself and his activities so as to eliminate the danger of exploiting others. Personal transformation can come through identifying oneself deeply and emotionally with group experiences. Various forms of "ritual magic" may attract the attention at this time. In any case, Pluto in the 8th House can encourage one to throw precedents to the winds in order to profit from the opportunities offered by modern business trends. One will, however, have to take complete responsibility for the results of the attitude he adopts. Pluto can call for a drastic showdown. At this time a person must be careful of shady financial schemes. The government or strong business or political groups can influence finances held in common. Money can be a bone of contention in one's intimate relationships as well, and financial re-arrangements with partners may become necessary. In certain cases this transit can provoke a test of the personal will or courage in the face of collective catastrophe or death. There can be a complete breakdown of the established life pattern, obliging one to strike out in a totally new direction. Generally speaking, however, Pluto's "influence" may manifest very little on the surface. A person's acceptance of occult or religious ideas or one's association with groups investigating the unseen side of life may now work important changes in one's entire attitude toward life.

When Pluto transits the 9th House, one's major contribution should come from his capacity to *understand* the new goals or principles necessary to establish a global consciousness and a new quality in interpersonal relationships. One can potentially become an example for others in a new style of life, or he can be an active promoter of the breaking-up of outmoded ideas, working actively toward the propagation of an idealism resulting from a new-found clarity of vision. Political developments on an international level or travel abroad can present dangers, although contact with foreign people can have an important effect on one's destiny. In a general way, Pluto in the 9th House asks one to contribute something new to the world according to his understanding of science, law, religion, philosophy or "occult" development. To this can be added astrology, spiritualism and depth psychology.

When Pluto crosses the Midheaven and transits the 10th House, a person should attempt to contribute meaningfully through his social or professional position. The test to be met is the *right use of power*. This is the time to consciously assume group responsibilities, to become a leader in a progressive movement aiming at human betterment. One will have to demonstrate his beliefs through his actions, and as usual with Pluto, there is a danger of becoming too fanatical or ruthless, either with oneself or with one's companions. During this transit there may be far-reaching changes affecting one's reputation, profession or social standing. One must prove through his actions that what he has become qualifies him for the public role he will play. The specific nature of that role is secondary and depends on one's hereditary possibilities. The important consideration is the *quality* of his performance. A person's spiritual status may well be decided now by the use he makes of the social power and authority at his disposal. Will he use it to further his own ends and personal ambition, or will he apply his power to further the ideal for which he worked while Pluto was in the third quadrant? Also, events outside one's personal control can bring about a loss of position and standing or trouble with government authorities.

When Pluto transits the 11th House, one's best contribution may be his innate desire to identify himself with all people or groups working toward greater human integration. A person should *act out* this ideal now and align himself with the forward-looking ideas and movements trying to lead humanity onward. In making a choice, a person should question the value of all social processes and be ready to reform himself as well as others. Radical changes in one's personal ambitions may alter the course of life, and a person may find himself plunged into entirely new social circles. He should be wary of new acquaintances or unusual offers from "friends" or groups. What matters most during this transit may be the contagion of one's total faith in the ideal he has made his own. The readiness to sacrifice one's all to that ideal, and the determination to promote essential human values, will be most important.

When Pluto transits the 12th House, one comes to the final phase in a full Pluto cycle, the phase during which the fruits of the old cycle, good or bad, are harvested. Out of those fruits the seed of the new cycle must be born. A person must therefore be prepared to meet without compromise those trials which always attend rebirth. He can only contribute something new to society at this time if he is prepared to totally repudiate the past and all outworn allegiances or sentimental attachments. There may be deep-seated rumblings in the subconscious mind, as present experiences demand change so that one may fit himself to more modern concepts of individual and social progress. The time may be ripe for exploration of little-known thought processes or occult theories. Such exploration can upset the findings of tradition and training, placing powerful new ideas in one's grasp. It can also leave one floundering in an ocean of metaphysical confusion, a dupe in the hands of unscrupulous charlatans. In spite of these dangers, many people can profit from the present psychological urge to make unknown realms of the universe or the psyche more tangible and familiar. They may be able to adapt ancient truths and symbols to modern understanding. For the more practically inclined, this transit can be used in a positive manner through a willingness to work for the underprivileged, either within one's own community or in the world at large.

INDIVIDUAL PLUTO CRISES. Aspects made by transiting Pluto to the natal Sun are quite important, particularly if there is an aspect between the Sun and Pluto in the birth-chart. Since Pluto symbolizes an individual's essential life-purpose in terms of his social destiny and the Sun refers to the creative spiritual power, then a transit of Pluto to the Sun can indicate a powerful and important transformation. Any aspect of transiting Pluto to the natal Sun can be significant, and especially the conjunction. The challenges at that time can utterly transform one's personal and social destiny. This may sometimes happen through the death of someone or through the establishment of an important personal relationship. Another important contact, although it does not always happen in a life-time, is the transit of Uranus over natal Pluto. Uranus is the symbol of social transformation and spiritual metamorphosis. It shows the way in which an individual can pass beyond the confining boundaries of his personal Saturnian ego, and therefore its stimulation of natal Pluto is a significant indication of the *opportunity* to fulfill a society-transforming destiny.

The crises which may come when transiting Pluto aspects natal Pluto refer more to a generic experience than to an individual one. They will be met by an individual in terms of the field of experience symbolized by the House position of his natal Pluto. This House indicates the best and most natural way for each person to meet the Pluto crises in his own life. *Real* Plutonian crises are never experienced by an individual in a significant way unless Uranus and Neptune have first prepared the way. In all other cases, Pluto simply indicates the collective pressures to which one is subjected as a passive specimen of society.

XI

The Retrograde Movement
of the Outer Planets

Retrogradation is a geocentric phenomenon. A planet at times appears to move backward in the sky as seen by an observer on Earth. The situation is similar to the case of two trains moving side by side at different speeds. If one is riding in the faster moving train and observes the slower moving one, the latter seems to slow down, then stop for a second, and finally appears to move backwards as the faster moving train overtakes it. Since the relationship of the Earth to the other planets is not of parallel lines but of nearly circular orbits, the illusion of retrogradation is only a temporary phenomenon and the true perspective is soon re-established. The traditional interpretations of retrogradation are more conditioned by the astrologer's reaction to the words "retrograde" and "backward" than by astronomical data and facts. Many points are ignored which can be very useful in interpreting the psychological meaning of retrogradation. Retrogradation occurs when the planet and the Earth are on the same side of the solar system and are about to form, or have formed, a straight line with the Sun. Thus all planets are their nearest to the Earth when retrograde and will appear at their brightest; their discs, when observed through a telescope, will be larger than at any other time in their cycles. This increase in light and size is most clearly noticeable in the cases of Mercury and Venus. What actually happens geocentrically when a planet goes retrograde is not a backward movement so much as an apparent loop in space which the planet describes as it moves nearer to the Earth. The planet seems to go out of its regular orbital path as if pulled toward the Earth, forming a loop directed Earthwards.

The relationship of a particular planet to the Sun at the time of retrogradation can be of two kinds. All those planets beyond the Earth's orbit, Mars through Pluto, are in opposition to the Sun at the mid-point of their period of retrogradation. Venus and Mercury, whose orbits are within the Earth orbit, are in *inferior* conjunction with the Sun at the midpoints of their retrogradation periods. Because their orbits are contained within the Earth orbit, Venus and Mercury — when observed from the Earth — always appear as close companions to the Sun. Geocentrically speaking they can never be in opposition to the Sun. A thorough interpretation of retrograde motion must take at least these basic points into consideration. They enable the astrologer to find a fundamental meaning which can be applied to the general case of retrogradation, at the same time allowing a differentiation between the motion of the interior and exterior planets. Rudhyar was the first astrologer to establish such a logical meaning and differentiation*, and he states that, of all the factors in astrology, retrograde movement is the one which openly stresses the difference between the geocentric and the heliocentric points of view. Planets are *never* retrograde heliocentrically speaking. Rudhyar believed that the study of retrogradation led to the change from the Ptolemaic and geocentric view of the universe to the heliocentric and modern world-viewpoint.

The significance of the discovery of heliocentricity is, according to Rudhyar, that thereafter Man became aware that there are two ways of looking at life, two ways of relating oneself to the universe. Astrologers cannot dismiss the geocentric point of view, for that is how the universe is seen directly and in terms of man's immediate experience. However, the heliocentric viewpoint adds a new dimension to man's consciousness of the universe. It symbolically represents man's present capacity to understand the universal laws of life in a detached, objective and impersonal manner. Although astrology can also use the heliocentric approach, it generally utilizes the geocentric point of view because it deals with direct and concrete human experience. It seeks to understand how human personalities develop, and what happens to them individually and in groups. Modern scientific and psychological knowledge has brought astrology to the realization that an individual personality can be understood as a field of energies, each of which has an independent existence and obeys its particular rhythm of development, regardless of whether one is aware of this fact or not. This field of energies is established within each particular organic structure. For this reason the human personality can be understood as an organic whole within which a complex harmony of opposite and complementary forces, impulses and desires operate. It never remains the same internally, even if it presents an external appearance which seems relatively permanent.

In astrology the planets symbolize the natural energies of life which animate and direct the personality. The rhythms of these energies are measured by the cyclic motions of the planets, and their interplay by the way the planets are inter-related by aspect and cyclic phase within the solar system. Rudhyar suggests that the heliocentric view of the solar system gives the astrologer a true picture of these life-energies within the human personality *could they develop freely according to their own natural*

---

*In articles in *World Astrology* magazine: January & February, 1944.

rhythms and without interference from the conscious will of man. These heliocentric planetary motions are constant, regular and always direct, revealing the rhythm of the energies of life in their natural and instinctive state. The geocentric point of view, on the other hand, reveals the things which *actually happen* within and around the individual. These actual happenings are the products, not of the unhindered development of the natural life-energies, but instead *as they are constantly being modified* by the will, the thought patterns and the emotions of the *conscious ego.* Because of this difference, Rudhyar has postulated that the geocentric motions of the planets represent the effect of "personality" upon "life," the effect of man's conscious will, thought and feelings on the energies within his body and psyche. The retrograde phases of the planetary cycles are therefore the outstanding indicators of man's conscious interference with the rhythm of the life-energies within his structured field. The loops in the geocentric paths of the planets are the signatures of man's interference, the signatures of *human needs,* needs which have arisen because of the fact that man wills, thinks and feels in a conscious and uniquely individual way.

When a planet is retrograde, its function is no longer active according to its own essential nature. In some cases this may seem to indicate a "retracing of one's steps"; however, this is not a true picture of what happens. As the planet describes a loop Earthward, symbolically one may *get a closer look at its life-energy and function,* and so perhaps learn how to gain a new perspective or to evaluate a situation in a new manner. It may mean putting right some injustice one has done, accepting the consequences of something wilfully done in the past, or preparing oneself deliberately for some new line of action. Whatever the actual circumstances, a retrograde planet is a planet ready to answer a personal need resulting from past activities and should be geared to a new cycle of self-expression. No one can say whether a person will make a constructive use of the retrograde phase of a planet's cycle or not. The possibility is always there; the need can and may be met and fulfilled at that time. That need, however, may also deepen if a person fails to face it objectively. In the latter event, the consciousness will become ever more a prey to fear and frustration, to feelings of failure and resentment.

The meaning and interpretation of the retrograde periods of the three "personal planets," Mercury, Venus and Mars, are discussed at length in the chapter devoted to them. This chapter will therefore be limited to the retrograde periods of the so-called "outer" planets, Jupiter through Pluto. The cycles of these outer planets (to which can be added that of Mars) deal essentially with the *outer* life of an individual. Jupiter and Saturn, the social planets, are concerned with the external manifestations of one's social life and their effects on his behavior. In the cases of

Uranus, Neptune and Pluto, the planets not visible to the naked eye and therefore generally beyond man's conscious awareness, the retrograde periods deal with attempts at spiritual transformation under the pressure of the social, religious or greater cosmic Whole in which the individual moves. As the mid-point of the retrograde periods of these planets is established by their opposition to the Sun, the major problem described by these periods is to understand as objectively and honestly as possible the meaning of the planetary function in one's conscious life. Through an understanding of the particular role which that energy plays in a given instance, a person may overcome whatever confusion the planet may have created.

Thus each year, whenever one or more of these planets is retrograde in the heavens, life demands an individual effort to become more objective toward the real meaning of one's external, social life. A person must try to adapt himself more effectively to the needs of his society and his interpersonal relationships, and to open himself to the wealth of possibly alien elements or unusual experiences which they now offer. At the same time, however, one must remain true to the structure of his essential identity and purpose as revealed by the birth pattern. As retrograde planets refer to the influence of the past, the opportunities they offer are always more or less fatefully conditioned by what has already happened in an individual life or on the world scene. The retrograde periods of the outer planets reveal crucial collective, social needs to which the individual should give his conscious attention and which he should try to fulfill. *This will be particularly true when the opposition of the Sun and the retrograde planet coincides with an important planetary placement or natal axis.* One's personal reaction to the needs of the moment will always be clearly indicated in terms of the circumstances and experiences of the House in which the transiting retrograde planet is found.

The foregoing is particularly relevant in the cases of Jupiter and Saturn. Uranus, Neptune and Pluto present astronomical peculiarities which made Rudhyar say forty years ago that they were, together, the basic challenge of our times to human consciousness. They are constantly trying to make us change our minds about things, and to seek and live a transpersonal life. (See Rudhyar's *The Sun Is Also A Star.*) There is practically no difference between the geocentric and the heliocentric positions of Uranus, Neptune and Pluto. What betrays their particular role is the fact that the satellites of Uranus and Neptune, instead of following the general west-to-east motion common to all other planetary bodies, move from east-to-west, and therefore in what might be called a retrograde motion. For this reason, Rudhyar has said that the obedience of these three most distant planets to the law of the solar system is only an external one because these planets move in the same direction as all other planets. They are *in* the world, but not *of* it. They are not only transcendent in the sense of being "beyond" the familiar Saturnian boundaries of human experience and human nature; they are *complementary* to the solar system and a perpetual challenge to its solar trends.

Uranus, Neptune and Pluto do not represent faculties normally inherent in human nature *as we know it today*. They are not ambassadors of the Sun, but of a galactic power and way of life which is basically different from our normal Sun-centered selfhood. Since the public discovery of these three planets, mankind has become ready to attempt the integration of his solar vitality and selfhood with the energies of the galaxy. This is an attempt to fit the individual into a Whole greater than that represented by the solar system. Thus, individually we must try to reach a more universal awareness of Spirit or of God through the conscious use of powers and functions which are not ours as a result of human effort, but rather have only become *available for our use* since the discovery of Uranus, Neptune and Pluto. These powers are "galactic", God-given gifts of the Spirit entrusted to man to be used wisely and for the good of all. Because of the apparent retrograde movement of their satellites, when Uranus and Neptune are retrograde they appear to move in the same direction as their satellites always do. Therefore they act according to their own "galactic" natures and not as visitors subservient to the law of motion of this solar system, although Rudhyar does not consider that they are necessarily more powerful at this time. From the point of view of the so-called "normal" personality, this may sometimes seem quite destructive, for when they are direct, what they offer is likely to be more easily acceptable.

These three planets are retrograde a little less than half of the time during any given year; therefore the fact of their retrogradation can only have a very general significance. In view of the distinction which has been made between their intrinsic meanings when direct and when retrograde, the most important times are when they change direction, either from direct to retrograde or vice versa. It would, however, be foolish to expect outstanding events to occur at the time of each planetary station. Being slow in movement, they can only indicate a general trend in events or a mass reaction. Nonetheless, people who aspire to public positions or who are already prominent in their community, because they are reacting more personally to the needs and trends of their time, are more often affected at the time of a change in the direction of these planets. Although it is impossible to establish a rule, experience has shown that it is just *before* a planet turns retrograde or direct that things come to a head. Here again, however, as in everything relating to progressions, directions and transits, nothing spectacular need happen if the progressed or transit indication does not tie in with the potential promise of the natal chart, although transit stations in the Angular Houses are often as marked as transit conjunctions or oppositions to natal planets.

While indications under Uranus are generally sudden and sharp, under Neptune the action is insidious and often imperceptible at the moment. Neptune's transit of a House or an important point in the natal chart is slow and therefore measures slowly changing social ideas and concepts. New responsibilities and obligations are introduced in terms of the needs of the times. There is a challenge toward a new social awareness, toward greater cooperation in group endeavours and toward detachment from limiting Saturnian attitudes. Pluto remains from thirteen to thirty years in a Sign, as its motion is very erratic. It has a broad mass influence and tends to stimulate obsessive ideas and power drives within a person. When Pluto is strong in a birth-chart, there is often a tendency to ruthless efficiency in following one's purposes, good or evil, and to put aside whatever and whomever is not absolutely necessary to the achievement of that purpose. The challenge then in all that such a person undertakes is to respect other people's integrity as individuals. Jupiter and Saturn in their transit cycles measure the type and degree of an individual's normal social participation in the world around him. At the time of their transit stations, before going retrograde or becoming direct again, they can present challenges to one's traditionally accepted social values and activities. Problems of adjustment arise or culminate in some decision affecting the scope and the place of one's normal activities.

In all these cases of retrogradation of the five outermost planets, the periods of a change in direction should be integrated with the general meaning of their transit cycles through the natal Houses of the birthchart, and also with the actual phase of development of the particular planet's cycle as measured from its natal position. These two cyclic situations will give the primary meaning of the planets' challenges to the individual. The times when the planet is stationary retrograde or stationary direct are again moments of focused activity in terms of this primary meaning, as are their transit contacts with natal planets or sensitive points. It must never be forgotten that humanistic astrology is not trying to pinpoint events, astronomical or circumstantial, but to relate them to the whole cycle of which they are a part.

As an example let us assume transiting Saturn is going through the natal 3rd House during 1976-1977. The reader will find the basic meaning of this transit in the chapter devoted to the Saturn Cycle. As the year 1977 opens, Saturn is retrograde and its opposition to the Sun occurs on February 2. This means that in terms of an approximate 12-month Sun-Saturn cycle, the opposition on February 2 was the culmination of what began on July 29, 1976 when the Sun and Saturn were conjunct. If

Saturn was transiting the natal 3rd House on July 29, 1976, circumstances near and following that date theoretically presented a new challenge in terms of the meaning of Saturn in the natal 3rd House. If, on the other hand, Saturn was still transiting the natal 2nd House at the time of the Sun-Saturn conjunction, then the challenge would have been in terms of 2nd House circumstances and experiences. If that individual met the challenge of the conjunction consciously and worked actively for a solution to the problems it posed, then the retrograde period and the opposition on February 2, 1977 could lead to the actual solution and freedom from some limiting condition in either 2nd or 3rd House terms, according to where Saturn was posited at the time of the conjunction. However, this actual solution and freedom from limitation would be, in both cases, in 3rd House terms. If the challenge was not met constructively, then the retrograde period which began on November 27, 1976 and lasted until April 11, 1977 would have built up a sense of frustration or disappointment which would have been most acute both near the time of the opposition on February 2, and also just before November 27 and April 11 when Saturn was stationary retrograde and stationary direct.

For those readers who use the Sabian symbols for the degrees of the Zodiac, the symbol of the degree on which a planet falls at the time of its opposition to the Sun will give a key both to the basic meaning of the confrontation experienced and to its potential solution as well. Of course, the meaning of this or any other *transiting* planetary opposition will be the same for everyone. It is a general challenge to all mankind. However, it will affect each individual personally according to the planets' House positions at the time. In the example given above, Saturn was at 14 Leo at the time of its opposition to the Sun. The symbol for 14 Leo is "A human soul seeking opportunities for outward manifestation", with the keynote, "the yearning for self-actualization". This is a general challenge to all people to try to let the soul manifest *through* the activities, thoughts and feelings of one's conscious ego in the everyday experience of life. The Saturn ego is that which most often hinders the manifestation of the soul. If transiting Saturn at 14 Leo is in the 3rd natal House at the time of the opposition, then 3rd House activities may be most hindering that soul's manifestation.

Conclusion

The humanist commitment is, above all, a commitment to become as fully as possible what one potentially is. Each person is born to express, in as pure a way as possible, the promise contained in his birth-chart. This naturally involves certain problems which must be solved and challenges which must be met. Rudhyar once said that we are all in some way both the expression of a problem and the possible solution to that problem. Therefore, an individual can only solve that problem if he really IS what his chart shows him potentially to be. From a certain point of view, this problem is life itself. There are, however, many more specific details to be added to this idea. We are all examples of what a human being *can* be, while at the same time each of us has something which the other lacks. This is true not only in terms of individual gifts and talents, but more especially in terms of the individual facet of truth which each person has to express. The whole truth will be all these facets put together. Therefore, each person must find his own way and his individual manner of expressing that truth.

The humanist commitment is not easy, because to live the conscious way means that one must become a true individual, and to be a true individual one must first of all take his distance from others, from what the unthinking majority accept. A person has to gain a perspective on what everybody else believes, feels and thinks. He must find out things for himself, rather than merely assuming the opinions of those around him. Thus, one must first isolate himself psychologically from the rest of the world. The process of individuation inevitably involves isolation as its first step. The individual must be born out of the psychic womb of family and society. This is generally the most difficult part of the whole process, freeing oneself from all the pressures and prejudices of one's environment and from all the ideas and values which are assumed by others and which must no longer be taken for granted. This does not necessarily mean separating oneself from one's feelings and emotions; however, one must learn to experience his feelings in his own personal way. Therefore, an individual must initially gain a perspective on the way his habitual feelings are conditioned by the feelings of those around him, on the way he has been made to feel and think according to the others' examples and standards. Once a person manages to separate himself from the accepted way of seeing and doing things, he will be in a position to determine how he can add something new.

How can an individual *use* his birth-chart as a guide to gain this new perspective? The first step is to live and work according to the meaning which one may find according to his specific age at that time (the Age

Factor). One's individual development is inextricably bound to the age factor, as it expresses the generic foundation for all individual variations. Before the age of 28, each person is trying, consciously or unconsciously, to bring himself up to date. In order to do this, a person must first go through the achievements of his racial and cultural past which have led up to the present moment. However, instead of continuing to live in the way indicated by the past, as so many people do, the humanist will try to USE that past as a starting-point for something new. In other words, he will not simply repeat what has already been done, with only superficial modifications which essentially change nothing. Rather, he will try to add something which did not exist before. The first 28 years of life should, therefore, represent a process of assimilation of the fruits of the past. Thus, an individual must become master of all the functions and talents at his disposal, of everything he possesses both outwardly and inwardly, in order to be himself. A person cannot truly become an individual in the psychological sense of the term before that time. A child prodigy is not yet a truly creative individual. He is an expression of his heredity, of his family or soul past, and unless he does something as an individual with his gift when he reaches maturity he will probably be forgotten. The real creative life, *as a true individual,* cannot begin before the age of 28.

There is no specific age at which it is too early to accept the humanist commitment, for everyone must start somewhere. A person may begin his study before the age of 28, just as a doctor begins his study of medicine well before that age. The proviso here is that one apply the humanist principles to *his own chart* in the beginning and not try to use astrology only for other people. *Humanist astrology must first be a PERSONAL experience.* All subsequent work in humanistic astrology will then stem from the initial commitment within oneself. Thus, when a person wishes to assume the humanist commitment, he should begin with his own birth-chart. After attempting to understand his natal pattern, he should then calculate the progressions and the transits from birth up to the present moment in order to see how his life, *as he has lived it,* fits into the humanistic pattern of such progressions and transits. This necessitates giving one's conscious attention to the deeper meanings which humanism applies to all astrological factors. Instead of studying one's transits and progressions in terms of events and the ups and downs of one's personal and social success and happiness, a humanistic astrologer will try to see them *and use them* in terms of their growth potential in both personal and social maturity.

To achieve a true personal maturity is a difficult task at any time, and today it is even more difficult because the whole of society is geared to the maintenance of all people in a state of perpetual immaturity, conditioned to buy what the economy has produced. Everything in the modern way of life caters to one's pride and stimulates his sense of greed and envy. It reinforces inherent laziness and complacency, and fosters a basic fear of insecurity. It supports a childish desire to depend on other people or to have one's own way at any cost. Social and moral principles of behavior have lost their authority, and therefore personal contact has become more and more irresponsible. Depth psychology, or a type of astrology which is truly psychological in its orientation, can help an individual to become a more mature person. In this case, astrology will only apply *provided* that it does not serve, as so much that goes by that name does, as an escape from personal responsibility through an unhealthy emphasis on external "influences" as being responsible for what one is, does and experiences. Humanistic, person-centered astrology is in a position to assist an individual to become mature because it fosters the ability to concentrate objectively upon the basic facets of that person's total personality, one after another, without evasion or unnecessary rebelliousness. It enables one to concentrate his attention purposefully on what is revealed astrologically at any time as the main focus of personal development.

A person who, during any phase of his life, does what is necessary for him to do, will have no time to indulge himself in the antics of a spoiled child. He will not see himself as a perpetual victim of the cosmos, constantly pondering why he was especially chosen for misery. An astrologer must realize that the basic problem for most people today is that they never know what it is that they *should* be doing. Because of the immense confusion of values in the modern world, life is no longer structured by worthwhile moral and spiritual principles of behavior. It is the task of the psychologist, or the astro-psychologist, to clarify the personal doubts, problems, fears and conflicts which beset 20th century individuals. The humanistic approach can add to this psychological work the knowledge of what an individual is meant to work toward, at any particular time, with reference to the *life-long task* of achieving full personal maturity. If an astrologer believes that the problems connected with adolescence or menopause are due to the transit of Saturn opposing its natal position at those times, and that it is the "influence" of that planet which is therefore responsible for the suffering and conflicts which often occur, then he will never be able to use astrology in a constructive psychological way. The question in astrology should never be how to employ one's "free will" in order to avoid the biological or individual crisis measured by planetary aspects. An astrologer should *know* that crises of growth *must* come in *every* life. Crises are necessary because they are essential to the development of personality. Individual freedom does not consist of trying to decide whether or not one will have a crisis, but in the *meaning* a person gives to it.

The ability to give meaning is the one basic spiritual characteristic of human beings. In his experiences in concentration camps during the Second World War, Victor Frankl discovered this uniquely human attribute. Humanistic astrology can develop this ability. For the humanistic astrologer, the value judgement which one gives to an experience or an event is not inherent in the experience or event itself. Those judgements of good and bad, favorable or unfavorable, are the result of what a person thinks and feels at the time. If one changes the values on which he bases his actions, feelings and thoughts, then the meaning of his experiences will also change. Therefore, when an astrologer labels a possible event or experience as "bad" because traditional astrological textbooks have stated that the planets involved are "malefic," or the aspects are "dire," or the degree involved is linked to a fixed star which brings catastrophic happenings, then his interpretation will have an obviously negative influence. The meaning which the person consulting him will extract from the experience or event will then also be negative, and that is a psychological crime. Thus, it is essential that the astrologer learn as soon as possible that *ANY astrological condition or aspect can correspond to a spiritual victory.* The astrologer who is unable to admit this fact and who, therefore, tends to hinder this victory through negative advice which stimulates fear or a sense of guilt and inferiority is a menace to society. The only way to avoid this danger is to make people at large realize, even if event-oriented astrologers will not, that astrological factors do NOT refer essentially to outer events or to forces external to the individual, but to phases of growth of the personality.

Opportunities for growth which are not fully met leave a residue of unfinished business which must inevitably be dealt with later. That is the real meaning of karma — unfinished business from the past. However, if one does manage to completely fulfill all that life demands of him, there need not be any residue of unfinished business. Achieving this leads to spiritual mastery. Spiritual growth does not stop there, however. If one comes to the point where he has fulfilled everything he was meant to do as an individual, then comes the moment when he will be asked to take on larger responsibilities, to take on the karma of groups, and eventually of humanity as a whole. This is the spiritual ideal exemplified in the life of Christ.

In order to successfully meet life's challenges and to grow as a conscious "I", each person must first *know* that he *is* an individual "I" with a purpose to achieve and a maturity to attain. If he does not know and feel this, then he will never be able to consciously and significantly *use* the energies and powers, both physical and psychic, conscious and unconscious, which his heredity and environment have offered him as a means of expression. Then these energies and powers will use him. Astrologically, the 2nd House will dominate the 1st House. A person will feel himself to be simply an expression of the various instincts, drives and desires which dominate him, one after another, as one planet after another is accentuated by progression or transit. For this reason, if an astrologer presents a birth-chart as being simply the picture of various drives and desires, neither his client nor the astrologer himself will ever learn to manage them constructively. This is also why humanistic astrology puts the accent on the self rather than on its powers. Its intention is to help a person realize that his life-purpose is to *use* his powers in terms of the spiritual quality of being which his birth moment meant him to reveal progressively through the years.

The astrologer has a *personal responsibility* toward his or her client in terms of the way in which that client will respond to (and perhaps follow) the advice given. It should never be a question of trying to "see" from a chart what *will* happen and then passing that information on to the client regardless of the consequences. That would not be psycho-astrological counseling, but simple fortune-telling, regardless of how sophisticated and "scientific" the means used. In every case, *before* speaking or writing, the astrologer should ask himself what the client can *do* with the information presented him. As *every* feature of a birth-chart including the progressions and transits can have a positive as well as negative potential, it is not the astrologer's function to crystallize this meaning as being "negative" when dealing with present and future possibilities. He must make the nature of the *challenge* clearer in terms of the overall life development and purpose. The *decision* to act positively or negatively must forever remain the responsibility of the client; and when I say "positive" or "negative," I mean a way leading either to spiritual fulfillment or to the loss of self in material values.

In closing, I would like to make it clear that when I speak of progressions and transits as revealing the way in which a person *should* act in terms of his "life-purpose", I am *never* referring to concrete actions or specific events. There is no fixed destiny for any individual. Possibilities of various kinds are constantly open to every person and at any age. Each possibility contains the latent energy to make it become an actual fact. The astrological factors describe the *type* of possibilities open to a person, and this is what the astrologer can make clear to his client. It is not for the astrologer to choose which possibility is to become an actual fact. Although he can make the client consciously aware that each possibility can materialize in a vast number of ways and on many different levels of reality, the final choice must be left to the client.

If a person fails to choose or feels unable to exert his will in a given direction, then what results will simply be the consequence of the momentum of that person's past. The future will then be determined by the unfinished business of his past, by his fears and frustrations, and by the pressure of influences issuing from his family, community or nation. If one fails to decide his own destiny, then the past will decide for him. This is especially true when one fears the recurrence of some difficult experience. By his own fear a person can actually call such experiences from the realm of possibility and make them actual. One has no right to blame astrology if, instead of exerting oneself in a consciously chosen direction, a person has waited passively for something to happen or has reacted without conscious purpose to what life presents.

Let us therefore learn to use astrology as a means to live more consciously, as a means to be fully awake and aware of what is at stake when moments of decision come in our lives. The critical phases — conjunction, semi-square, square, sesqui-quadrate and opposition — in all planetary and inter-planetary cycles always represent moments of decision, moments in our lives when we should be awake to the need to break away from some attitude or situation which tends to limit our growth, or which keeps us in bondage to the past. We always face life with what, *at the time,* seems to us the best that we are capable of. Whatever attitude we take, we take it because the total balance of our nature at the time inclines us to act in that way and because we believe that it will be for the best. Through crises and the many partial defeats in all lives, we learn slowly to change this "total balance" of our natures. And so we grow. There is no other way.

CRCS PUBLICATIONS also distributes the following:

JIM MAYNARD'S CELESTIAL INFLUENCES CALENDAR & ALMANAC **$3.95**
The best and most accurate astrological calendar. Many illustrations, full instructions, and a complete ephemeris included. Aesthetically designed, and available in either Eastern or Pacific Time.

THE POCKET ASTROLOGER (small version of Celestial Influences) **$1.95**

JIM MAYNARD'S CELESTIAL GUIDE **$3.95**
Pocket-size, week-at-a-glance astrological engagement calendar. Nicely-designed and extremely useful, with large spaces for notes and appointments. Includes all important astrological data and complete ephemeris.

THE PLANETS & HUMAN BEHAVIOR by Jeff Mayo **$3.75**
Excellent, well-written work based primarily on Jungian psychology. Unifies astrology and psychology.

ASTROLOGER'S ASTRONOMICAL HANDBOOK by Jeff Mayo **$3.50**
For students or practitioners, well-organized and clear.

WISDOM IN THE STARS by Joan Cooke (Hodgson) **$3.00**
A study of the signs of the zodiac from a spiritual perspective, based upon the evolution of consciousness and reincarnation. A unique and insightful book by a well-known British clairvoyant, easily understood by laymen as well as astrologers.

ASTROLOGICAL ASPECTS by C. E. O. Carter **$3.95**
After 45 years, this book still ranks as one of the most thoughtful studies of aspects. Based on case histories rather than mere speculation, it illuminates the principles involved in each aspect and the positive qualities of the "difficult" aspects.

MODERN TEXTBOOK OF ASTROLOGY by Margaret Hone (hardcover) . **$10.00**
One of the most complete, thoughtful, and well-written textbooks of astrology. Extremely clear and organized.

APPLIED ASTROLOGY by Margaret Hone (paperback) **$6.50**
The sequel to her *Modern Textbook*, this is the first paperback edition of one of the few works which help the intermediate student to master interpretation in a systematic way. Using many case histories and combining both natal chart factors & progressions, this book has aided many students to put the fundamentals to practical use.

LECTURES ON MEDICAL ASTROLOGY by Dr. William Davidson **$14.50 per set**
A set of 5 mimeographed booklets based on transcripts of Dr. Davidson's course for astrologers. Explaining the basic principles of applying astrological factors to health problems, this is the best treatment of this subject available.

COUNSELING & INTERVIEWING TECHNIQUES FOR ASTROLOGERS by Dr. Marvin Layman **$3.50**
Practical, clear, informative guide to the common problems encountered in professional or semi-professional practice, including excellent ideas about structuring one's practice properly & handling problematical clients.

BORN TO HEAL by Ruth Montgomery (special value hardcover)............... **$2.50**
Fascinating biography of a healer which gives new insight into the energy dimension of both astrology & healing.

For more complete information on our books, complete book list, dealer's discount schedule, or to order any of the above publications, write to:
CRCS PUBLICATIONS
Asbill Court Building
111 G Street, Suite 29
Davis, California 95616